FASCISM

Paul M. Hayes

THE FREE PRESS
A Division of Macmillan Publishing Co., Inc.
NEW YORK

The Free Press
A Division of Macmillan Publishing Co., Inc.
866 Third Avenue, New York, N.Y. 10022

Library of Congress Catalog Card Number: 73-13448

4 - 18 - 74

Printed in the United States of America

printing number

1 2 3 4 5 6 7 8 9 10

To all my friends at
Queen Elizabeth House, Oxford

Contents

Introduction

No completely satisfactory definition of fascism has yet been produced, and it is not the purpose of this work to attempt such a definition. Although there is lack of agreement about the true nature of fascism, both of the past and present, this has not prevented widespread use of the term 'fascist'. The fact that it is a term used almost always in a pejorative fashion has made the task of distinguishing its meaning still more difficult. One example of such misuse should suffice. During the years immediately preceding the Second World War Soviet leaders and the Soviet press consistently referred to Hitler's Germany as fascist. This description of the Third Reich would in all probability have been accepted by Hitler himself—certainly it was not generally challenged. Yet in the 1970s Soviet leaders and the Soviet press have stigmatized the present West German government as fascist—a description which is as false as it is alarming. What do the German governments of 1940 and 1970 have in common, what is it that makes them 'fascist'? To all but the wilfully blind the answer is clear—the only substantial common factor is that both governments were German. The term 'fascist' has in the case of Herr Brandt's government been misused for the purposes of propaganda and the achievement of certain political goals.

While the term 'fascist' is still used in this way, and there is little reason to suppose such usage will cease, it should not be a cause of surprise that there is much confusion as to the exact nature of fascism. Those liberals of the intellectual Left who found fascism easy to define in the days of Hitler found their definitions challenged by revelations of the nature of Stalinism. The peace of their comfortable world was violated once again in the 1960s with the rise of the New Left. To their dismay, horror and confusion the liberals of the past now heard themselves dismissed as 'fascists'. To use the term 'fascist', therefore, has become standard technique among all those who wish to make some controversial comment on political developments and at the same time to place those whom they oppose beyond the pale of human sympathy. Frequently this misuse of the term is successful, but happily not always; observers of British politics will recall with distaste Churchill's 'Gestapo' gaffe of 1945 and Wedgwood Benn's likening of Powell to Hitler during the election campaign of 1970. It should not, therefore, be a matter for surprise that members of the general public and, more particularly, students of politics, history, economics and sociology remain confused as to the precise nature of fascism.

It would perhaps be easier to state what fascism is not rather than what it was or is, but this is surely the wrong way to approach the problem. The method used in this work is an examination of the background to fascist theory and a short analysis of those régimes, past and contemporary, which are generally believed to have had or to have 'fascist' characteristics. There is one major exception and that is all governments which have described themselves as 'communist'. There are many who believe that Stalin's Russia was every bit as fascist as Hitler's Germany, or that the present régime in power in Russia is as worthy of the description as that of the colonels in Greece. The reader may, of course, judge this matter for himself by comparing the account of fascism in this work with any standard text on government and politics in the Soviet Union. However, there are two reasons why the political experience of the Russians in the last half-century has not been examined in this work. The first is lack of space—to try to compare political, economic and administrative trends in those countries which call themselves 'communist' with those generally believed to be 'fascist' would far exceed the purpose of this work. In the second place any definition of the term 'fascism' is likely in practice to be so loose that to regard it as a suitable description also for explaining modern Marxist forms would be unrealistic. A loose term would become even more elastic. Any study of totalitarianism would be bound to take into consideration the communist as well as the fascist experience, and would be able to find many common aspects, but the purpose of this work is to discuss the phenomenon of fascism rather than analyse competing forms of totalitarian ideology.

In this book the discussion of some issues has necessarily been brief or, on some topics, altogether omitted. Space does not permit the constant insertion of contrary points of view or cautionary advice, though it must always be borne in mind that the opinions of many of the writers quoted are the subject of acute historical controversy. This is certainly true of the writings of Hegel and the critical comments of Popper. Popper's analysis of Hegel has been subjected to very serious criticism from eminent scholars. It would not be advisable for the reader to accept uncritically the views presented here—he must read some of the *critiques* of Popper's thesis in order to judge properly its merits. Similarly, Herder, Nietzsche, List and many others are controversial writers and it can hardly be claimed that the interpretation put on their views in this book is definitive. Most of those quoted in the following pages were men of broad interests and frequently their works display characteristics of inconsistency or internal conflict. Obviously, in these cases it is a question of judgement as to the relative weight to be assigned to their different assertions. Nor should they be thought of merely as precursors of fascism. They must be seen in the context of their overall importance as economists, politicians, philosophers or historians.

Unfortunately it has also been necessary to omit, for the most part, references to the artistic background of fascism. This is in itself a topic worthy of a major study. Most readers are aware of the contribution of Wagner to an exotic and exaggerated Teutonic romantic nationalism. They may be less conscious of the very powerful link between the arts and fascism. Many influential poets, novelists, artists, sculptors, photographers and musicians have been associated with fascism in one way or another. Many became associated in their youth and after repented their folly. Others have never publicly repudiated their commitment. But the important fact is that men and women in the public eye, apparently unconnected with politics in any formal way, were associated with fascist movements. This fact in itself was a valuable asset to fascist parties. Some mention has already been made of the connection between music and fascism. The link between poetry, literature and fascism is even stronger. Names such as D'Annunzio, Pound, Lawrence, Marinetti, Benn, Céline, Eliot, Wyndham Lewis and Yeats leap immediately to mind. Not all of these were fascists, but it is of interest that their works were of comfort to fascists and were used by fascist propagandists. In their assault on decadent materialism writers such as Céline opened the door to the fascist catharsis. The despair of Céline ran so deep that he was prepared to witness the triumph of those, like the Jews, whom he detested, in the hope that ultimately a reaction would ensue. Fascism's structured society appealed greatly to those who had lost their balance in the whirlpools of emotion which flooded intellectual activity and creative composition in the early twentieth century. Fascism, wrongly, was believed not only to satisfy basic human urges but also to approach problems from a sharper and more intellectual viewpoint. The combination of intellectual arrogance and belief in earthy or primitive values which was so typical of many literary figures in the 1920s and 1930s thus propelled them in the direction of fascism.

While valuing the contributions of those writers who helped undermine the values hitherto so deeply entrenched in Western democratic societies, the fascists held the contributions of other artists in still higher regard. On the whole they preferred the arts with greater physical contact—music, photography, drawing, sculpture—for these could reach a wider and less literate audience. Music and sculpture reached a wide audience and the fascist laid great emphasis on the importance of 'relevant' music and sculpture. The experiences of Speer, whose rise to power began through his skill as an architect, are eloquent testimony to the value attached to work which would lend itself to fascist interpretation. Similarly, the fascist journals employed skilful artists and cartoonists, those who were able to capture in a few lines the essence of the political aspirations of fascist movements. Photography, both as an art form and as an adjunct to political use, reached new heights under the fascist régimes. Leni Riefenstahl, the director of the films of the Nazi rallies at Nuremberg, played a vital part in the establishment of Nazism as a vital force in Germany. The examples that could be cited are almost endless; it must suffice to say that no student of the phenomenon of fascism should remain unaware either of the contribution of the artists to the rise of fascism or to its grip on the popular imagination.

Finally, there is no real discussion of the well-established viewpoint that fascism is unique and specific, both in cultural and historic terms. At one time this belief was widely held and has been persuasively argued by some distinguished scholars, among them Hannah Arendt and Carl Friedrich. In one sense this whole book tries to undermine the position taken up by these writers and the case must rest upon the persuasiveness of the evidence adduced. But it would be wrong to imagine that there is a complete conflict of views. The difference of opinion lies not in the nature of the facts but in how they should be interpreted. Friedrich wrote in the introduction to his book on totalitarianism that it 'is the most perplexing problem of our time. It has burst upon mankind more or less unexpected and unannounced. There are antecedents, to be sure, both in thought and in action, but they do not add up to the reality with which the mid-twentieth century finds itself confronted and by which it finds itself persistently challenged.' In essence, these few words summarize the position taken up by a whole group, almost a generation, of distinguished writers. It is a view with which I cannot agree, for it seems to me that there is ample evidence to show that if the precursors of fascism did not quite know the shape of the beast they were helping to create they did at least have some idea how it would behave. The enemies of the open society cannot have been so naive that they could not envisage the type of society that would replace it—at least not all of them. Further, as I hope is shown, fascism is derivative and imitative and must, therefore, be predictable to a certain degree. That a contrary viewpoint has been so widely held may, I think, in part be attributed to the fact that many of its supporters wrote soon after or even during the horrific events of 1922–45. Having lived so recently through such an experience it must be difficult to persuade oneself that such an occurrence was not unique and not related to a set of non-recurring historical factors. The mere passage of time can sometimes help to place a series of events in a more accurate historical context. It can, of course, also mislead.

This book, then, does contain much opinion that is controversial. It is not deliberately intended to be so and, indeed, I deeply respect the quality of the work of those authors with whom I disagree. Fascism is one of those 'isms' for which every person will find his own definition and hence this book should be seen as an attempt to argue the case for one major interpretation of its historical and sociological significance, not as a definitive statement of what fascism is or was. Disagreements of interpretation are inevitable at every level, even when the facts are clear, and no reader should believe otherwise, save at his own peril.

PART I

The Intellectual Origins of Fascism
and the Development of Fascist Theory

I Some General Comments

> 'Begin at the beginning,' the King said, gravely, 'and go on till you come to the end: then stop.' Lewis Carroll, *Alice in Wonderland*.

'Fascism', wrote George Mosse, 'originated in the attack on positivism and liberalism at the end of the nineteenth century.'[1] Ernst Nolte, on the other hand, has suggested that 'if fascism can be defined as a new reality which did not exist before World War I, or only in rudimentary form, the next obvious step is to declare it to be the characteristic political trend of an era in which . . . Europe can be regarded once more as the focal point of the world.'[2] The difference between the approaches of these two eminent scholars highlights the problem of determining the origins of fascism. Is it possible to 'begin at the beginning' when one group of historians sees fascism as a movement with political roots in the nineteenth century and another sees it as an essentially twentieth-century phenomenon?

The intellectual basis of fascism is a strange mixture of theories, ranging from the radical to the reactionary and encompassing ideas about race, religion, economics, social welfare and morality which are at the very least dissonant. In addition to the diverse origins of the body of doctrine that may be termed 'fascist' there also exists a further complicating factor—the clash between the ideological basis of fascism and the adaptations to that ideology made in order to suit the differing institutional requirements of those countries which adopted fascist solutions to their problems. These essentially practical modifications in due course became enshrined in fascist doctrine and were applied to different situations, not infrequently without success. A characteristic example of unsuccessful modification of fascist doctrine may be seen in the Italian acceptance of German theories of race, in particular those regarding the Jews. Italian anti-Semitic legislation of the late 1930s was recognized as an unpleasant irrelevance even within the ruling hierarchy of the Italian Fascist Party. This phenomenon is not unfamiliar to those who have studied ideologies. In his definitive study of communism,

R. N. Carew Hunt wrote: 'There is no doubt that communists do believe that they are applying to political situations a theory which they fervently accept and which they hold to be scientific . . . We are apt to forget that there is any theory behind our own institutions. But communists never forget their own theoretical principles. In part this is a question of age, for younger movements are always more conscious of theory than older ones. But it also reflects the belief that marxism is a science, and that communist strategy and tactics derive from it by strictly logical deduction.'[3] Much of this is equally applicable to fascist theory and practice.

In retrospect, therefore, fascism must be seen as a curious combination of ideology, often self-contradictory, and practical modification of theory in order to accommodate important institutional, administrative, economic or social demands. In this sense both Mosse and Nolte account satisfactorily for the origins of fascism. Fascism was, and is, a blend of theory and action. The intellectual basis of fascist theory has roots deep in European culture; the energy which stimulated the growth of fascism in the twentieth century was created by the collapse of the hitherto apparently stable national and international political systems that had existed before 1914.

To turn first to an examination of the intellectual origins of fascism is justifiable in terms of chronology. Many of the ideas that were to have an impact in the 1920s and 1930s had been the subject of discussion and controversy long before the First World War. However, before placing too much weight upon the influence of the ideas of the men of letters, it is as well to remember that some of the most energetic and successful fascists, Hitler and Mussolini among them, had little time for the theorists when in power and not much more during the course of their political struggles. The influence of the theorists was much stronger among the men of the second rank—upon Rosenberg,[4] Doriot[5] and Farinacci.[6]

Fascism is international in one sense and that is that those whose views are generally believed to have been influential in the formation of its theories have come from many countries. They include Gobineau,[7] Sorel,[8] Herder,[9] Darwin,[10] Nietzsche,[11] Marinetti,[12] Spengler,[13] and Chamberlain.[14] Some of these men, such as Herder and Darwin, were immensely influential during their own lifetimes; others, like Gobineau, became influential after death when their writings were dragged out of darkness and oblivion by those who saw contemporary applications (or misapplications) for their theories.

It should readily be apparent from the diverse nature of the writers and thinkers already mentioned that fascist theory is not a tightly-knit bundle of ideas, interdependent and interrelated. It is, in fact, rather untidy and inchoate. It is composed of a large number of diverse ideas, drawn from different cultures. To make matters still more complex there exists no fascist equivalent of *Das Kapital*. Hitler's *Mein Kampf* is an important and fascinating document but it does not contain either a blueprint for action or a coherent theory of socio-political-economic development: the fascists had no Marx.

As there exists no obvious text upon which to base analysis and criticism it might be thought that the task of explaining fascist theory is almost impossible. That this is not the case is largely owing to the fact that the theorists wrote about contemporary problems and wove their ideas about them. A simultaneous examination of their ideas (in some cases far removed from fascism) and the historical circumstances surrounding their development can give a surprisingly coherent picture of fascist theory. For the sake of convenience the main impact of fascist ideas has been divided into eight sections:

(a) the myth of race;
(b) the idea of the élite and the leader;
(c) the totalitarian state;
(d) nationalism;
(e) socialism;
(f) militarism;
(g) economics;
(h) the concepts of morality and might in international affairs.
While these categories are by no means exhaustive they cover the main topics which writers who were allegedly fascist frequently covered. In many cases there is a considerable overlap between the different sections.

2 The Myth of Race

'The physical development and racial improvement of the people
form the necessary basis of lasting progress.' Vidkun Quisling,
Russia and Ourselves

The concept of racial superiority was a constituent part of fascist
ideology. Because of the particular forms racial theory took during
the period of Nazi ascendancy on the continent of Europe—the
campaigns for the systematic elimination of the Jews and the Slavs—
the myth of race is perhaps the most widely known fascist theory. It
overlapped at several points with the idea of élitist government and
also with more common national and military objectives. It is often
stated that there was much that was essentially German rather than
fascist in these theories. The Italians, for example, on the whole
showed little enthusiasm for the idea of racial superiority, except
under German pressure in the years immediately preceding the
outbreak of the Second World War. However, even among the
Italians there were firm believers in racial superiority, not only
among the full-blown fascists such as Farinacci but also among
nationalists. In a letter of 1895 D'Annunzio[1] wrote: 'I glory in the
fact that I am a Latin, and I recognize a barbarian in every man of
non-Latin blood. . . . If the Latin races are to preserve themselves, it
is time they returned to the healthy prejudice which created the
grandeur of Greece and Rome—to believe that all others are
barbarians.'[2] The step from D'Annunzio to Rosenberg was but
small.

In fact, the notion of racial superiority was of a much older
vintage than the close of the nineteenth century. At the beginning of
the century, under pressure from the aggressive French nationalism
spearheaded by Napoleon, many Germans responded by consoling
themselves for the defeat of Austria and Prussia with the thought
that Germans were bound to triumph over disaster in the long run
through their natural superiority as a race. Thus the term '*Volk*' came
to have a particular meaning for Germans—one which was associated
with endeavour, struggle, reward and domination. As the German

Volk remained disunited the concept of the destiny of the *Volk* paradoxically gained rather than lost ground.

One of the earliest enthusiasts for the concept of racial superiority was Fichte[3] who, in 1807, declared in a lecture at Berlin that not only were the Germans an '*Urvolk*' (original folk) but furthermore it was 'quite plain that only the German ... truly has a folk and is entitled to depend on one; he only is able to feel real and rational love for his nation.'[4] This theme was to be taken up by many other Germans, even among his contemporaries. Some of these were men of real ability, others crude and uneducated. Most prominent among the latter group was Jahn[5] who combined his opinions of the physical and mental attributes of the German people into a strange and incoherent philosophy of race. On a more sophisticated level, Arndt[6] (an early believer in the destiny of the Nordic races) and von der Marwitz[7] (an early campaigner against the Jews) brought many members of the educated classes, particularly in Prussia, over to Fichte's views.

The propagation of Fichte's ideas, albeit in a more complex form, owed much to the ability of Görres,[8] a publicist and author. His main work was *Das Wachstum der Historie* in which he elaborated the concept of the myth of the folk. At one time he was editor of the *Rheinischer Merkur*, using his position to campaign for a greater, united Germany. His views were not, however, merely nationalist but also racialist—he was a firm believer in the purity and strength of the German race: 'Like cannot dissociate itself from like, nor can blood of the same mixture belie itself, even though it may have branched off from the main stream into smaller vessels.'[9] His work was repeated by many minor figures during the following decades.

By the middle of the nineteenth century the concept of racial superiority was well established in the European cultural tradition, although, curiously, most of the thinkers who had embraced the doctrine fervently had been German. It is thus easy to see why for so many Germans the concept of the '*Herrenvolk*', delineated by Hitler in the 1920s and 1930s, should have been so attractive. It was familiar—a part of the German literary and historical tradition. It had become a doctrine sedulously fostered by generations of instructors, in the schools, universities and in the armed forces. The concept had received further reinforcement from the military victories of 1866 and 1870-1 and the economic prosperity of the following half century. The chosen race was that of Germany.

However, the leading apostle of race theory was not a German, but a French diplomat, Count Arthur Gobineau. Gobineau stressed the importance of race as the essential factor in the process of civilization, although many of his opinions were later distorted by twentieth-century fascists in order to suit their own purposes. He was a man of intensely pessimistic social outlook, viewing the decadence of contemporary society with resignation and loathing. His opinions of the virtues of certain races was never very consistent, varying according to his mood and his diplomatic postings. For example, early in his career he declared in the *Essai sur l'inégalité des races humaines* that society in Latin America was decadent, principally because of miscegenation between Europeans and natives. Yet a few years later, when in correspondence with Pedro II of Brazil, he took a very different stand.[10] Again, he was at first sympathetic to Prussia, later to Austria. His work was thus neither consistent nor systematic.

It was Gobineau's view of the hierarchical structure of races that was to have so much influence upon later writers. He believed that the most important peoples were to be found among the white races, followed by the yellow races and then the black. Among the white races were some of great ethnic purity which, therefore, had considerable potential for the development of civilization. There were others of different stock within the white races whose main capacity was the ability to transmit ethnic decay and hence to accelerate the collapse of civilization. The race which possessed the maximum potential for civilization was that of the Teutons. The most degenerate were the Slavs and the Celts. The preferred race of Teutons varied according to his moods, being at different times the Germans, the Scandinavians and the English.

Many of Gobineau's ideas were ignored or glossed over by later writers. He was not particularly anti-Semitic, believing that the debasement of the Jews arose from miscegenation with the black races rather than from racial faults inherent in themselves. This aspect of his thought was studiously ignored by Rosenberg and many other devotees. Similarly, he was hostile to slavery, but even in his own lifetime two American publicists—Henry Hotz and Josiah Nott —perverted his views for their own propaganda purposes. More predictably, he was anti-egalitarian and anti-democratic. He believed in an ordered, hierarchical society. He was hostile to materialism and cherished the institutions of the family and aristocracy. He regarded an élite as essential to the preservation of a civilized society. The influence of these and other ideas among the Junkers and other members of the educated classes in Germany was particularly strong and bred many imitators.

Within Germany the concept of race was further strengthened by the writings of Schemann, the founder of the Gobineau Society in 1893, Wagner,[11] Dühring[12] and Lagarde.[13] All of these men flourished in the second half of the nineteenth century and some were very influential, Wagner in particular, because his appeal stretched beyond the literary circles in which his contemporaries were almost exclusively active. Strangely enough, the views of these men had in part been stimulated by the progress of scientific analysis. Darwin's ideas and researches, which were of inestimable scientific importance, soon acquired a political dimension when they were claimed by the apostles of race. A new and more powerful form of racialism arose—dubbed Social-Darwinism.

Enthusiasts for this cult were by no means confined to Germany. Indeed, three leading writers were of English origin—Houston Chamberlain, Pearson[14] and Kidd.[15] Chamberlain developed the concept of the folk-nation, destined to triumph because of its superior genetic gifts. His devotion to the Aryan race, in particular the German branch, was extraordinary. He was frequently guilty of grossly inaccurate historical statements in defence of his ideas. He believed, for example, that the Renaissance had been the result of an upsurge in the German spirit. The unfortunate fact that many of the earliest Renaissance scholars and artists had come from Italy was explained in terms of the heavy preponderance of Teutonic blood in northern Italy (settled by the Lombards, Franks and Goths). Chamberlain's views thus antedated those of Farinacci by some forty years. Furthermore, Chamberlain regarded physical and mental superiority as complementary attributes: ' . . . horses and dogs give us every chance of observing that the intellectual gifts go hand in hand with the physical; this is specially true of the moral qualities; a mongrel is frequently very clever, but never reliable; morally he is always a weed.'[16] Chamberlain thus helped create a strange and perverted mixture of the theories of Darwin and Gobineau. He found a highly receptive audience in Imperial Germany.

While Chamberlain's ideas fell on fruitful soil in Germany, Pearson was engaged upon similar work in England. In 1905 he

wrote that 'A nation . . . is an organized whole . . . kept up to a high
pitch of external efficiency by contest, chiefly by way of war with
inferior races, and with equal races by the struggle for trade-routes
and for the sources of raw material and of food supply.'[17] Pearson's
contribution to the theory of race was to emphasize the importance
of the 'tribe' as distinct from the 'individual'. In the 1890s his ideas
gained ground not only against the orthodox views of Darwin but also
perversions of those views by Germans such as Haeckel.[18] Pearson's
main rival in Britain was Kidd, whose major contribution to racial
theory was his *Social Evolution* of 1894. Kidd was not liked or
respected by Pearson, for he was not only anti-socialist (and Pearson
claimed to be socialist) but also a devout Christian. However, they
both agreed that it was essential for the Empire to be maintained, if
necessary at the expense of inferior peoples. Kidd had written that
'In the North American Continent, in the plains of Australia, in
New Zealand, and South Africa, the representatives of this vigorous and virile race are at last in full possession.'[19] Pearson echoed
these sentiments when, at the height of the Boer War, he declared:
'This dependence of progress on the survival of the fitter race,
terribly black as it may seem to some of you, gives the struggle for
existence its redeeming features; it is the fiery crucible out of which
comes the finer metal.'[20]

The myth of race found powerful allies in the period preceding
the First World War. The economic and social pressures generated
in Europe by changing industrial patterns found a ready outlet in the
drive towards imperialism. Powerful groups in Germany and
England adopted the arguments of the racial theorist to suit their
own political ends. Similar movements existed in both France and
Italy, but they were less strong, perhaps because of the checks to
imperial policies sustained by these countries at Fashoda in 1898 and
Adowa in 1896.

It was in England and Germany (and later the United States) that
the influence of the concept of race, conjoined with imperialism, rose
to a peak. A number of otherwise apparently incompatible ideas
became united in a strange combination of Social-Darwinism
Social-Imperialism, religious mysticism and the theories of racial
destiny. Politicians and writers were carried away by the heady
doctrine. It is easy to see how Sorel's views on the importance of
myths in history were developed during these years of frenzied
activity.

In 1902 Lord Rosebery[21] explained that 'the true policy of imperialism ... relates not to territory alone, but to race as well. The Imperialism that, grasping after territory, ignores the conditions of an Imperial race, is a blind, a futile, and a doomed Imperialism.'[22] Rosebery's voice was not alone in either the Liberal Party or the country. His views were reinforced by those of Mackinder,[23] Joseph Chamberlain,[24] Rhodes,[25] and Kipling.[26] These men were not racialists in the sense that Rosenberg was a racialist, but they believed that the English (or the Anglo-Saxon) race had certain duties to perform and that its ability to fulfil these tasks depended in part at least on its character as a race. A semi-mystical belief in destiny—their own and that of their country—drove them on. The major share of the white man's burden was, Kipling believed, to be borne by the English:

> God of our fathers, known of old,
> Lord of our far-flung battle-line,
> Beneath whose awful Hand we hold
> Dominion over palm and pine—
> Lord God of Hosts, be with us yet,
> Lest we forget—lest we forget![27]

Crude racial ideas became inextricably mingled with consideration of important social and economic questions of the day. Imperialism, the destiny of the race, national prosperity and the spread of Western civilization all became interrelated. The writers and politicians who initially believed in only one of these ideas were often induced to accept the validity of the others, frequently without undue exercise of their critical faculties. In many cases other influences were responsible for changes in political positions. Joseph Chamberlain's original faith in the virtues of the English was transformed into an ardent imperialism not so much by the growth of public opinion, for which he himself was in a large degree responsible, but through long and continued contact with the Conservative Party and the industrial interests of the Midlands. Rhodes' experiences with the Boers and the native races of South Africa urged him along the road to aggressive nationalism and racial superiority. Mackinder, the Liberal Imperialist, derived new ideas from his political experience and constructed a whole new theory of geo-politics, which was seized upon with enthusiasm by believers in the myth of race. Thus dawned the age of the Yellow Peril and the Slav Menace.

Much the same process took place in Germany, although in that country opposition to these powerful new ideas was much less strong and articulate. The beliefs of the Social-Darwinists in England were challenged strongly by certain sections of society, particularly among the scientists, traditional conservative circles and in radical and socialist groups. In Germany the voices of men like Virchow,[28] a traditionalist Liberal, were generally raised in vain. The opposition in Germany was perhaps weaker because of the slightly different nature of the Racial-Imperialist myth. In England it was, although apparently chauvinistic and aggressive, essentially a defensive phenomenon. The nation already had an empire; it was the duty of the race to preserve it. For the Germans there was no empire, save that in Germany itself, so much more emphasis was placed upon the destiny of the race and the rightful place of the race in the future world.

In Germany the public was inundated by a torrent of racial, imperial and military propaganda. Leading figures in all sections of society professed the same aims. In 1887 the Colonial League was founded, the All-German Association in 1891 (the precursor of the Pan-German League), the Navy League in 1898 and the Bureau for Publicity and Parliamentary Affairs, which was under the control of Admiral Tirpitz,[29] in 1897. The Pan-German League was of these organizations the most active in propagating racial myths. Its propaganda was directed at first by Hasse and later by Class,[30] both enthusiasts for nationalism and racial superiority. The influence of these bodies was very strong in the armed forces, from which, in consequence, many able writers were drawn. Most notable was Bernhardi,[31] who wrote in 1911 that 'War is a biological necessity of the first importance, a regulative element in the life of mankind which cannot be dispensed with, since without it an unhealthy development will follow, which excludes every advancement of the race, and therefore all real civilization.'[32]

In Germany the combination of racial and imperial propaganda was of particular effect because of the separation of the German folk. To write in glowing terms of the desirability of reunion was a certain recipe for success. The concept of a super-state, founded upon the great block of German-speaking peoples in Central Europe, came to dominate political writings. The theories of Mackinder gained ground rapidly and attained a popularity in Germany far exceeding the attention given to them in Britain. Before the war of 1914–18,

Ratzel[33] and later Haushofer[34] provided an intellectual justification for pan-German expansion. The frustrations of Germany's pre-1914 position were dramatically expressed by Naumann[35] in 1915 when he wrote: 'We are a folk; we have learned and discovered our folk economy in an economic straitjacket amid a world of enemies. That is the background of everything which may happen subsequently.'[36] As well as these practical schemes for the unification of the folk there was also a strong element of mysticism present in many writings. Houston Chamberlain was the foremost writer in this vein, noting in 1901, in a letter to the Kaiser, that 'Science, Philosophy and Religion can today take no onward step save in the German tongue . . . God builds today upon the Germans alone.'[37] In reply Wilhelm II wrote: 'You sing the High Song of the German, and, above all of our glorious tongue, and pregnantly summon the Germans to . . . take up the task of being God's instrument for the spreading of this *Kultur*, of His teachings.'[38] It can scarcely be wondered at that the racial propagandists were successful in Germany when they were so well endowed with support from the highest in the land, leading naval and military men, professors and even apparently sanctified with the blessing of religion.

The war of 1914–18 proved to be a serious setback for imperialists in both Germany and England, but for the racialists it added the notion of catharsis to their theories. The concept of a revivified Germany, cleansed of impurity and rising from the flames, became a favourite image of writers like Rosenberg. In defeated Germany belief in racial doctrines, fanned by opportunists and encouraged by economic depression, grew swiftly and led to the formal incorporation of the racial myth in Nazi doctrine. Rosenberg's clumsy prose was by no means the most influential in inter-war Germany. More important was Haiser, who wrote in 1923: 'A nation which lacks a ruling class of pure stock can only be governed by an absolute master . . . all Germans await such a master and the rest of the Occident will soon come to their way of thinking. Germany needs the man who will knock down all unmanageable fellows, all personalities.'[39] Still more significant was Spengler, who wrote in 1934 that: 'It is high time that the "white" world, and Germany in the first place, should consider these facts. For behind the world wars and the still unfinished proletarian world-revolution there looms the greatest of all dangers, the coloured menace, and it will require every bit of "race" that is still available among white nations to deal with it.'[40]

Another sinister component of the racial myth was anti-Semitism. It was not until well into the nineteenth century that quite widely-held, anti-Jewish feelings were first erected into a comprehensive doctrine. It was always much stronger as a movement in Germany than in England, France or Italy. In most of Southern Europe and Scandinavia there were so few Jews that any attempt to make propaganda through anti-Semitism was a largely pointless exercise. In Russia and Germany there were large Jewish communities and in Russia anti-Semitism became a regular aspect of governmental policy for the last half-century of Romanov rule.

In Germany anti-Semitism soon became part of the racial myth. All the failures of German policy, the inability to transform economic into political domination, could be attributed to the pollution of Aryan society by the Jews. It was at this level that the theories of Darwin and the eccentric views of Gobineau became popularized in bastard versions. Anti-Semites ranged from men of the people, like Stöcker,[41] to intellectuals such as Dühring, Houston Chamberlain, Driesmans and Wilser. Dühring's *Die Judenfrage als Racen-, Sitten-, und Kulturfrage* was the classic exposition of anti-Semitic theory. Beside this massive work of excoriation the attempts of men like Wilser to prove Aryan supremacy by means of genetic analysis paled into insignificance. Dühring asserted that 'society is in many places so paralysed by moral poison that it can no longer stir its limbs to reaction.... Now what part have the Jews played in this corruption? ... Where the Jews are to the fore, there is there most corruption. This is a basic fact of all cultural history and cultural geography.'[42] Dühring's viewpoint was to some extent formed by his hatred of France and England, in which countries Gambetta and Disraeli were influential, and the press, in which Jews were frequently very powerfully established. Dühring's economic views, which were hostile to free trade, further reinforced these sentiments. In fact some of his suggestions merely antedate Hitler's actions by half a century—'the commonplace and short-sighted pretext of toleration is no longer relevant ... [there should be] ... social defence against marriage with those belonging to the Jewish race.... Requisites of an effective agitation with the reduction and extinction of the powers of the Jews as the final target.'[43]

Dühring's crude anti-Semitism was shared by Wagner and many other influential Germans. Houston Chamberlain, however, was hostile to the Jews not because of a belief in their racial impurity but rather because they formed a major obstacle to German domination of Europe, through their economic and industrial influence. The views of others were less sophisticated, being based on greed, envy, religious intolerance or any of a number of other social factors.

If anti-Semitism was rife in Germany, Russia and their Eastern European dependencies it also existed outside these areas. In Austria, where many Jews had settled, Schoenerer[44] and Lueger[45] made political capital out of anti-Semitism. In Romania, Bulgaria and Serbia the Jews faced regular attacks from right-wing, nationalist bodies. At the end of the nineteenth century the small Jewish community in France came under hostile public inspection because of the false allegations against Dreyfus. Leading the anti-Semitic agitation was Drumont,[46] whose political influence did not decline until the Dreyfus Affair had been finally settled in favour of the accused. Even in Britain, where the Jews were exceptionally well integrated, strange anti-Semitic echoes were occasionally heard. During the constitutional crisis of 1909–11 Belloc[47] described the House of Lords as 'by its constitution a committee for the protection of the Anglo-Judaic plutocracy'.[48]

It was, however, the collapse of German society in 1918 and the following years which gave new life to anti-Semitism. To the minds of the general public, right-wing propaganda about Jewish betrayal seemed a plausible explanation for the misfortunes which had overtaken Germany. The prominence of Jews amid the ranks of the Social Democrats in Germany and among the Bolsheviks in Russia confirmed these beliefs. The economic and social problems that faced industrialized Europe after 1918 paved the way for a general revival of hostility to the Jews.

It was in this period that Drexler,[49] soon to be succeeded as leader by Hitler, founded the Nazi Party and adopted a policy of systematic anti-Semitism. The Fatherland Party of Tirpitz held similar views, as well as a whole host of splinter groups. Soon Hitler's anti-Semitism began to attract important recruits, Ludendorff[50] and Houston Chamberlain. Keyserling, while declaring that anti-Semitism might appear irrational, suggested that 'it must have some justification, for Jews are, as they always have been, equally despised throughout the world'.[51] Von Beck's bogus *Protocols of the Elders of Sion* strongly influenced Rosenberg and Streicher.[52] Moeller van den Bruck[53] linked Marxism and Judaism with the formation of anti-German combinations in Europe. In anti-Semitism Hitler and the Nazis found the well-nigh perfect weapon, combining the strength of mass working-class support with intellectual and upper- and middle-class prejudices, with which to attack and destroy the weak structure of German democracy.

The theories of race thus were spread through many lands, though flourishing most strongly in Germany. The apostles of race could be found among all classes of men, in conditions of economic strength and of economic weakness. The theories derived strength from popular misinterpretation of important scientific discoveries and from resolution born of defeat. The desire for a pure Aryan race seems to have gained ground in Germany despite the defeat of 1918. Race theory embraced snippets of many different ideas; it was derived from nationalism, militarism, Darwinism, socialism, élitism and romanticism. Those who supported the theories ranged from pillars of society, like Milner,[54] to those who believed in a new form of social dynamism, like Hitler. The element of the irrational was very strong, as of course it needed to be, and thus belief continued for some long time after favourable evidence had ceased to exist. Perhaps examination of this subject may be concluded with one final example—despite widespread hostility to racial theory in the 1930s in Britain, Mosley[55] was able to suggest (and expect the public to believe) that 'We have created the Empire without race mixture or pollution. . . . It should only be necessary by education and propaganda to teach the British that racial mixtures are bad.'[56] In the same pamphlet he also asserted that it would become necessary to breed children in order to protect the national interest. Race theory was by no means just '*le vice allemand*' as so many of the post-war generation would like to think.

3   The Idea of the Élite and the Leader

'The man of the future in Germany must be a man of action, he must have something in common with adventurers and captains of brigands.' Franz Haiser, *Die Judenfrage vom Standpunkt der Herrenmoral*

Élitist theories have a long and respectable history. Among the ancient philosophers both Plato and Aristotle believed in the excellence of some form of aristocracy. Their views on these topics were on the whole accepted without too much criticism during the Middle Ages, for they could be adapted to fit in with the prevailing social patterns of the time. During the Renaissance and the following centuries political analysts looked rather more closely at these ideas. Once free discussion of the political concepts involved was permitted, two very different schools of thought emerged. On the one hand emerged the prophets of democracy, who saw no justification for an aristocracy, save that of talent. On the other hand there were a number of thinkers who saw that any logical extension of the principle of aristocracy would lead to rule by one man. In the former group were men such as Locke, Godwin, Marx and a whole host of liberal, radical and revolutionary writers. In the second camp were Machiavelli, Hobbes, Fichte and Hegel. Within these camps there were very diverse views but the principal issue which separated the types was the significance of the doctrine of pure reason. The former, by and large, believed that application of reason to problems, be they political, economic, social or philosophic, would inevitably produce a just and viable solution. The latter group took a more pessimistic view of society and its institutions.

It was in the eighteenth century that the age of reason and enlightenment reached its peak. In the chaos wrought by the French Revolution, initially hailed as the culmination of the process of pure reason, it was inevitable that there should be strong reactions against radicalism in all its diverse forms. In many countries the reaction was simply conservative—the reaction of men like Burke; in others it led to a gradual extension of democracy, as in the case of the United States. In Russia the reaction was the imposition of still tighter control. The Tsar was even willing to wage war to defend his fellow monarchs from attack by the revolutionaries. The stage was set for the emergence of new political disputations.

It was Herder who first successfully linked three separate political concepts into a meaningful whole, these concepts being nationalism, the élite and the rejection of rationalism. In the Germany of the Napoleonic Wars his ideas fell upon receptive ears. The Germans, through their nationality, were destined to be the ruling élite in Europe once they had achieved the goal of national unity. Herder rejected the age of reason with contempt: 'Again I cry, my German brothers! Now! The remains of all real thought of the folk is hastening towards the gulf of oblivion in one final burst of speed. The aura of the so-called Enlightenment is consuming itself like a cancer. For the last half century we have been ashamed of everything relating to the Fatherland.'[1] Herder's views on these topics brought him into open conflict with Kant,[2] who attempted to rebut them in a number of lectures and books. Other German figures of the time, such as Schiller,[3] preserved an ambivalent attitude.

Herder's views were quickly taken up by other writers and soon attained a complexity undreamed of by the author of the movement. In the early nineteenth century Herder's ideas were developed by Hölderlin,[4] Hegel[5] and Fichte. It was Hegel who first asserted that reason must be identifiable with reality, thus introducing a note of pragmatism into the whirlpool of conflicting theories. It was Hegel's method which provided the plan for future theorists of the élite and the leader. Hegel recognized the need for leaders to stand out from the multitude and he termed such men 'world-historical individuals'. Their life was one of duty not just of pleasure and command. Such a person 'is not so jejune as to wish this and that and to take many things into consideration, but he is related quite ruthlessly to the One End. Thus it is also the case that they treat other great, indeed sacred, interests in a frivolous manner, which conduct is certainly subject to moral blame. But such a great form must trample underfoot many a guiltless flower, must destroy much in its way.'[6] Hegel was the first to seek out the superman; many others, particularly Germans, were to continue the search with enthusiasm.

Development of the themes of élite and leadership was slow until the publication of Darwin's theories in 1859. Darwin's theories of the survival of the fittest could be adapted not only for racial purposes, as it was in both Germany and England, but also for proving the value of aristocracy and leadership. The combination of Darwin and Gobineau (neither, incidentally, properly understood) led ultimately to Hitler's assertion that 'The best constitution and the best form of government is that which makes it quite natural for the best brains to reach a position of dominant importance and influence in the community.'[7]

If it was publication of the theses of Darwin and Gobineau that triggered off interest in élitism, the soil was already fertile. In Germany the influence of Hegel and Fichte had already been felt; in England there were those who saw the English race as an élite. Carlyle,[8] in his *Essay on the Nigger Question*, published in 1849, had viewed the interests of the English working class as paramount. The Eyre case of 1865–8[9] showed that Carlyle was supported by Dickens,[10] Ruskin[11] and Kingsley.[12] Although Carlyle was hostile to Darwinism his views were readily taken up by the Social-Darwinists. In Germany, although there was not quite the weight of literary talent in support of élitism as in England, élitist ideas made a still more profound impression. The influence of Haeckel and Lassalle[13] was particularly strong. So, too, was that of Wagner, who, in addition to his anti-Semitic outpourings, eulogized anti-democratic social patterns. In his writings, as in his operas, the heroes had to overcome the incomprehension of the common herd.[14]

However, the leading figure in the establishment of the theory of the élite and the theory of the leader was Nietzsche. Nietzsche hated what he called the 'slave morality', he hated Christianity because it promoted that slave morality, he despised the weak and the tolerant. Nietzsche declared: '. . . men are not equal: so speaketh justice. And that which I will they cannot will.'[15] Nietzsche looked forward to the replacement of mankind by a race of supermen: '. . . now love I God; mankind I love not. Man for me is a thing far too imperfect. Love of mankind would destroy me.'[16] Nietzsche, in common with Carlyle, worshipped personality and saw history in terms of the actions of great men. However, the German carried these ideas further, becoming the champion of instinct in man and violently hostile to anything that stood in the way of instinctive reactions. Thus it was he hated all forms of morality, religion and all institutions which fettered natural energies.

If Nietzsche propounded an élitist view of society in *Also sprach*

Zarathustra, in *Ecce Homo* he left scarcely any values of existing society unscathed. The reign of violence and nihilistic terror was the destiny of civilization: 'Life itself is essentially appropriation, infringement, the overpowering of the alien and the weaker, oppression, hardness, imposition of one's own form, assimilation and, at the least and the mildest, exploitation. There is neither "spirit", nor reason, nor thinking, nor consciousness, nor soul, nor will, nor truth: they are useless fictions. It is not a question of "subject" and "object", but of a particular species of animal, that prospers only under a certain relative correctness, above all regularity, of its perceptions (so that it can capitalize its experience).'[17]

Redemption could only come through the new race of Supermen. The only nobility was to be that of birth and blood, and here Nietzsche was referring to a neo-Darwinist process of selection by ability to survive, not a hereditary aristocracy. In some of his writings Nietzsche even made suggestions as to the methods of breeding that would be necessary, ruthless though they might be. 'Ah, where in the world have happened greater follies than amongst the compassionate? And what in the world hath done more harm than the follies of the compassionate?'[18] It was Nazi acceptance of these doctrines that led to the concentration camps and the medical experiments to determine the nature of Aryan genetics. The need of society for some outlet in violence, so obviously a part of Nazi doctrine, was also expressed by Nietzsche when he wrote: 'At the bottom of all noble races lies unmistakably the beast of prey, the magnificent blond beast, greedily prowling after prey and victory; from time to time an explosion is necessary, the beast must break out again, must go back to the wilderness.'[19] No other country had a writer as powerful as Nietzsche nor one whose writings seemed to provide as much comfort in the years of humiliation and anguish through which his nation passed.

Although Gobineau could qualify as an élitist of a rather special type, the French were little subjected to élitist propaganda until towards the end of the century. Espinas'[20] *Les sociétés animales,* published in 1877, enjoyed a limited amount of success, but made little permanent mark. By the 1890s the situation had changed completely, the rise of anti-Semitism was paralleled by the revival of élitist theories. Men of widely different political beliefs, Sorel, Le Bon,[21] Barrès[22] and Déroulède[23] subscribed at one time or another to these theories. Sorel was the most influential of these, at least in the long term. His true radicalism was frequently concealed by his aristocratic disdain for vulgar opinion and his devotion to anti-rationalism. Chiefly remembered for his advocacy of myths in history, and in particular his syndicalist view of the value of the general strike, he shared many of Nietzsche's views, although his élite was the proletariat. As the best of his biographers wrote: 'There is another side to his thought, a mystical, religious side, that led him to deify the proletariat, and it was the propagation of this faith, with all its emotional overtones, that truly makes him the father of communist socialism and even, in a somewhat different way, of national socialism.'[24] His belief in the role of unconscious motivation in human decision was closely similar to that of Nietzsche and proved to be a stimulus to the work of Freud.[25]

Barrès, nationalist and militaristic, was perhaps the most conventional élitist among these Frenchmen. He valued many traditional elements in society despite a temporary enthusiasm for Boulangism. Déroulède, founder of the *Ligue des Patriotes* in 1882, hastened the process by which nationalism in France was to become increasingly the distinctive characteristic of a clerico-military élite of the Right rather than an ardent revolutionary spirit of the Left, as it had been during the war of 1870-1. Déroulède's view of society became increasingly Bonapartist, that is to say he believed that it was possible for a leader with charisma to dominate the people, or, if one leader was lacking, a certain elevated section of society. Le Bon derived much of his social and political thought from Darwinism and sought to explain the disintegration of society in psychological and biological terms. His solution was, inevitably, élitist. Le Bon's influence was considerable for, as a writer, he was prolific and some of his works, particularly *Les lois psychologiques de l'évolution des peuples*, published in 1894, caught the public's imagination.

In the United States, the concept of élitism was, in a sense, built into the social and political system. Élitism was based upon two notions, both widely accepted by Americans (and sometimes by Europeans)—firstly, that the best and most adventurous spirits had migrated from Europe, and, secondly, that anyone possessing sufficient energy and determination could reach the highest peaks of society. In combination these assumptions came in practice to mean that the dominant classes were dominant because they had emerged through a rigorous process of natural selection. In the 1880s a cleric of uncertain mental stability, Josiah Strong, seized upon many of

Darwin's ideas and forced them into a framework of chauvinism, imperialism, racism and élitism.[26] One of the pioneers of sociology in the United States, Sumner,[27] wrote: 'The millionaires are a product of natural selection, acting on the whole body of men to pick out the requirement of certain work to be done ... the bargain is a good one for society.'[28] Logically enough these beliefs led to veneration for outstanding figures, indeed a strong form of the cult of the leader. This was prevalent not only in the nineteenth century when semi-religious respect was paid to figures such as Washington and Lincoln, but extended to the present age, when Franklin Roosevelt and Kennedy were also deified.

Elsewhere in the Western world the theories of Darwin, particularly those expressed in *The Descent of Man*, had much less impact. The influence of the Catholic Church restricted uninhibited comment in many countries, although in Italy there were signs of an incipient élitist party, albeit heavily dominated by conventional nationalists. Leaders of this Italian party were Corradini,[29] later to be a Fascist Party senator, Sighele,[30] De Zerbi[31] and the little-known Turiello.[32] In 1895 Sighele launched a comprehensive attack on democracy in his *Contro il parlamentarismo*, in which he also outlined a racialist-élitist alternative. Corradini followed an orthodox path from nationalism and the destiny of the race to support for fascism and its ideas of heroic leadership and élitism. De Zerbi, who was an ardent nationalist, eventually developed into a rabid racial theorist, extolling the desirability of shedding blood to purify the nation. Turiello's masterpiece was entitled *National Virility and the Colonies*, in which he not only glorified wars between nations and the extension of imperialism but also extermination of the weak, for the future lay with the strong.

The attack upon the philosophy of idealism spread throughout Europe, and as the progress of liberalism was checked by the disasters of the First World War so did the doctrine of leadership and the élite become more popular. The misty vision of Houston Chamberlain was replaced by the more precise image of Lamprecht, who wrote prophetically in 1904, 'expansion into a super-state, concentration of all social forces in the state in order to gain influence abroad, the leadership of a man and a hero; these are the most pressing requirements of the expansionist state'.[33] Spengler and Moeller van den Bruck reiterated these sentiments after 1918 and, in the economic climate of the 1920s, with increasing effect.

Not long after the war of 1914–18 the heroic leaders began to emerge. First and most splendid was Mussolini. Exaltation of his virtues was by no means confined to his own country. Cardinal O'Connell of Boston declared that 'Mussolini is a genius in the field of government given to Italy by God to help the nation continue her rapid ascent towards the most glorious destiny.'[34] Lord Rothermere declared through the columns of the *Daily Mail* in 1928 that Mussolini was 'the greatest figure of our age'.[35] In the years 1922–39 there was comparatively little criticism of Mussolini, despite increasingly capricious approaches to the solution of Italian and international political problems. He was flattered and imitated by dictators and would-be dictators throughout Europe, by Dollfuss,[36] Degrelle and Mosley.

However, it was not in Italy but in Germany that the greatest opportunity arose for the implementation of élitist theories. The influence of Haiser and Rosenberg grew ever stronger. The Nazi Party was founded upon the cult of leadership, indeed Hitler declared: 'No, my party comrades, we shall not discuss the growth of a new upper class. We shall create it, and there is only one way of creating it: battle. The selection of the new Führer class is my struggle for power. Whoever proclaims his allegiance to me is, by this very proclamation and by the manner in which it is made, one of the chosen. This is the great revolutionary significance of our long, dogged struggle for power, that in it will be born a new Herren-class, chosen to guide the fortunes not only of the German people, but of the world.'[37] It can hardly be assumed that the great bulk of the German people who voted for Hitler remained totally unaware of his views on leadership and the élite. Indeed Hitler went out of his way to put his views on these topics before the public, for he knew of their strong appeal. In a society racked by uncertainty, economic misery, declining social status and a multitude of lesser problems Hitler's answers were highly attractive. He offered the German people the opportunity to regain their self-respect by thinking of themselves as the new élite, the group destined to rule Europe and, ultimately, the world.

Hitler's own words became a source of inspiration to others. The dictators began to spawn imitators, as Le Bon had predicted in his *Le déséquilibre du monde*. In Norway Quisling[38] set up his own movement and cheerfully digested the whole of Nazi theory on race and leadership. It was the same story in many other European countries.

Fortified by example and by the existence of strong intellectual support, the admirers of élitist theory began to put that theory into practice. In conjunction with existing social pressures, nationalism, expansionism and anti-Semitism, a new and terrifying powerful impetus was given to the doctrines of leadership. The scientific analysis of Darwin and his disciples, misunderstood and misinterpreted at almost every turn, was transformed into a cult which provided all the answers for its disciples.

4 The Concept of the Totalitarian State

> 'The democratic nations must disappear, because they put their trust in illusions, more particularly the illusions of truth and justice. There is only one reality in the world—force. If you listen closely you can already hear the tramp of the Caesars who are coming to take over the world.' Oswald Spengler, *Der Untergang des Abendlandes*

Totalitarianism is one of the oldest political philosophies in the world. For a state to be deemed totalitarian it is sufficient that the functions of the state and society be the same. The nation is integrated into the state, so that elements of choice or divergence disappear, be they moral, political, economic or religious. In practice, of course, there has as yet been no totalitarian state—totality of integration has never been achieved. Even under Hitler or Stalin there was a lack of total control of the minds, and even behaviour, of their subjects. However, the philosophies of these states at those times may fairly be deemed totalitarian, for it was the ultimate purpose of their leaders to fulfil their destinies by creating the perfect totalitarian state.

Hitler wished to sweep away all opposition. Once in power he purged his party of potential rivals, abolished other political parties, controlled the press and radio and emasculated the trade unions. For a long time the army was the only significant alternative organ of power in Germany and, until the army turned against Hitler he had, in practice, total control. In the end the army (or, rather, significant sections of its officer class) revolted, but by then it was too much compromised to have any real credibility as an alternative power. Only external factors—the progress of the war, shortage of raw materials, etc.—provided any limitation on Hitler's totalitarian state between the failure of the plot of July 1944 and surrender in May 1945.

Naively, many observers have believed that the totalitarian state is not only modern in practice, but also in theory. Nothing could be further from the truth. While it is true that modern means of control and communication have facilitated the rise of totalitarianism, the ideas behind the theory of totalitarianism are extremely ancient. Franz Neumann asserted that 'National Socialism has no political theory of its own . . . has no rational political theory . . . has no theory of society . . . is incompatible with any rational political philosophy.'[1] The last of these assertions has a considerable amount of truth in it—for fascism sprang from anti-rationalist reactions. The first three assertions are false. National Socialism in particular, and fascism in general, derived important political concepts from a very ancient political tradition, reaching back into the distant past for support and intellectual justification—to Plato and Heraclitus.[2]

It should not be imagined that Mussolini or Hitler were devoted students of Greek philosophy, for they were not. In fact, they drew their inspiration from the political conditions and theories of their own times. Others who helped mould these political theories certainly studied the Greek philosophers and those who followed them; the really important factor, however, was the widespread availability as part of the cultural heritage of the nineteenth century of a political and social case for totalitarianism. Karl Popper characterized this popular and heady doctrine as a mixture of Hegel and Haeckel. Popper rightly saw Hegel's commitment to the negation of doctrines of moral responsibility and Darwin's biological discoveries (as interpreted by Haeckel) as the seminal factors in the rise of totalitarian philosophy and fascist practice. In his *The Open Society and Its Enemies* Popper saw Hegel as the link between totalitarianism of the past and of the present: 'Just as the French Revolution rediscovered the perennial ideas of the Great Generation and of Christianity, freedom, equality and the brotherhood of man, so Hegel rediscovered the Platonic ideas which lie behind the perennial revolt against freedom and reason. Hegelianism is the renaissance of tribalism.'[3]

Ignoring, for the moment, the suggestion that Hegel was the vital link in the chain of totalitarian thought, it is worth while examining briefly some of the suggestions of the ancient philosophers and their heirs so that they may be contrasted with fascist practice. Heraclitus believed in the totality of the world—that is to say, he believed that everything in the world was part of an ordered whole.[4] The modern fascist would believe that such was the goal of the totalitarian state. The enthusiasm for strife, warfare and competition was also present in Heraclitus' philosophy: 'One must know that war is common and right is strife and that all things are happening by strife and necessity.'[5] It is no accident that Spengler, Ranke, Hegel and Lassalle all showed great interest in Heraclitus; indeed, Lassalle declared that 'The heart of the philosophy of Heraclitus . . . is the true concept of what is to be, the oneness of being and non-being.'[6] The mysticism, the concepts of destiny and totality were present in the ideas of both the Greek and the German.

The views of Plato were also easily adaptable by the fascists. In *The Republic* he declared, for example, that 'those who keep watch over our commonwealth must take the greatest care not to overlook the least infraction of the rule against any innovation upon the established system of education either of the body or of the mind.'[7] The theory of the élite was put forward with great elegance: 'If a state is constituted on natural principles, the wisdom it possesses as a whole will be due to the knowledge residing in the smallest part, the one that takes the lead and governs the rest. Such knowledge is the only kind that deserves the name of wisdom, and it appears to be ordained by nature that the class privileged to possess it should be the smallest of all.'[8] Rigid control of education and the exaltation of the *Volk* (the elite) were characteristic features of Hitler's fascist experiment.

Plato's greatest contribution to the theory of totalitarianism was, perhaps, made in the discussion on the unity of the state. In this section he asked: 'Does not the worst evil for a state arise from anything that tends to rend it asunder and destroy its unity, while nothing does it more good than whatever tends to bind it together and make it one?' He answered in the following fashion: 'Are not citizens bound together by sharing in the same pleasures and pains, all feeling glad or grieved on the same occasions of gain or loss; whereas the bond is broken when such feelings are no longer universal, but any event of public or personal concern fills some with joy and others with distress? . . . The best ordered state will be the one in which the largest number of persons use these terms in the same sense, and which accordingly most nearly resembles a single person.'[9] It would be possible to continue with more quotations to show how deeply Platonic political philosophy was committed against the concept of an open society, but these seem sufficient to serve the purpose.

In Aristotle's writings there may also be discerned some basic characteristics of totalitarianism. His ideal state (the *polis*) formed a fully integrated system of social ethics, claiming their full allegiance. 'It remains to discuss whether or not the felicity of the state is the same as that of the individual or different. The answer is clear: all are agreed that they are the same.'[10] Barker, in his *The Political Thought of Plato and Aristotle* commented that 'there is in Aristotle an identification of the State and the individual. . . . It is the old thesis of Plato, that the virtues of the State are the virtues of the individual writ large.'[11] Aristotle also held significant views upon the question of slavery, which he justified not only upon biological (as did Haiser) but also on moral grounds (as did Stapel).[12] 'It is obvious that we should all agree that the inferior class ought to be slaves of the superior,' wrote Aristotle. 'And if this principle is true when the difference is one of the body, it may be affirmed with still greater justice when the difference is one of the soul; though it is not as easy to see the beauty of the soul as it is to see that of the body.'[13]

If the ancient philosophers made important contributions to the concept of totalitarianism it must also be remembered that at this distance in time misinterpretation of their writings is easy. Heraclitus was essentially concerned with cosmic rather than political forces. It is not altogether clear to what extent his views on the *cosmos* would have been applicable to the *polis*. Plato foresaw no conflict between the interests of the individual and those of the state in its ideal form, for he believed that the characteristics of a state were derived from those of its citizens. However, the ideas of Plato, Heraclitus and Aristotle were interpreted by Hegel, Spengler and other totalitarians and are, therefore, important. Nor were they always misstated—it must not be forgotten that Plato and Aristotle believed that the rulers of their states were entitled to deceive their subjects. This in itself was a major contribution to totalitarian theory.

Despite the existence of totalitarian elements in the political philosophies of Plato and Aristotle there remained one important theoretical limitation. These philosophers, and their medieval heirs, set their ideal states in a moral framework, though this moral framework was entirely different in the pre- and post-Christian eras. It is to Machiavelli[14] that one must look for the first convincing public justification of amorality. Machiavelli had little respect for the benevolence of human nature or for the notion of the invincibility of reason. Machiavelli insisted that political power alone was the end of the state; force and deceit were legitimate political tactics to aid the preservation of power. In *Il Principe* he was writing of course for a particular situation in conditions of great social turbulence. His ideas were, however, to have a much greater impact on post-Renaissance political thought. In the *Discorsi* he captured the essence of the totalitarian outlook when he asserted that 'when it is a question of saving the fatherland, one should not stop for a moment to consider whether something is lawful or unlawful, gentle or cruel, laudable or shameful; but, putting aside every other consideration, one ought to follow out to the end whatever resolve will save the life of the state...'[15]

Although in the case of Machiavelli's writings there was no mystical content, only a harsh pragmatism, political thinkers did not at once abandon the medieval framework of religion and geomancy. Bodin,[16] whose definition of sovereign power as inalienable and absolute heralded a new approach to politics, was nonetheless pre-occupied with the task of expressing his revolutionary doctrines in conventional form. For Bodin order was the paramount goal of the state, lest there grow up 'a licentious anarchy which is more dangerous than the most violent tyranny on earth'.[17] In the twentieth century Rosenberg developed this theme to its logical conclusion in his *Ordenstaat*.

In the middle of the seventeenth century Hobbes[18] threw off the last shackles of the medieval approach to political analysis of the form of the state. Hobbes it was who justified the utilitarian power of the sovereign state. In his *Leviathan* Hobbes depicted the state as essentially non-moral; the significant test of the standing of a state was whether or not its power was effective. The totality of sovereign power formed a fundamental part of Hobbes' argument: '... because every Subject is by this Institution Author of all the Actions, and Judgments of the Soveraigne Instituted; it followes, that whatsoever he doth, it can be no injury to any of his Subjects; nor ought he to be by any of them accused of Injustice ... every particular man is Author of all the Soveraigne doth; and consequently he that com-plaineth of injury from his Soveraigne, complaineth of that whereof he himselfe is Author; and therefore ought not to accuse any man but himselfe; no nor himselfe of injury; because to do injury to ones selfe, is impossible.'[19] The full implications of the power conceded to the sovereign were not clear to Hobbes, except in the context of his own times. It was impossible for him to conceive of a twentieth-century version of his sovereign power, unlimited by moral laws and actively assisted by contemporary techniques. Yet Hobbes did recognize how all-embracing the power of his sovereign would have to be. He saw that the sovereign would be obliged to control education and the propagation of news and opinions. He saw too that there could be no intermediary authorities in the state, unless such were controlled by the sovereign rather than acting as a check on his power. The impersonality of the twentieth-century authoritarian and totalitarian state was, no doubt, far from Hobbes' ideal, but his definitions and arguments in the hands of others proved to be a strong encouragement for its development.

During most of the eighteenth century the views of Hobbes and his predecessors were rejected by political thinkers. Two schools of thought, representing the conservative and liberal traditions, held sway in Europe, both of them valuing rationalism as a method of procedure. By the end of the century the impact of the French Revolution had wrought great changes in the ranks of those who had followed Locke, Voltaire, Hume, Spinoza or Rousseau. A revival of old ideas, suitably adapted to meet new conditions, took place. At the head of those who sought a new approach to politics (albeit based upon some ancient concepts) was Hegel.

In a devastating indictment of Hegel, Popper wrote: 'There is nothing in Hegel's writing that has not been said better before him. There is nothing in his apologetic method that is not borrowed from his apologetic forerunners. But he devoted these borrowed thoughts and methods with singleness of purpose, though without a trace of brilliancy, to one aim; to fight against the open society, and thus to serve his employer, Frederick William of Prussia. Hegel's confusion and debasement of reason is partly necessary as a means to this end, partly a more accidental but very natural expression of his state of mind.'[20] This judgement, harsh though it is, is fundamentally sound. In any consideration of Hegel's importance as a political philosopher it must not be forgotten that he acquired much of his fame and influence from the adoption of his views as the official philosophy of the state of Prussia. The testimony of Schopenhauer[21] and Schwegler[22] has made it clear that political influence and personal importance were strong elements in Hegel's approach to the analysis of political problems. Had Hegel's influence not been so all pervasive his selfish domination of the Prussian school of philosophy after his elevation to the Chair of Philosophy at Berlin in 1818 would perhaps later have been challenged as strongly as was Wordsworth's acceptance of Poet Laureate by Browning:

Just for a handful of silver he left us,
Just for a riband to stick in his coat.[23]

There was no German Browning to launch such a savage attack on Hegel precisely because his officially approved philosophy had been so effectively penetrative not only in Prussia but in much of the rest of Germany as well. The reservations and criticisms put forward by Schopenhauer were even suppressed for a long time and, when finally revealed, were derided as un-German, which in the period of the Empire was fatal to their acceptance.

It was Hegel who introduced into the mainstream of German political thought those elements of earlier approaches to the subject that are most easily recognizable as totalitarian. There are elements of mysticism, universalism, aristocracy, anti-democracy and utilitarianism, synthesized into a strange and incoherent, but powerfully attractive, philosophy. Hegel's approach to politics was so readily adaptable to modern conditions that it was embraced not only by the fascists but also by the Marxists. Characteristically, Hegel was hostile to the prevailing (eighteenth-century) concepts of reason and freedom. His hostility was to become deeply rooted in both German society and indeed in fascist ideology. I. A. R. Wylie recorded a conversation in the 1930s between herself and a young Nazi, which revealed the deep influence of these concepts among Germans: 'I remember an illuminating conversation I had with a young Nazi after Hitler's rise to power. He expressed himself as ecstatically happy because he said he was at last free. "Free from what?" I asked in astonishment. "Free from freedom", he retorted exultantly.'[24] In one phrase was summarized the major gift of Hegelianism to fascism—the liberation of the mind from rationalism and freedom of expression.

Some of the concepts which Hegel took from the ancient philosophers have already been mentioned. It was Hegel who exalted the state as the end and sole purpose of existence: 'In the existence of a Nation, the substantial aim is to be a State and preserve itself as such,' or 'The State is therefore the basis and centre of all the concrete elements in the life of a people: of Art, Law, Morals, Religion and Science.'[25] The affinity of these ideas with Platonic philosophy is clear. In the case of fascism the connection may be traced through crude nineteenth-century nationalism and Social-Darwinism to exaltation of the *Volk*. The duty of the folk was to create the all-powerful state. Hegel was not responsible for the perversion of the concept of spirit into race, but he provided the framework. Furthermore, by asserting that 'The State must be comprehended as an organism,'[26] Hegel revived the (again essentially Platonic and Aristotelian) concept of the organic state. Popularized in the late nineteenth century, this idea came to form an essential element in fascist theory. Writing in 1934, Rosenberg declared: 'We know that a genuine outlook on life cannot confine its expression to theoretical principles or confessions of the soul, but that it must assume a form of cult . . . capable of expression only in the true state.'[27]

If Hegel advocated the abasement of the individual before the state he also attributed certain other qualities to the state which were to have almost as profound an effect upon the formation of fascist ideology. Hegel saw the state as an organism free from moral obligation, the enemy of all other states, committed to warfare against other states and subject only to the test of success. Many of these ideas may be clearly discerned in the writings of Plato, Aristotle, Machiavelli and Hobbes. They may also be found in contemporary fascist ideology, most notably among German writers. The notion of the totalitarian state, sustained by commitment to strife and free from conventional moral assumptions concerning the conduct of affairs both internal and external, was to reach its highest peak with the mysticism of Stapel, who declared 'The God of Our Force and Our Pride, far from being a guarantor of objective morality, even has the function of easing Our Path wherever it suits us to wrong others or those among Us who are less genuinely We.'[28] Stapel's theory was plainly a cover for the right of the state and its leaders to undertake any action deemed necessary, irrespective of individual or corporate rights, and, further, designed to sanctify such oppression in the name of religion.

There has already been some discussion of the role of Hegel in the promotion of the concept of the heroic leader, but this digression on his influence would be incomplete without some further reference to this topic. Hegel's exaltation of the 'world-historical person' was tailor-made for adaptation not only by nationalists who created their own Valhalla of heroes in virtually every Western country at the end of the nineteenth century, but also for acceptance among the totalitarians. At one time or another Hitler, Mussolini, Marx, Lenin, Trotsky, Stalin and Khrushchev have been held up to admiration as 'world-historical persons'. Hegel unconsciously predicted the political tactics of Hitler when he wrote: 'In public opinion all is false and true, but to discover the truth in it is the business of the Great Man. The Great Man of his time is he who expresses the will of his time; who tells his time what he wills; and who carries it out. He acts according to the inner Spirit and Essence of his time, which he realizes. And he who does not understand how to despise public opinion, as it makes itself heard here and there, will never accomplish anything great.'[29] The strength of this aspect of Hegelianism was greatest under Hitler, when the exaltation of the leader reached new heights. 'Whoever feels a glimmer of faith in God himself, must recognize Providence in the drastic and evident preference shown for the German cause because of the Führer, which should teach even a blind man.'[30] Finally, the streak of nihilism in Hegel's philosophy, the outlook on the world of the gambler, attained great popularity among modern German thinkers, including Jaspers,[31] Heidegger,[32] Husserl,[33] Gogarten[34] and Scheler.[35] It was also a feature of fascism, reflected in Hitler's and Mussolini's wild ventures in foreign policy and Hitler's ultimate commitment to the idea of the 'Götterdämmerung'.

Many of those whose names have already been mentioned in connection with the fascist concepts of the leader, the race and the élite derived inspiration from Hegelianism. The relevance of the writings of Hegel to the infiltration of totalitarian concepts into German political, cultural and literary life can easily be imagined. The list of those indebted to Hegel stretches from Lassalle to Rosenberg; it includes some thinkers, although not many, outside the German tradition, Pearson, Kidd and Sorel among them. Totalitarianism in Germany also drew inspiration from sources other than Hegel and his disciples, as it did in other areas of Europe.

In Germany another influential figure whose ideas were not markedly affected by those of Hegel was Müller.[36] A romantic conservative, he expressed his views in a way that was highly acceptable to some of the reactionary figures of his time, most notably Metternich. His enthusiasm for conservatism and romantic nationalism did not extend, however, to supporting the anti-Hardenberg clique, which was at that time influential in the internal politics of Prussia and instrumental in supporting the elevation of Hegel to the Chair of Philosophy at Berlin.

Müller also believed in the organic nature of the state—he saw it possessing essentially personal elements, being a living and growing body. He saw nationalism and individualism as almost interchangeable concepts in his organic state. It was a view that was to be revived in the 1920s by Aall, [37] the political mentor of Quisling, and was to gain a number of important adherents. 'So long as state and citizen serve two masters', wrote Müller, 'so long as hearts are internally rent by a double desire, the one, to live as a citizen in the state . . . the other, to extract himself from the whole civil order, to cut himself off from that same state along with his domestic and whole private life and with his most sacred feelings, indeed even with religion'[38] it would be impossible to achieve real freedom. This doctrine was readily acceptable to the fascists.

It would be easy to trace the influence of Hegel and his disciples in the development of totalitarian thought in much more detail, in particular with reference to Germany. However, the point is, I think, already clearly demonstrated and only one contribution to fascist theory needs some further explanation. That contribution is the theory of the organic state, the very fundament of modern totalitarianism. It was this theory, classically put forward by Plato and Aristotle, and given contemporary relevance by Hobbes, Bodin, Machiavelli and Hegel (all of whom were writing in times of social and political upheaval), that was the subject of most attention by writers and thinkers of the nineteenth and twentieth centuries.

The abasement of the individual and the exaltation of the state were necessary premises for belief in the state as an organism. The theory attained a new dimension in the era of the Social-Darwinists with the advent of the biological state. Theorists asked themselves, in the light of Darwin's theories of evolution and survival (or rather in the light of their interpretation of Darwin's theories), the question: How might the state be best equipped to survive as a successful entity? To the state was attributed a life cycle of its own, with certain types of state doomed to extinction as the march of evolution passed them by. It was a doctrine to which Hitler himself subscribed: 'The day of the small states is past, in the west as well. I shall have a Western Union too, of Holland, Flanders, Northern France, and a Northern Union of Denmark, Sweden and Norway.'[39]

The foundations for Hitler's views had been laid by the Social-Darwinists. Pearson, for example, urged that 'every citizen must learn to say with Louis XIV, "*L'état c'est moi*".'[40] It was Pearson too who declared that 'An offence against the state ought to be looked upon as a far graver matter than the offence against the individual.'[41] Pearson was a true totalitarian in that he saw the state and society as ideally identical and he carried this view to its logical conclusion. 'No tribe of men work together unless the tribal interest dominates the personal and individual interest at all points where they come into conflict', he declared.[42] It is easy too to see how Pearson thought of the state as a biological entity once it is appreciated that he not only identified the state and the individual but also continually empha- sized the importance of good hereditary qualities. The successful state would be that populated by those races destined to be successful and by appropriate measures that state could secure its own future through the operation of essentially biological factors. Pearson believed in the necessity of certain eugenic methods—the elimin- ation of the unfit, the insane, the mentally handicapped, the criminal and the workshy. Pearson was hostile to medical efforts to preserve lives: 'The death-rate is selective, and if we check Nature's effective but rough-shod methods of race betterment, we must take her task into our own hands and see to it that the mentally and physically inferior have not a dominant fertility.'[43] In Pearson's state, therefore, the sovereign power was indeed 'as great as possibly men can be imagined to make it'[44] for the state had the power to limit and to permit life—it had taken on a biological existence of its own.

Pearson's views were popular among Social-Darwinists, although many did not hold them in such extreme form. Bernhardi, for example, wrote that 'the social system in which the most efficient personalities possess the greatest influence will show the greatest vitality in the intrasocial struggle'.[45] In the case of Bernhardi these views were connected with the biological progress of the nation as a whole: 'The State will not be to us merely a legal and social insurance office, political union will not seem to us to have the one object of bringing the advantages of civilization within the reach of the individual; we shall assign to it the nobler task of raising the intellectual and moral powers of a nation to the highest expansion . . . this highest expansion can never be realized in pure individualism. Man can only develop his highest capacities when he takes his part in a community, in a social organism, for which he lives and works.'[46]

Bernhardi's opinions were derived not only from the Hegelian tradition and the influence of the Social-Darwinists but also from the writings of Treitschke[47] and Schleiermacher.[48] Treitschke was immensely influential during the period between 1874 and his death in 1896 and his veneration for the state was reflected in his teaching. 'The State', he wrote, 'is a moral community. It is called upon to educate the human race by positive achievement, and its ultimate object is that a nation should develop in it and through it into a real character; that is, alike for nation and individuals, the highest moral task.'[49] Earlier in the century, Schleiermacher had taught that 'The State alone can give the individual the highest degree of life.'[50]

The doctrines of subjugation of the individual and the glorification of the state as a biological entity reached their apogee not in Germany but in Sweden. During the opening years of the twentieth century Kjellén[51] fully developed this concept and was, through his anti-Russian and anti-British writings, soon widely read in Germany. In his *Staten som livsform*, published in 1916, he declared that 'States are super-individual organisms which are as alive as individuals, although they are far larger and far more powerful in their processes of development . . . theirs alone is the power to reproduce the life cycle in its highest form.'[52] Consequently Kjellén's view of society was essentially opportunistic, amoral, anti-democratic and anti-individualistic. It was, in fact, the theoretical precursor of the fascist totalitarian state.

5 Fascism and Nationalism

'Either a German God or none at all. The international God of Christendom is a patron of the Treaty of Versailles. We cannot bend our knees to a God who neglects us for the French.' Ernst Niekisch, *Gedanken über deutsche Politik*

The influence of nationalism upon fascist doctrine and practice has been so strong that fascist and nationalist have on occasion been regarded as virtually interchangeable terms. There are, of course, strong similarities between certain aspects of many fascist and nationalist movements. The nationalists and the fascists of both Italy and Germany believed in forward and aggressive foreign policies. They believed in annexation and *Machtpolitik*. The same was not true in all countries. In Spain, for example, the fascists prompted Franco to enter the Second World War, but his natural prudence and his evaluation of the national interest dictated a course of action other than submission to the will of Hitler. His decision was strongly supported by nationalists in Spain, and as the war progressed their viewpoint was vindicated and Franco's fascist allies were removed from their positions of influence. Franco was able to achieve in Spain what von Papen had failed to do in Germany —the suffocation of the fascists by the nationalists.

However, it is not the purpose of this study to place on record the manifold differences between fascism and nationalism, but rather to examine the significant contribution made by nationalism to fascist theory. Those who contributed handsomely to fascist theory included many ardent nationalists, among their number Spengler, Herder, Novalis,[1] Pearson, Kidd, D'Annunzio, Mackinder, Milner and Déroulède. All these men were ardent supporters of nationalism; this, in turn, generated passions which could be, and were, seized upon by the fascists. Milner, for example, declared that 'This country must remain a great Power or she will become a poor country; and those who in seeking, as they are most right to seek, social improvement are tempted to neglect national strength, are simply building their house upon the sand.'[2] Sentiments of this type were conventionally nationalistic, but Milner also asserted that 'I have emphasised the importance of the racial bond. From my point of view this is fundamental. It is the British race which built the Empire, and it is the undivided British race which can alone uphold it.'[3] Nationalism opened the way for the fascist theory of the race in a fashion that was much more comprehensible to the general public than the Social-Darwinism of Pearson.

The views of Milner were reflected in almost every European country in the last few decades before the First World War. In some countries much nationalist sentiment was generated over colonies; this was true of Germany, France, Britain and Italy. In other states nationalist sentiment increased because of poor economic or social conditions or because of domination by alien races; some, or all, of these factors were present in Norway, Poland, Finland, Serbia and Romania. To this formidable movement could also be added historical antagonisms between nations, such as those between Germany and France, or Russia and Austria-Hungary. Nationalism was on the march and was a major factor in contributing to the outbreak of war in 1914. As Lloyd George recollected: 'The populace caught the war fever. In every capital they clamoured for war. The theory which is propagated today by pacifist orators of the more cantankerous and less convincing type that the Great War was engineered by elder and middle-aged statesmen who sent younger men to face its horrors, is an invention. The elder statesmen did their feckless best to prevent war, whilst the youth of the rival countries were howling impatiently at their doors for immediate war. I saw it myself during the first four days of August 1914. I shall never forget the warlike crowds that thronged Whitehall and poured into Downing Street, whilst the Cabinet was deliberating on the alternative of peace or war.'[4]

In view of the disappointments suffered by most, if not all, of the European nations during and after the First World War it should hardly be a cause of surprise that nationalism emerged in many cases stronger and more belligerent from the disasters of 1914–18. Conventional nationalism of the nineteenth-century style became an essential basis for fascist movements—particularly within the defeated countries.

The principal components of the new and vigorous nationalism were, in general, resentment against the terms of the Versailles settlement, fear of violent economic or social revolution while admitting to a desire for activity and change (in ways that were not Marxist) and a search for that comradeship and community of interest that had existed in wartime. In due course all these features were adopted by fascist parties in varying degrees, according to national and party political requirements.

Resentment against the existing pattern of international affairs was an extremely consistent feature among fascist groups in the inter-war years. In Italy, for example, dislike of Versailles was particularly strong and it was this which enabled D'Annunzio to take action over Fiume. Of this incident Vincenzo Nitti, son of the Italian premier, wrote: 'My father was by no means dismayed at D'Annunzio's action, because it gave him more strength in his international dealings.'[5] Nitti himself later admitted as much by stating that he 'was aware of the fermenting spirit in the north, and I instructed General Diaz to make a close inspection of the occupation zone'.[6] After Mussolini's accession to power nationalism was still further glorified, becoming the major elements in Italian diplomacy. The bombardment of Corfu, the acquisition of Fiume, the resettlement of Libya, support for Dollfuss, the occupation of Abyssinia, assistance for Franco, the seizure of Albania and the invasion of Greece followed one another in rapid succession between 1923 and 1940. All of these actions were justified in terms of a rabid nationalism: 'We have a right to Empire', said Mussolini, 'as a fertile nation which has the pride and will to propagate its race over the face of the earth, a virile people in the strict sense of the word.'[7] It is almost unnecessary to stress the common intellectual origins of Mussolini's and Milner's robust patriotism.

Nationalism in Germany, already strong, was given a further stimulus by the humiliations of the post-war period. The occupation of the Ruhr by the French in 1923 did little to secure the international position of the French in the short term and much to weaken it in the long term. But rampant nationalism was already abroad before the French blunder. As early as March 1919 the 'Juni-Klub' had been founded by a number of nationalist intellectuals.[8] The club sponsored a weekly journal, *Das Wissen*, which received regular contributions from among others Ernst,[9] Grimm,[10] and Moeller van den Bruck. The weekly paper was hostile to Versailles, Marxism, the Weimar Republic (and, indeed, democracy in any form) and the League of Nations. Spengler characterized the Treaty of Versailles as being 'not intended to create a state of peace but to organize the relation of forces in such a way that this aim could at any time be secured by fresh demands and measures.'[11] In 1928 Hitler was quite explicit in his opposition to the settlement: 'National honour requires that we restore the borders of the year 1914. This is the tenor of the discussions at the beer evenings which the representatives of national honour hold on all sides.'[12]

On countless occasions Hitler reiterated his hostility to the League and to the political and territorial framework which it was designed to protect. So effective was his voice that he gained the tacit support of Hugenberg[13] and his Nationalist Party. In fact, it was not until Hugenberg made an alliance with Hitler in the autumn of 1929 that the Nazi Party began to make a significant advance. In the election of 1928 the Nazis secured only 12 seats in the Reichstag, in 1930 the number rose to 107. Hitler and Hugenberg held in common a detestation of Versailles, the Dawes and Young plans and Locarno. In consequence Hitler was given much favourable publicity in the Hugenberg-controlled news media. The Nazi/Nationalist line appeared daily in *Der Tag* and the *Berliner Lokalanzeiger*, weekly in *Die Woche*, and at regular intervals in the *Ufa Wochenschau*, the weekly newsreel. Nationalism made an unequalled contribution to the popularity of Nazism and its political success. Thyssen,[14] who financed the Nazi Party at a critical time in its fortunes, later admitted that he did so solely because of his wish to defeat the Young Plan.[15] Without the strong nationalistic sentiment of the Germans, composed of a blend of pre- and post-war frustration, Hitler's movement would never have enjoyed success.

The hostility to the settlement so obviously apparent in Germany and Italy was also a feature of politics in many other European nations. In those which had suffered under the terms of the settlement, such as Hungary, Austria or Bulgaria, the reason was plain enough. If men such as Horthy and Seipel contrived to stifle the worst excesses of nationalist sentiment they were successful only at the price of a gradual erosion of liberty in their countries. Dollfuss, in 1920 an ardent adherent of the Bardolff circle,[16] was compelled to accept the internal political influence of the semi-fascist Heimwehr in order to maintain an independent line in foreign affairs. The Arrow Cross in Hungary held a similar position in relation to the regency of the pro-British Horthy.[17]

Less comprehensive, perhaps, is the rise of nationalist and then fascist sentiments in countries which had benefited from the territorial settlement. In Romania the Iron Guard, which became the third largest party at the election of 1937, relied heavily upon a tradition of romantic nationalism. In spite of large acquisitions at the end of the war (Transylvania, Bessarabia and confirmation of the Dobruja) Codreanu[18] and his colleagues wished for still more. This nationalism, in conjunction with agrarian radicalism, formed the basis of fascist appeal in Romania in the 1930s. Poland, also a great beneficiary from the treaty, was, by 1939, ruled by men of at least quasi-fascist inclinations. In part this may be seen as a nationalist response to the threat of a resurgent Germany, in part as a nationalist and anti-Marxist response to the revival of Russia. Disappointment at the failure to secure Polish claims to the whole of White Russia had led to war, thus further inflaming nationalist and irredentist feelings. Additionally, in the words of Paderewski, the failure to be ceded Teschen 'dug an abyss between the two nations',[19] and led to the sad participation of Poland in the rape of Czechoslovakia two decades later. If Poland's foreign policy in the inter-war years (and some aspects of her internal policy) bore a marked resemblance to that of fascist powers, this similarly was largely derived from the frustration of pent-up nationalist ambitions immediately following independence.

Even in neutral countries the rise of fascism may be seen as an offshoot of nationalism. In the cases of Clausen[20] in Denmark and Quisling in Norway their nationalism sprang not only from traditional and romantic sources but also from specific grievances. Clausen believed that Denmark should have received more German territory at the end of the war. Such small popularity as he ever attained in Denmark was derived almost entirely from his vigorous beating of the nationalist drum. Ironically, his poor performance in elections forced him to abandon conventional methods of obtaining power and to seek German aid. The support of the Nazis was only given at the price of Clausen's abandonment of his territorial claims, thus knocking away his last domestic political prop. In Norway Quisling moved more gradually towards a fascist position. In his early years as a politician he derived popularity from several conservative groups through his insistence on strong defence forces and the cession of part of Greenland by Denmark. By 1939 he was a thoroughgoing fascist, believing that war had already been declared between nationalism and Bolshevism and that the starting point of this struggle was 'the march on Rome of 28 October 1922, when the

European revolution began—against democracy, Bolshevism and the mastery of the Jews'.[21] In Quisling's case, as in so many others, nationalism was but the prelude to fascism.

The second major reaction of nationalists in the inter-war years was fear of violent social or economic change. This, too, played a large part in creating a suitable climate for the rise of fascism. It is, perhaps, Italy which furnishes the best example. In Italy the nationalists and fascists shared common ground in their hostility to neutrality during the period 1914–15. Despite the reverses sustained by Italian armies during the war these groups did not entirely lose their influence. The possibility of collaboration was badly shaken by the fascist conference at Milan in 1919, at which Mussolini not only demanded Dalmatia but simultaneously advocated support for the League of Nations, already a body much detested by nationalists. However, internal developments soon produced an end to these differences. In November 1919 the Socialists won 156 seats and the Catholic Popular Party 100. Their opposition to centrist government made the advent of a stable administration impossible. The failures of Nitti and Giolitti[22] in the following eighteen months convinced both nationalists and fascists that Italy was about to fall victim to a revolution. Mussolini was astute enough to capitalize upon the fears of Giolitti and in May 1921 secured some 35 seats as part of the governmental electoral list. The aura of respectability the fascists gained through association with Giolitti was to stand them in good stead during the troubles of the next year or so.

The inability of Giolitti, Bonomi[23] and Facta[24] was abundantly demonstrated during the following months. Every failure and every increase in unrest among the Italian people (often encouraged by the fascist squads) led to an increase in Mussolini's influence. Albertini,[25] editor of the *Corriere della Sera*, even advocated the elevation of Mussolini to power in the summer of 1922. At one time or another the fascist campaigns against socialist revolutionaries were supported not only by conservative but also radical and liberal newspapers.[26] The general strike of August 1922 provided Mussolini with still more support. Agrarian, financial and industrial interests flocked to support the fascists as it became increasingly clear that their privileged positions were threatened. Mussolini's mouthpiece, *Il Popolo d'Italia*, received heavy investment as fascist counter-revolutionary forces swung into action in Leghorn, Ancona, Genoa and Milan. The prominent industrialist, Pirelli, later admitted that on 26 October 1922, just a few days before the fascist seizure of power, a committee of the General Confederation of Industry visited Mussolini at the offices of the party newspaper. The pressures which pushed Thyssen and other German industrial barons in the direction of support for Hitler in the early 1930s were discernible in Italy a decade before. Hatred of the 'Reds' was a characteristic common to many Italians who were not members of these interest groups and Mussolini's firm stand against Marxism (exemplified by the immobilization of socialist propaganda through the destruction of *Avanti*) won him much support in the autumn of 1922. The road was thus paved by essentially conservative forces for Mussolini's coup of October. Just as Kerensky underestimated the danger from the Left in 1917, so the decent, middle-of-the-way democrats in Italy failed to perceive the danger from the radical Right only five years later.

Many of the same points are illustrated by the history of Germany in the 1920s and early 1930s. For all his much-vaunted commitment to a party of the working class, in practice Hitler reflected the social attitudes of the middle and upper classes. In 1922, for example, he refused to allow his supporters to participate in a Bavarian rail strike. At no stage did he advocate the expropriation of the property of the House of Hohenzollern. Hitler soon saw the political advantages he could draw from an exhibition of social and economic conservatism. The most tangible form of support consisted of subsidies from the important industrial barons of Germany. After 1929 Hitler was to receive, according to Funk[27] and Schacht,[28] considerable aid from industry, banking and big business. If Hitler never became their puppet, as Thyssen, Vögler[29] and Krupp[30] had hoped, he was, nevertheless, much indebted to them for their support at a vital stage in his career.

The unrest of 1918–19 and the financial collapse of the 1920s were instrumental in engaging the interest of business circles in Hitler in the period after 1929. Kirdorf[31] wrote to Hitler, after attending a Nazi Party rally, saying: 'Anyone who was privileged to attend this session will, even though he may doubt or decisively reject particular points in your party programme, nevertheless recognize the importance of your movement for the rehabilitation of our German fatherland and wish it success.'[32] His views were echoed by other magnates—for them Hitler represented a way of controlling the unrest which grew as the unemployment figures spiralled. Their error of judgement was repeated by conservatives in other countries.

In France conditions were rather different. The innate conservatism of the Third Republic hindered challenges mounted against orthodox governments in the inter-war years. The administrations supported by the *Cartel des Gauches* and the Popular Front were not distinguished by a radical approach to the solution of problems: indeed, dominated by figures such as Briand[33] and Chautemps,[34] their policies could hardly be anything other than gradualist. Despite the soothing effect of this approach, antipathy to violent social or economic change was generally influential in the rise of many, though not all, fascist movements. It was during 1933–4 that this fact became clear for the first time. The administrations of Boncour[35] and Daladier[36] had tried to pursue orthodox deflationary policies, in the face of socialist opposition as sterile of ideas as the British Labour Party of 1931. The complex political manoeuvres of allegedly radical groups eventually disgusted a sizeable party of deputies (mainly members of Blum's[37] Socialist Party) who, led by Déat,[38] Marquet[39] and Renaudel,[40] openly rebelled. This rebellion provided a major impulse to the development of fascism. The following year, in February 1934, fascist movements became a serious threat to the French government; thereafter the situation worsened rapidly.

In the elections of 1936 the Socialist Party manifesto declared that 'It is now two years since the appearance of fascism in France. The great capitalists, dogged by declining profits and threatened privileges, fear lest the suffering people free themselves from their domination. They have subsidized and managed fascism.'[41] While this manifesto can scarcely be regarded as a totally detached survey of the developing political situation, there was a strong element of truth in its denunciations. The inability of the Centre and the Right to protect business interests from the rising tide of popular discontent led a number of industrialists and bankers to seek help from the various fascist groups. The differences between conservatism and fascism thus became blurred. Leaders of the rebellion of 1933 soon took their place at the head of essentially conservative social forces. Déat, writing in 1942, stated: 'The necessary rescue of our middle classes will be one of the happiest effects, one of the most essential objectives of the National Revolution.'[42] The views of Déat were also those of Drieu la Rochelle,[43] Maurras,[44] Brasillach[45] and Bardèche.[46] Their blend of élitism, social conservatism and intellectual revulsion from Marxism proved to be a powerful political force in the France of 1934–40.

Elsewhere in Europe the fear of revolution promoted the cause of fascism. In most of Eastern Europe the combination of a fear of Russia and a hatred of Marxism was far too powerful for democratic, non-fascist governments. The history of Austria, Hungary, Romania, Poland, Greece and Finland in the inter-war years indicates how widely the conservative forces of society fell under the spell of fascism. In Austria, for example, Chancellor Seipel naively declared that 'In our land of Austria there exists a mighty mass movement which wants to liberate democracy from party rule. The pillars of this movement are the *Heimwehr*.'[47] In Austria too the apologists for fascism were stimulated by a genuine intellectual movement, led by Spann[48] and Steidle.[49] Elsewhere in Eastern Europe the fascists adopted the conservative social philosophies of peasant societies for their own purpose.

In Norway Quisling's party initially attracted support through his identification with movements of a patriotic and conservative nature. In the first few years of the existence of *Nasjonal Samling* it received backing from figures such as Aadahl,[50] the editor of *Nationen*. However, the poor quality of Quisling's leadership and his early avowal of support for fascism frightened many Norwegians away before they were too heavily committed to withdraw.

It was in Spain that resistance was perhaps strongest to any idea of social revolution and it was in that country that the fascists seemed at first to enjoy an unequalled triumph. However, as the history of the *Falange* in the period after 1936 makes clear, it was the conservative forces, led by Franco, who used the fascists rather than becoming fascist tools themselves. In 1936 the formation of the National Bloc (in which the *Falange* played no part whatsoever) was in appearance a concession to fascism, but as Robles[51] correctly pointed out, the responsibility for the growth of fascism was governmental inaction in the face of a revolutionary situation. The Socialist, Prieto,[52] admitted to similar views. Therefore, many of the Spanish who supported the *Falange* were by preference conservative in their political instincts, and it was the political skill and determination of Franco that first contained and then stifled the threat from the radical Right. Thus Spanish conservatives were not, in the end, confronted with the wreck of all their hopes, as was to happen in Italy and Germany. In Spain traditionalism and conservatism proved too strongly-based for the fascist storm to uproot.

The comradeship of the First World War also proved an

important link in uniting nationalist and fascist sentiment. It was, of course, Hitler who was the most effective in his use of this feeling. After 1918 there were many war veterans who sought to revive the comradeship of the war years as compensation for the economic indignities to which they were then subject. The genesis of the *Freikorps* proved also to be the critical factor in the survival of Hitler's party and in its formative years. Many of Hitler's future associates, Göring,[53] Röhm[54] and von Epp[55] began their political careers as discharged and discontented soldiers. The importance of these men has been singled out for attention by Alan Bullock, who wrote: 'When Hitler began to build up the German Workers' Party, Röhm pushed in ex-*Freikorps* men and ex-servicemen to swell the Party's membership. From these elements the first "strong-arm" squads were formed, the nucleus of the S.A. In December 1920 Röhm had persuaded his commanding officer, Major-General Ritter von Epp—himself a former *Freikorps* leader and a member of the Party—to help raise the sixty thousand marks needed to buy the Party a weekly paper, the *Völkischer Beobachter*. Dietrich Eckart provided half, but part of the rest came from Army secret funds. Above all, Röhm was the indispensable link in securing for Hitler the protection, or at least the tolerance of the Army . . . without the Army's patronage, Hitler would have found the greatest difficulty in climbing the first steps of his political career.'[56]

Hitler was always aware of the value of this link for the purposes of propaganda. He was always willing to pose for pictures together with Hindenburg, just as he was eager to co-operate with Hugenberg and his party of nationalists. The notion of association with the military was always attractive to Hitler—he spoke frequently of his duty to protect the interests of those who had made such sacrifices during the war. In 1928 he said: 'The only part to which an army can have an inner relationship in a militarily valuable sense, is that nationally conscious core of our people which not only thinks in a soldierly manner out of tradition, but rather, out of national love, is also the only part ready to wear the grey tunic in defence of honour and freedom.'[57] This theme proved a constant source of success to Hitler in his attempts to convert conventional nationalists to support of his movement. In the end, with the aid of Oskar Hindenburg, even the haughty and aloof President himself was brought to believe that regeneration for Germany might be achieved through the agency of national socialism.

There were similar, though perhaps less strong, tendencies in Britain, France and in Italy. In all these countries programmes based upon remembrance of the sacrifices and the comradeship of the war had some attraction for the disillusioned of the inter-war years. Outside Germany feeling was most strong in Italy, where Badoglio[58] warned Nitti, 'a kind of fever has invaded the younger elements of our army, due, it seems, to a dislike of ordinary, grey, everyday life and the constituted order; a scorn for goodness and saving, for the family, tradition, religion.'[59] D'Annunzio spoke of 'A million dead, a million wounded, together with the ruin of our finest provinces of the Veneto . . . Now, having borne the yoke of war, we bear the yoke of peace.'[60] In his biography of D'Annunzio, Anthony Rhodes has aptly summed up the discontent of the times, upon which fascism flourished: 'As in all the European countries, there was the problem in Italy at the end of the war of demobilizing soldiers who, in economic terms, are simply large masses of men accustomed to receiving food from the state. There was the difficulty of converting war industry to peace uses. There were strikes; the devaluation of the currency; a civil service still partially disorganized; a housing shortage. Ex-soldiers always remember the advantages of military life, when the war is over—the regular salary, the jolly companionship, the songs, the stars on the sleeves, the gun at the belt, the feeling of Power. Moreover, one of the great Italian maladies has always been *reducismo*, soldiers returning from some great enterprise that has made the state, and who now believe they can unmake it. The Rubicon has never really been forgotten in Italy.'[61]

If there was discontent in Italy there was some unrest too in the undefeated and undeprived countries, such as Britain and France. Herbert Tint saw dissatisfaction among ex-servicemen and a desire for a return to the ideals of 1914–18 as important factors in the rise of fascism in France; 'the generation which grew to maturity after the war could be just as hostile to the parliamentary system as was a large number of ex-servicemen. The former resented the privileged position claimed by the latter, and tended to despise them for the flabbiness with which they used it, while the ex-servicemen felt let down by the politicians who had promised them the things politicians promise servicemen.'[62] The *Croix de Feu*, which became an important and influential organization in the 1930s, was originally founded in 1927 as an ex-servicemen's movement. Under De La

Rocque[63] it rapidly became anti-communist and anti-democratic. By 1934 it had a membership of over 30,000 and, according to Alexander Werth, 'De La Rocque, a friend of Foch and Lyautey, had many friends in the army, and he also has many Reserve officers among his followers.'[64] In the period after 1940 the army was to prove a fertile breeding ground for collaborators and fascist activists. The *Action Française* and the *Croix de Feu* had done their work well.

The patterns of political development in Italy, Germany and France were common, allowing for local mutations, throughout most of Europe. The spirit of comradeship made itself felt through organizations and parties claiming to represent the interests and the ethos of the war veterans. In all of these countries para-military bodies came into existence, ranging in size from the S.A. in Germany to the Legion of the Archangel Michael in Romania. Large or small these movements were symptomatic of a deep malaise in and dissatisfaction with contemporary society. What was more natural than that the warriors should return to war ? The fascist movements were more suitably placed to take advantage of this upsurge of nationalist feeling than were the conventional parties of the Right. In some cases the fascist leaders seized their opportunities with gusto, in others their failure was abject. In Austria, Dr Pfrimer,[65] a leader of the *Heimwehr*, was able to declare in 1930 that 'On all sides the conviction was evident that here in Austria only fascism could now save us. We must make an attempt to seize power; then the leaders of our movement will be able to take the business of government in hand.'[66] In Scandinavia, on the other hand, the legions never marched—the post-war conditions were never the same as those in countries that had participated in the war. In Hungary the fascist movement was controlled by energetic conservative forces. Only in Britain were there opportunities in theory which in practice never arose. The conservatism of the British electorate, if it contributed to appeasement in the 1930s, had in credit a total repudiation of nationalist-fascist militancy. This factor alone made it easy for nationalism to become a rallying call for anti-fascist action by Britain in 1939, when in most of the rest of Europe vigorous nationalism had proved to be a Trojan horse through whose agency the fascist legions had been admitted to the citadel of power.

6 Fascism and Socialism

'Socialists have to inculcate that spirit which would give offenders against the State short shrift and the nearest lamp-post.' Karl Pearson, *The Moral Basis of Socialism*, p. 307

The socialist aspects of fascism are those most commonly ignored, perhaps because they conflict with the convenient explanation that fascism was a right-wing movement. However, the conventional Marxist interpretation of fascism is as erroneous on this subject as was Marx's theory of increasing misery among the industrial proletariat in Western Europe. But, if the Left overlooked the socialist items in fascist programmes, so too did the Right. In view of the origins of many of the leading fascists of the twentieth century this is a surprising phenomenon in itself. Hitler came from a poor Austrian family and lived for some years in squalid conditions in Vienna. Mussolini was first an ardent socialist; so too were Déat and Mosley. Doriot was a leading member of the French Communist Party and Quisling's Bolshevik sympathies in the 1920s were well-known in Norway. It would be a further cause of surprise if some of the original ideas held by these leaders had not affected their later political programmes. In fact, there was a considerable socialist content in the programmes of most of the fascist movements, particularly in Germany, where the party was, after all, the Nationalist Socialist German Workers' Party.

Yet the connection between fascism and socialism is much older than the twentieth century. Mussolini and Déat merely followed an already well-trodden path. It was the conditions of the time which made the intellectual mixture of socialist ideas and conventional nationalist assumptions so significant. The distress of the post-1918 period provided the incentive for millions to swallow the heady brew of fascism, which was a combination of nationalism and socialism. In 1877 Virchow asked a German audience to 'picture to yourself the theory of descent as it already exists in the brain of a socialist. Ay, gentlemen, it may seem laughable to many, but it is in truth very serious, and I only hope that the theory of descent may not entail on us all the horrors which similar theories have actually brought upon neighbouring countries.'[1] Virchow's vision was to receive substance in Germany only sixty years later and, already, it had begun to take shape in the brain of Dühring.

Socialist ideals were particularly influential among European intellectuals during the second half of the nineteenth century. The enthusiasm of many, however, was dimmed by excesses during the revolutionary days of the Paris Commune and by the regular assassination of leading figures in the world of politics. Liberals could understand, if not approve, the attacks on autocratic politicians from Eastern Europe, but attempts on the lives of politicians in France, England and the U.S.A. were more difficult to explain away. Many self-confessed socialists began to turn away from internationalism towards a new and fiercer form of nationalism.

In Germany there already existed a readily assimilable doctrine, composed of a strange mixture of socialism, romanticism and nationalism. As early as the beginning of the century Müller had declared that if the state were ever to be totally united then it would be necessary for all property to be held in common. He saw money as an expression of the human need for a relationship with others, but his socialism was intended to preserve the national state and not to fulfil international goals.[2] Later in the century Rodbertus,[3] while challenging the proletarian movements of his time, nonetheless sought to achieve a goal which he defined as national socialism. As Butler has pointed out: 'His own prescription for the solution of the social problem would appear to have been regulation by the state of all wages by means of authoritative arbitration between employers and workers.'[4] It is perhaps merely an unfortunate coincidence that this device is held in such high regard by progressive economists in the second half of the twentieth century; indeed, it is now widely believed to be essential to the achievement of planned economic growth and prosperity.

Much more influential than either Müller or Rodbertus was Lassalle, who was mainly concerned to make converts to his ideas among members of the working class in Berlin. In the early 1860s he became a prominent figure, founding the General German Workers' Union in 1863. Lassalle even corresponded with Bismarck, urging him to grant universal suffrage: 'Give me universal suffrage and I will give you a million votes,'[5] he wrote, and again: 'Above all I blame myself for having forgotten yesterday to impress once more upon you that eligibility for suffrage must be conferred upon positively all Germans. An immense means of power.'6 Socialism thus began that distinctive journey towards nationalism and the deification of power so characteristic of fascism in Germany.

Lassalle's movement continued after his premature death under the leadership of three minor German politicians, Schweitzer, Hasenclever and Hasselmann. The scope of this group's activity and influence was, as time passed, much reduced by the group being outmanoeuvred at the Gotha Congress of 1875. However, in the 1880s Stöcker revived and rejuvenated some of Lassalle's ideas, but he was in turn supplanted by the man who was to become the leading figure in the contemporary national socialist movement—Dühring. Dühring's socialism was based not upon the Marxist class struggle but on the self-sufficiency, both economic and ethical, of the national community. His views, because of their anti-Semitic colour, often conflicted with those of his precursors on important points. The influence of Dühring's *Wert des Lebens* was profound, not least upon philosophers, like Spengler, and a whole generation of immensely powerful businessmen and industrialists.

These views were further developed by Naumann in the early years of the twentieth century. He sought to unite conservative authority and social reform in a new theory of political progress. Bismarck had, of course, already taken some hesitant steps in this direction some two decades earlier. Naumann was acutely conscious of the process of change and development within German society and industry during the period 1870–1914. He wrote that 'Despite all the strife between the many associations of opposing interests we are yet a uniform folk, grandly uniform in this method of constituting practical life and work. To this end national schools, universal conscription, the police, science and socialist propaganda have worked together. We hardly know that fundamentally we all wanted the same thing: the regulated labour of the second capitalistic period, which can be described as the transition from private capitalism to socialism, provided only that the word socialism is not taken to mean the phenomenon of purely proletarian big-business but is broadly understood as folk-ordering with the object of increasing the common profit of all for all.'7 The essentially anti-liberal nature of Naumann's vision of society foreshadowed actual developments in Germany during the inter-war years.

It was, however, in the period of the Weimar Republic that

socialist ideas became firmly established in nationalist mythology. The path of German socialism in the 1920s was particularly tortuous, being complicated by the political decisions forced upon its leaders in the period immediately preceding and following the Versailles settlement of 1919 and by the economic problems of the whole era. Ebert,[8] Noske[9] and their political allies were not socialists in the sense that they feared revolution at least as much as the parties of the Right. In January 1919 this 'socialist' government permitted the murder of Liebknecht[10] and Luxemburg;[11] in June of the same year Bernstein[92] was strongly censured by his 'socialist' party colleagues for venturing to express some mild criticism of German leadership during the recent war. The spirit of nationalism had so thoroughly penetrated the socialist parties that these events were tamely accepted, almost without challenge. More slowly and at first almost imperceptibly, the spirit of socialism continued to penetrate the nationalist parties.

Within the Nazi Party one of the most influential figures at this time was Feder,[13] one of whose lectures proved instrumental in the recruitment of Hitler. Feder denounced the greed and the weaknesses of capitalism in a terminology composed of a mixture of Marxist and anti-Semitic concepts. If it was principally anti-Semitism that initially attracted Hitler it should not be imagined that socialism had no appeal to the former inhabitant of the Viennese slums. The party programme of 1920 included a number of statements of intent which might generally be regarded as impeccably socialist in origin. Among these were the nationalization of major industries and industrial combines, the abolition of unearned income, profiteering and speculation, the provision of equal opportunities in education and employment, the institution of workers' shops, acknowledgement of the right to work and encouragement of work in the communal interest. In addition, of course, there were many elements of crude nationalism, including the formation of a large standing army, the abolition of the Versailles settlement and the concept of a Greater Germany. However, the fact remains that the Nazi Party in its period of growth and development as a social force (1920–33) was fully committed to a social and economic programme of a radical nature. If the influence of Feder soon waned it was replaced by the still more powerful and active pressure of the Strasser brothers[14] and Röhm.

Among those who helped create a favourable intellectual climate in Germany from which Hitler and his party were able to benefit were some influential figures, notably Spengler and Rathenau.[15] The essentially anti-liberal concepts of these two men played a significant part in the promotion of the apparently impossible reconciliation between nationalist and socialist views of society. Rathenau, according to Butler, had great influence upon Drexler and, through him, on the newly-born N.S.D.A.P. It was Rathenau who popularized the concept of rule by a popular élite. Mann[16] had a very similar vision, conceiving of the future of German politics as 'the thing which would be necessary, which could be finally German, would be a union and pact between the conservative idea of culture and the revolutionary idea of society'.[17] Spengler had much in common with Mann and Rathenau: he saw the true significance of socialism not in 'Marx's theory but Frederick William I's Prussian practice which long preceded Marx and will yet displace him—the socialism, inwardly akin to the system of Old Egypt, that comprehends and cares for permanent economic relations, trains the individual in his duty to the whole, and glorifies hard work as an affirmation of Time and Future'.[18] Socialism thus became in Spengler's eyes 'not a system of compassion, humanity, peace and kindly care, but one of will-to-power'.[19] Socialism became a philosophy of toughness, resourcefulness, brutality and scepticism. Its internationalism was replaced with the concept of domination by one race over all other peoples.

Moeller van den Bruck echoed many of these viewpoints when he wrote that 'when we talk now of German socialism, we do not of course mean the socialism of the social democrat . . . neither do we mean the logical Marxist socialism which refuses to abandon class war and the Internationals. We mean rather a corporative conception of state and economics which must perhaps have a revolutionary foundation, but will then seek conservative stability.'[20] This view was prophetic, for only a few years after his death the clash between the orthodox socialist opinions of Otto Strasser and the national socialism of Hitler came to a head. The year 1930 witnessed the final breach. Otto Strasser accused Hitler of wishing 'to strangle the social revolution for the sake of legality and your new collaboration with the bourgeois parties of the Right'. Hitler retorted: 'I am a Socialist, and a very different kind of Socialist from your rich friend, Reventlow. I was once an ordinary working-man. I would not allow my chauffeur to eat worse than I eat myself. What you understand by Socialism is nothing but Marxism. Now look: the great mass of

working-men want only bread and circuses. They have no understanding for ideals of any sort whatever, and we can never hope to
win the workers to any large extent by an appeal to ideals. We want
to make a revolution for the new dominating caste which is not
moved, as you are, by the ethic of pity, but is quite clear in its own
mind that it has the right to dominate others because it represents a
better race: this caste ruthlessly maintains and assures its dominance
over the masses.'[21]

The electoral success of Hitler and the total failure of Strasser and
his breakaway group during the next few years demonstrated the
relative attraction of the rival socialist appeals to the German people.
If Hitler's socialism contained many features common also to Virchow's nightmare these features were reflected in the mirror of
public opinion. When Hitler came to power he implemented a
number of socialist measures; he was not just a drawing-room
revolutionary. If the impetus for fulfilment was, perhaps, prompted
by Schacht (for the soundest of economic reasons rather than for
doctrinal reasons), this was of little import. Hitler certainly saw that
socialist measures designed to improve the lot of the working class in
Germany, far from being incompatible with his national socialist
views, were, in fact, an essential element, based on a well-established
social and cultural foundation.

Socialism as a force conducive to the rise of fascism was by no
means confined to Germany. In France, Italy, Spain and England as
well as in much of the rest of Western Europe the connection between socialism and fascism may also be seen. In France it was
particularly strong, although the fascist movement there had a less
direct link with the culture of the past. Fascism in France was
essentially a product of the 1930s and a movement for young men,
although many of them derived inspiration from the French radical
tradition. Among these may be numbered Bardèche, Brasillach,
Déat, Doriot and Drieu La Rochelle. They shared a common hatred
for bourgeois society and for its values, they wrote and spoke in
bitter terms of the dull conservatism which was the prevailing
political characteristic of the Third Republic. They often chose to
appeal to the radicalism of the past—to Proudhon[22] and Sorel. It is
impossible not to recognize the immense contribution of radical and
socialist thought to their political development and hence that of
their movements or parties.

In part, confusion about the precise nature of the contribution of socialism to fascism in France has stemmed from the actions of the fascists during the period 1938–45. Because many of them collaborated with the Germans during the war and still more had advocated a policy of appeasement before the outbreak of war, it has been too easy to dismiss French fascism as a phenomenon of conservatism. As has been suggested already the French fascists were violently hostile to this *immobilisme*. If Laval[23] believed that 'One must never start out on the Right. It is bad. You should start from the Left . . . as far left as possible . . . and then keep coming back, coming back . . . not too fast. One must begin by inspiring fear. It is a condition of success',[24] this was certainly not the motivation of the fascists. There was, however, confusion among the ranks of the fascists themselves, which has also helped to obscure the true origin of much of their ideology. This confusion was not derived merely from rivalry but from a basic divergence of opinion about the nature of fascism. Some saw French fascism as a movement based upon the national traditions of the past; others believed it to be a French version of a European revolutionary phenomenon. When anti-Semitism became a serious element in fascist ideology, after Blum's succession to the premiership in 1936, one group saw anti-Semitism as a contemporary continuation of the anti-Semitism of the Dreyfus era. Others saw anti-Semitism as a proletarian upsurge of feeling against monopolistic big business, cartels and plutocracy. The socialist content in fascist ideology was much greater among adherents of the latter point of view.

On occasions the revolutionary note was particularly strong. The fascist programmes contained promises to control the activities of big business and to promote the welfare and social aspirations of the working class. Perhaps this is not wholly surprising in view of the Communist background of Doriot and the Socialist origins of Déat. Drieu La Rochelle, who was extremely hostile to contemporary society, wrote in 1934, 'fascism is a socialism of reform, indeed a reformist socialism which has, apparently, more energy and fire than the traditional parties'.[25] In the same year Doriot, who had just defected from the Communist Party because of its failure to make common cause with the Socialists, declared his belief in the proletarian offensive against capitalism and advocated political unity of the Left. Doriot clung to the cause of revolutionary defeatism long after it had been abandoned by the parties of Blum and Thorez.[26] It is significant too that his political base was Saint Denis, in the Paris

Nord region. In 1938 Doriot was still criticizing the Popular Front for its failure to suppress cartels and monopolies.[27]

The views of Drieu La Rochelle and Doriot were shared by others. Déat believed that fascism would end the class struggle and that the end of totalitarianism was 'reconciliation and the inauguration of class co-operation'.[28] Indeed, he predicted political representation through syndicalist corporations and there was some attempt made to implement this proposal under Vichy. In the cases of Bardèche and Brasillach there is considerable evidence of that particularly pernicious form of élitism found amongst Western European socialists. Brasillach in his *Je suis partout* regularly denounced servility among the working classes and urged the development of individual qualities of leadership which would benefit the masses. Brasillach was an intellectual, a romantic and as much of a socialist as Pearson. Bardèche, related by marriage to Brasillach, shared many of his points of view. More fortunate than the other French fascists, he survived both the war and the peace and in 1961 published *Qu'est-ce que le Fascisme ?*, in which he reiterated many of his opinions held in the 1930s. Again and again he placed great emphasis on the role of socialism in the formation of fascism, seeing it as essentially a marriage between socialism and nationalism and drawing attention to contemporary phenomena such as Nasser's Egypt. If in practice socialist ideals were rarely achieved by French fascists this was perhaps more a function of the problems caused by the operation of fascism under wartime conditions than an admission of the impracticability or inappropriate nature of socialism as a constituent element in fascism.

In Italy Mussolini was acutely aware of his socialist background. He was conscious of the fact that he had worked as a manual labourer in Switzerland and had been treated as a common criminal by the police. During the years 1909–14 it seemed as if he had shaken off his early commitment to anarchism. He became a socialist editor and organizer, clinging to a rigid Marxist ideology which was only destroyed under the pressure of war. Before this stage had been reached, however, Mussolini had attempted, in partnership with the anarchist Malatesta,[29] to organize a revolutionary 'red week' in June 1914. Can it be assumed that Mussolini's radical youth was totally insignificant in the development of his political ideas only a decade or so later ?

On close inspection it becomes fairly clear that there was a large element of socialist and revolutionary idealism incorporated in Italian fascist doctrine. The party contained a number of left-wing syndicalists who, in the 1920s, became staunch supporters of the corporate state. They wished to see a popular state organized from the base and in constant contact with the people. They expected fascism to lead to the abolition of class conflict and the achievement of social justice. As late as December 1924 it was suggested that Mussolini should give up his governmental post and fight new elections as 'the chief of a revolutionary party'.[30] Mussolini, however, was astute enough to muzzle these potential critics by providing them with a version of guild socialism. While some industries were returned to the control of business interests, others, such as the railways, were left in the control of the state. In all probability the influence of Farinacci and his followers was so strong in this particular case that the Duce would not have dared to de-nationalize the railways.

Mussolini was himself very eager to demonstrate the socialist elements in his corporative state. In 1930 a National Council of Corporations was set up, as a result of which workers were placed in suitable categories, designed to assist the protection of their interests. In 1933 it was suggested that at some point in the future this deliberative assembly would replace the Chamber of Deputies. In 1939 this actually happened. In fact, as the end of the fascist régime approached so did the fascists revert towards the radical party programme of 1919. Starace[31] and his supporters became ever more influential. Government expenditure rose sharply, nearly tripling between 1935 and 1940. During the whole period of the depression the policy of heavy government spending was fairly effective in controlling unemployment, which was rife in most other Western European countries. Labour disputes were settled by a process of compulsory arbitration and not by the traditional strikes and lock-outs. Welfare services, controlled rents and subsidized holidays were introduced for certain sections of the community.

Mussolini did not, therefore, entirely ignore his socialist background during his years of power. He was not just the tool of conservative and business interests. In his first administration he included a Socialist as a minister, and in 1924, after his election victory, apparently even contemplated a return to normal political life. In the summer of that year he was ready to include two Socialists in his cabinet, a scheme which fell to the ground only after the ill-advised murder of Matteotti.[32] However, Mussolini's post-war socialism always bore the stamp of the élitism of Pareto[33] and Mosca.[34] In this sense his commitment to socialism was very limited and thus proletarian participation in government was restricted. Mussolini cared for the backing of the Italian people and was prepared to introduce radical measures on a limited scale in order to ensure a certain level of support. The influence of socialist ideas on the fascists in Italy was, therefore, largely to contribute to the enlightenment of fascist pursuit of self-interest. Once in power there occurred a rapid retreat from revolutionary dogma.

In Britain socialist contributions to fascist doctrine were derived from two major different sources—social-imperialist and social-Darwinist theories prevalent at the close of the nineteenth century, and, secondly, the political beliefs of Mosley. Among the most vocal socialists could be found a group, principally among the Fabians, dedicated to the ideal of national socialism. Prominent among this group were Webb[35] and Shaw.[36] It was no accident that Spengler later wrote: 'Materialism, Socialism and Darwinism are only artificially and on the surface separable. It was this that made it possible for Shaw in the third act of *Man and Superman* (one of the most important and significant of the works that issued from the transition) to obtain, by giving just a small and indeed perfectly logical turn to the tendencies of "master-morale" and the production of the Superman, the specific maxims of his own Socialism. Here Shaw was only expressing with remorseless clarity and full consciousness of the commonplace, what the uncompleted portion of the *Zarathustra* would have said with Wagnerian theatricality and woolly romanticism.'[37] Spengler saw Shaw as one of the seminal figures in the development of what was subsequently dubbed fascism, and he was right to do so.

A number of the Fabians linked together nationalist expansion and domestic reform as the principal aims of a progressive society. During the Boer War Shaw urged Fabian support for a 'lofty and public-spirited Imperialism'[38] against Hobson's[39] wish that 'the Society disassociates itself from the Imperialism of Capitalism and vain-glorious Nationalism'.[40] The supporters of Shaw won the day, later justifying their position in a tract entitled *Fabianism and the Empire*. The next few years were to witness a fusion of national and socialist aspirations and the emergence of a type of pre-fascist ideology. Shaw's goal was 'the effective social organization of the whole Empire, and its rescue from the strife of classes and private interest'.[41] Webb and Shaw called for a party of national efficiency, to include in its programme the reform of housing, elimination of slums, the reform of education and the poor law and the establishment of a minimum wage. All these might be described as socialist measures and they attracted support from a wide cross-section of men in public life. Wells[42] in his *The New Machiavelli* drew a bold and clear picture of the élitist social assumptions made by many of the members of this group, known as the 'Coefficients'. They were socialists, but socialists tormented by doubt as to the capacity of the people to make the right decisions.

As may easily be imagined the influence of a group which included in its membership not only Webb and Shaw but also Mackinder, Wells, Amery[43] and Maxse[44] was profound. Its effect on the newly-born Labour Party was much greater than was realized at the time, and in the 1930s many of the disasters suffered by that party may be attributed to failure to resolve the internal contradictions that had been in existence almost from the movement's foundation. The contradictions were well illustrated in the person of Blatchford,[45] who regarded himself as a working-class patriot. In his *Merrie England* he set out to promote the interests of the working class; he believed in progressive education, the protection of industries, the abolition of poverty and the strength of agriculture. In France Blatchford would have found many who sympathized with his views, both before and after the war of 1914–18, but in England the structure of politics hindered the growth of a dynamic fascist party based upon national efficiency and expansion and socialist reform.

It was Mosley who attempted to channel the immense volume of intellectual national socialism into a fascist party. In his attempt he imposed the mark of his own personality and his own beliefs upon English fascism. Without Mosley fascism in England was a plant doomed to perish through lack of sustenance. If Mosley came from a conventional conservative background his political aspirations were influenced much more by his experience as a socialist in the years 1924–30. Mosley was not merely a member of the Labour Party he was also generally regarded as being on the left-wing of the party, being a member of the I.L.P. It was Mosley, together with Strachey[46] and Cook,[47] who advocated the policy of the living wage. It was Mosley who drew up plans for the nationalization of the banks, advocated state planning and the elimination of a pool of unemployed. In 1925 Mosley and Strachey worked together on a pamphlet, later expanded into a book, entitled *Revolution by Reason*. The socialist was well to the fore in this work: '. . . poverty, when joined to our modern capacity to produce, is a twice-cursed evil. It curses the humble because they cannot buy. It curses the great and the rich because they cannot sell.'[48] Mosley believed in the necessity of state control of the economy, in particular the regulation of the money supply. He believed in governmental compulsion of industry, both employers and workers, in order to advance the national interest. These views, slightly altered, were to form the basis of his fascist corporative doctrines in the 1930s.

In the mid-1920s Mosley was the darling of the miners and of other militant forces within the party, though he was not so popular with the leadership. In 1929 he became Chancellor of the Duchy of Lancaster in the newly-elected Labour Government. In office as in opposition he tried to put forward consistent ideas for betterment of social conditions. In January 1930, being extremely dissatisfied with the performance of the administration, he put forward a series of economic proposals, later known as the 'Mosley Memorandum'. When this document was rejected by the party leadership Mosley resigned. A failure later in the year to convince the annual party conference that he was right led to his withdrawal from the party and the foundation of the New Party in early 1931. Among those who greeted the formation of this political group with sympathy were the future Lord Nuffield,[49] Bevan,[50] Brown[51] and Oliver Baldwin.[52] The claim that the party sought to incorporate talent from all the old parties was not mere bravado.

The New Party based its political platform upon the *Mosley Manifesto*, which claimed that its signatories surrendered 'nothing of our Socialism'.[53] In the circumstances of 1931 its emphasis on unemployment and the disastrous economic climate gave the manifesto particular appeal. In May 1931 the main aim of the movement was seen to be the ending of class conflict: 'The trouble is not that we have a class war so much as that we have a class deadlock. That deadlock must be unlocked. We shall try to do something towards unlocking it', wrote C. F. Melville.[54] Others were less confident of Mosley's devotion to the causes of political endeavour or the achievement of socialism. Beatrice Webb wrote: 'I doubt whether Mosley has the tenacity of a Hitler. He also lacks a genuine fanaticism. Deep down in his heart he is a cynic. He will be beaten and retire.'[55]

Bevan was more worried by the likely political future of the New Party. 'Where is the money coming from? Who is going to pay? Who is going to call the tune? I tell you now where you will end up ... as a Fascist party.'[56]

The fascist movement in England thus owed its formal existence to Mosley, at least as a powerful force. There had been earlier attempts to create fascist parties, notably by Miss Linton-Orman[57] in 1923 and Leese[58] in 1929. The formation of Mosley's British Union of Fascists in 1932 killed all the rival groups as well as sounding the death knell for the New Party. As time passed and as the prospect of power faded, owing to the strong grip of the National Government upon the country, the fascists gradually abandoned more and more of their radical programme, ending as a discredited political splinter group. In its origins it was socialist and revolutionary in outlook, owing a great deal not only to Mosley's commitment to socialism but also to a climate of opinion generally in favour of social progress. Rather unusually it is perhaps possible to identify the moment when Mosley's enthusiasm for the proletarian revolution evaporated. In April 1931 at a by-election in the constituency of Ashton-under-Lyne, faced with a hostile crowd, Mosley declared: 'That is the crowd that has prevented anyone doing anything in England since the war.'[59] Mosley too had taken the path of élitism which led inexorably to fascism.

The patterns visible in the major Western European countries were repeated elsewhere. In Norway Quisling attempted to found a political movement based upon a heady mixture of romanticism, racism, socialism and nationalism. In 1930 Quisling wrote that the important political task in Norway was 'to free the fatherland from class warfare and party politics, and to carry through national revival and unification upon a basis of sound political and economic principles'.[60] Later that year Quisling attacked another politician for wishing 'to hit the workers on the head and then to talk to them from a bourgeois standpoint'.[61] Quisling's enthusiasm for socialism and revolution, already dulled by his experiences in Russia in the 1920s, was finally stilled by his experiences as Minister of Defence between 1931 and 1933.

In Spain the fascist party claimed to be a movement based on syndicalism, deriving support from the long tradition of Spanish anarchism and radicalism. While Primo de Rivera[62] led the party this claim enjoyed considerable validity. The *Falange* would not participate in the mass grouping of the Right in the elections of February 1936. It was dedicated to ending the class struggle, parties, parliamentary democracy, separatism and social injustice. Many of its aims were socialist and, initially, many of its members were drawn from the ranks of the socialists, revolutionaries and syndicalists. The decline of the *Falange* into a meaningless, arid and conservative, corporative movement stemmed largely from the political skill of General Franco. Even before the end of the civil war its pretensions as a radical organization had been destroyed.

Eastern European politics repeated many of the characteristics of the West. Fascism owed much in virtually every European country to socialism as well as nationalism. When the orthodox parties of the Left or Left-centre came to power in the years between the wars disillusionment was frequently rapid, although the desire for radical change remained. Fascist parties stepped in to fill the breach, drawing upon diverse traditions to attract popular support. Agrarian radicalism was one of the most common political movements in these economically underdeveloped areas and fascism usually traded upon these and similar political phenomena. That fascist movements once in power almost everywhere deserted the radical principles they had formerly supported must not be allowed to obscure the fact that socialist ideas nearly always played a major part in the achievement of that power. It was socialism too which frequently provided the intellectual justification for the élitist theories adopted universally by fascist leaders.

7 The Influence of Militarism

'War means the state in its most actual growth and rise—it means politics.' Professor Max Scheler, *Der Genius des Krieges und der deutsche Krieg*

The contribution of a tradition of militarism to the rise of fascism seems so obvious that it would scarcely seem to warrant further investigation. However, this first impression is somewhat misleading It is true that the trappings of militarism formed a prominent part of fascism in action; the most vivid memories of fascism are usually associated with violence by military or para-military bodies. Mosley's Blackshirts, Mussolini's *Squadristi* and Hitler's Stormtroopers seem, in retrospect, to have projected a true public image of the philosophy behind the organization. Wherever fascist movements existed in Europe there could be found violence, militarism and an army of the streets. It mattered little whether the country was monarchist or republican, from Northern or Southern Europe, Catholic or Protestant, Latin, German or Slav. All those with fascist movements paid some respect to militarist traditions and these traditions in turn contributed to the rise and development of fascism.

However, when a closer examination is made the strength of militarism in the various countries is seen on the whole to have been weak. Perhaps then the association of fascism with violence and para-military bodies had more to do with the social upheavals of the years after 1918 than the strength of militarism as part of the cultural life of most countries prior to 1914. It is true that war fever existed in many major European countries in 1914, but was this strictly militarism? Was England, for example, a militarist country even in the years immediately preceding the outbreak of the Great War? The answer seems, fairly obviously, no. There was an abundance of anti-German feeling and a rather better-concealed hostility towards Russia. There was a strong pride in Empire and a belief in the destiny of England, but these, while helping to create the atmosphere of the Boer War and the Dreadnought Crisis, hardly amounted to a vigorous tradition of militarism. Indeed, there is a considerable volume of evidence which points in a very different direction. The debate about the introduction of conscription was to cause a bitter rift within the Liberal Party, even during the war itself. Before the war only a few had advocated the introduction of conscription or the need for a larger standing army. The Labour, Liberal and Conservative parties were opposed to schemes put forward by Blatchford and Lord Roberts.[1] These and other enthusiasts for a larger military establishment were treated with a kind of indulgent contempt by the influential sections of government and society. Indeed, it seemed as if politicians in England had taken Taine's[2] prophetic words to heart: 'Universal military service by conscription, with its twin, universal suffrage, has mastered all Continental Europe—with what promise of carnage and bankruptcy for the twentieth century!'[3]

It is difficult to discover a true tradition of militarism in the countries of Scandinavia, Belgium, the Netherlands, the Baltic states or most of Eastern Europe. In Italy there were many bombastic claims to imperial greatness and advocacy of army colonialism, but these hardly amounted to a militarist tradition. In fact, Italy was of all European countries the one perhaps least suited to the habit of marching towards the sound of gunfire, as both D'Annunzio and Mussolini were to discover. In Spain and Portugal there existed the tattered remnants of past imperial glories, but political leaders of all shades of opinion in these countries were well aware of their military weakness. Nor were these patterns essentially different in the whole of the rest of Europe, except for Germany and France. In these two countries alone was there a real tradition of militarism and it was only their fascist movements which derived appreciable benefit from deep-rooted cultural and intellectual commitments to militarism in their societies.

The militarist tradition was most strong in Germany. Militarism had formed an essential part of German intellectual and cultural history during the whole period of Prussia's rise to ascendancy in Germany. The effect of constant military success was visible at an early date to acute political observers: 'We shall wait in vain for the awakening in our land of that public spirit possessed by the English and the French and other nations, unless we imitate them in defining for our military leadership certain limits and restrictions which they must not disregard,'[4] wrote Baron Stein.[5] Not all those who were anxious to advance the cause of Germany by military means were militarists in the wider political sense. This was true of Clausewitz,[6] the father of military science, for he appreciated that war should be used by policy-makers rather than be used as an instrument to create policy. It was his view that 'The first, the grandest, and most decisive act of judgement which the Statesman and General exercises is rightly to understand ... the War in which he engages, not to take it for something, or to wish to make of it something, which by the nature of its relations it is impossible for it to be.'[7] Clausewitz, like Darwin and Gobineau, was to be the victim of much misinterpretation in the years immediately preceding the war of 1914–18.

During the nineteenth century there grew up in Germany a tradition of deference to the army, born out of respect for its highly successful leaders. The century 1814–1914 may be dubbed, not entirely inaccurately, in terms of international politics, as the age of the Prussian general. As this was the age also of great German expansion and development it is hardly surprising that militarism penetrated education at all levels. Only a few men inside Germany and not many more outside perceived the dangerous path that was being followed by the leaders of Germany. It was too late to write in 1914 that 'inspired and led by Prussia, Germany has staked its whole existence, its presence and its future, on military power'.[8] The war of 1914–18 as well as that of 1939–45 owed its inspiration, at least in part, to the pernicious influence of militarism.

Among the leading figures in Germany who valued militarism were Ranke,[9] Treitschke, Bernhardi, Banse[10] and Nietzsche. In his *Politisches Gespräch* Ranke makes his character, Friedrich, say '. . . if the community is to become universally significant moral energy is above all necessary . . . you will not be able, as a matter of fact, to recount the names of many important wars from which it may not be deduced that true moral energy was the determining factor in victory'.[11] The tradition of Ranke was made still more honourable by the Saxon, Treitschke, who wrote in the period of Germany's greatest military successes. As well as being an advocate of the abasement of the individual before the state he also observed that 'Just where, to the superficial observer, war appears as something brutal and inhuman, we have learnt to discern its moral force . . . a man must sacrifice not only his life, but also the profoundly just and natural impulses of the human soul. He must renounce his whole ego for the sake of the great patriotic idea. Therein lies the moral sublimity of war.'[12] Treitschke had enormous influence. As Professor of History at Berlin from 1874–96 his lectures helped determine the political outlook of those who were to lead Germany into war in 1914 and into the disaster of 1933. It was Treitschke too who demanded that the state be run by strong men, who were either loved or detested, and not by political mediocrities. Nietzsche strongly influenced Germans of a slightly later generation, in particular those Nazi Party members who were interested in the occult and mysticism. It was Nietzsche who wrote: 'Ye have heard men say: Blessed be the peacemakers; but I say unto you: Blessed are the warmakers, for they shall be called, if not the children of Jahwe, the children of Odin, who is greater than Jahwe,'[13] or, again, 'Do ye say that a good cause halloweth even war? I say to you a good war halloweth any cause.'[14]

The growth of fascism among military men was fostered by two writers of considerable reputation—Bernhardi and Banse. Bernhardi, a soldier himself, produced an intellectual justification for the feelings so commonly held in the German Army before 1914. It was he who asserted that there was danger in 'the false and ruinous notion that the maintenance of peace is the ultimate object, or at least the chief duty, of any policy'.[15] He also proclaimed that 'Military service not only educates nations in warlike capacity, but it develops the intellectual and moral qualities generally for the occupations of peace. It educates a man to full mastery of his body, to the exercise and improvement of his muscles; it develops his mental powers, his self-reliance and readiness of decision; it accustoms him to order and subordination for a common end; it elevates his self-respect and courage, and thus his capacity for every kind of work.'[16] Bernhardi also advocated the introduction of a very positive educational policy: 'The government will never be able to count upon a well-armed and self-sacrificing people in the hour of danger or necessity, if it calmly looks on while the warlike spirit is being systematically undermined by the Press and a feeble peace policy preached, still less if it allows its own organs to join in with the same note, and continually to emphasize the maintenance of peace as the object of all policy. It must rather do everything to foster a military spirit, and to make the nation comprehend the duties and aims of an imperial policy.'[17] The views of Bernhardi not only strengthened the aggressive elements on the German General Staff, thus contributing to the outbreak of war in 1914, but through their implementation in the fields of education, propaganda and publicity insidiously moulded the political outlook of a whole generation of the German people. It was this generation to which Hitler was able to appeal so successfully.

The military reverses of 1914–18 strengthened rather than weakened the spirit of militarism. The overthrow of the Empire and the advent to power of the Social Democrats confirmed many Germans in their belief that Bernhardi had been right in his condemnation of toleration for those who preached peace policies. In this time of despair the writings and lectures of another militarist became extremely popular. The fascist nature of Banse's views is clear: 'How utterly different is the peace-loving man, the pacifist! Peace is the only state for which he is fitted; and he will do everything to preserve; he will endure any humiliation, including loss of liberty and even the most severe damage to his pocket, in order to avoid war. His dim lustreless eyes betoken servility (which does not rule out impertinence), his clumsy body is obviously built for toiling and stooping, his movements are slow and deliberate. This type is the born stay-at-home, small-minded, completely flummoxed by the smallest interruption of the normal course of events, looking at the whole world from the standpoint of his little ego and judging it accordingly.'[18] The glorification of war had a strong appeal to the veterans of the trenches, who sought to recapture the comradeship of bearing arms together. It also appealed to those who had lost wealth or status during the chaos of the 1920s and who wished to re-establish themselves and their nation at the expense of others.

Banse united political, military and moral justification for these beliefs in his writings. In 1932 he wrote: 'War means the highest intensification not only of the material means but of all the spiritual energies of an age as well . . . indeed war provides the ground on which the human soul may manifest itself at its fullest height, in richer forms and surging from more profound wells than it might in any scientific or artistic exploit.'[19] Nor was Banse a lone voice. His propaganda was popular among the members of the Nazi Party and the army but it also gained recruits among teachers, lecturers and a whole host of influential professional men. In these cases the fact that Banse was writing in the German tradition was of great significance. He could not be dismissed as a crank or eccentric. In 1911 Kaufmann[20] had observed that 'not a community of men of free-will but victorious war is the social ideal—it is in war that the state displays its true nature'.[21] The moral conclusion to be drawn from these statements was clearly stated by Lenz:[22] 'Far be it that humanity should, in our minds, refute war; nay it is war that refutes humanity.'[23] The drive towards war was further reinforced by the official organ of the German Army, which declared: 'War has become a form of existence with equal rights with peace. Every human and social activity is justified only if it helps prepare for war. The new human being is completely possessed by the thought of war. He must not, he cannot, think of anything else.'[24]

It is hardly necessary to outline further the immense contribution made to the rise of fascism in Germany by the existence of this militarist tradition. It was recognized even by those who had at one time sought to close their eyes to the existence of fascist imperialism. In an attempt to explain to the station-master of Grantham why his mission failed, Henderson wrote: 'Though but few of the actual leaders of the National-Socialist Party are Prussians by origin, it is the Prussian ideology, and particularly their methods, which are no less dominant today in Germany than they were in 1914 or in 1870.'[25] Nor was the contribution of militarism forgotten after the end of the war of 1939–45. At the trial of the war criminals in Nuremberg Colonel Taylor observed that 'The military defendants will perhaps argue that they are pure technicians. This amounts to saying that military men are a race apart from and different from the ordinary run of human beings—men above and beyond the moral and legal requirements that apply to others, incapable of exercising moral judgment on their own behalf.'[26] Was this not what Stein had feared and what Bernhardi had sought to promote?

There was also a tradition of militarism in France, though it was not as strong as in Germany. Militarism was given a new energy by the humiliations of the unsuccessful war against Germany. There were those in France who saw failure as a function of imperfect leadership, lack of a properly educated population, a declining birth-rate and a number of other plausible and implausible causes. However, the most popular and significant explanation was that France had been betrayed by a lack of military preparation and that only through the inculcation of militarist ideas and aspirations would it be possible to regain the lost provinces of Alsace and Lorraine. Soon the notion of the inviolability of the army became an important feature of French politics. How dangerous this belief was may be seen from the sordid disclosures of the Dreyfus Affair. The tradition was already well established by the 1890s. As early as 1877 Gambetta[27] had declared: 'Who are they, then, these people who dare associate the name of the army and the sacred interests it represents with some infamous conspiracy!'[28] In 1882 Déroulède founded the *Ligue des Patriotes*, a militaristic and proto-fascist organization. It was never intended that this body should work through the accepted institutions of political life, but rather the League was expected to mobilize and manipulate the masses in order, if necessary, to overthrow governments hostile to Déroulède, who urged his audience to 'develop everywhere and in everyone the spirit of patriotism, which makes for the passionate love of one's country; the military spirit, which makes one serve it with patience and valour; the national spirit which is the exact and reasoned knowledge of the interests and needs of the whole nation, and which must be allowed neither to crumble away, at home, into a particularistic spirit, nor to dissipate itself, abroad, in a humanitarian spirit'.[29]

The League became an accepted part of French life. It organized rifle clubs, physical training and parades. It had its own newspapers, pamphlets and meeting houses. It organized inquiries into economic and industrial changes produced by the loss of the provinces. Above all it was revanchist. It was the League which created the situation from which Boulanger[30] was able to benefit. Throughout the period from 1882–1914 patriotic organizations continued to play a central part in every major French political crisis, whether led by Barrès, Drumont or Déroulède. But by the early years of the twentieth century all these bodies had vanished, being replaced by the *Action Française*, founded in 1899 by a number of young intellectuals, the most prominent of whom was Maurras.

Militarism became an ever more familiar part of French intellectual life as the danger of war loomed larger. The foundations of the *Union Sacrée* were being laid. In 1904 Barrère, a leading French diplomat, wrote to Delcassé,[31] asking him: 'How will you conduct diplomacy when the world knows or believes—which is the same thing—that we no longer have either an army or a navy?'[32] Discussion of conscription, the relative strengths of rival armed camps, the implementation of alliances and military conventions were the dominant themes of French diplomatic and political activity in the decade preceding 1914. As Bernhardi justly remarked, ' . . . if France thinks she has all the trumps in her hands, she will not shrink from an offensive war, and will stake everything in order to strike us a mortal blow. We must expect the most bitter hostility from this antagonist.'[33] During the crisis of 1911 the French Minister of

Finance, Klotz, made a speech in which he referred to 'the inviolability of the military tradition of France . . . the necessity of preparing for war, for it is only through war that the destiny of our country will be achieved'.[34] Klotz was by no means an extreme figure in France. He held views which were mild in comparison with those, for example, of Paléologue.[35]

Militarism penetrated even the ranks of French socialists, having already conquered the radicals. In 1913 Péguy[36] saw France as the beleaguered fortress of civilization—'this is in fact a state of war in peacetime . . . I do not believe that since the beginning of the world there has ever been a situation like that through which we are living now. It is an armed vigil without end.'[37] Péguy's views were echoed by Bourget in the *Echo de Paris*, when he wrote: 'War is truly regenerating, adorned by that seduction which the eternal bellicose instinct has reawakened in the hearts of men.'[38] The radical, Delcassé, positively gloried in the outbreak of war: 'Everything is going according to plan. The system of alliances and friendships which I had instituted or made secure is coming into play.'[39] The French were filled with 'that mysterious frenzy of the millions which can hardly be described in words but which, for a moment, gave a wild and almost rapturous impetus to the greatest crime of our time'.[40]

The ultimate justification of French militarism lay in victory in the war of 1914–18. As in the case of Germany, the war promoted militarist feeling in certain circles, although in France there was a more general revulsion from the concept of military glory. Instrumental in producing this reaction were the mutiny of 1917, the slaughter of Verdun and the Nivelle offensive, the policy blunders of the early post-war years and the wish to remain in step with England. In these circumstances militarism became increasingly the property of the fascists, who, in the face of political defeat, were ultimately to betray their own nationalism, patriotism and militarism, as Barrès had predicted long before: 'The day will come when it will be the conservatives who will accept and call in the foreigner. Yes, those who today are the patriots, the proud, will become tired of living in a France that is decayed, a life full of humiliation, and they will call for the intervention of the foreigner who can give them at last the joy of participating in a great, collective life.'[41]

The height of fascist influence in France, until the period of Vichy, was achieved in 1934. The riot of 6 February 1934 represented the revolutionary element in French fascism and was almost entirely sustained by para-military fascist organizations and their supporters. These bodies were collectively termed the Leagues. The principal participants were the *Action Française*, the *Jeunesses Patriotes*, the *Francistes*, the *Croix de Feu* and the *Solidarité Française*.

The most obviously fascist of these groups was that led by Bucard,[42] the *Francistes*. Bucard had met Mussolini and participated in the international fascist congress at Montreux later in 1934. His movement was heavily subsidized by the Italians, but it never attained the political or numerical significance of its rivals. Nor were either *Solidarité Française*, founded in 1933, or the *Jeunesses Patriotes*, founded in 1924, of great importance, though they claimed to share a quarter of a million members between them in 1934. The most important of these Leagues was the *Croix de Feu*, which had the strongest military tradition. When founded in 1927 membership had originally been confined to those cited for gallantry on the field of battle. Although this qualification had later been waived, it was still essentially an ex-servicemen's organization in 1934. It was led by Colonel de la Rocque and, after being proscribed by the Popular Front government of Blum, was reconstituted into the *Parti Social Français*. Later in the 1930s emerged the *Cagoule*, led by Deloncle,[43] which was a fully fledged para-military body and looked towards Italy for support.

Without the League fascism in France would have been very much weaker than it was. If these groups, including the *Croix de Feu*, often regarded themselves as non-fascist this was an illusion. The *Croix de Feu*, through its periodical, *Le Flambeau*, claimed to accept order and discipline, but not 'brutal repression, not force in the service of private interests, opinion stifled, regimentation, militarism . . .'.[44] These and similar claims were certainly not valid by the middle of the 1930s. The Leagues and French fascism flourished on absorption of the French traditions of political violence, militancy and militarism. It was difficult to believe in a process of national regeneration without believing in the necessity of having shock troops to achieve such a revival. The fascists were not so inconsistent and they seized upon the tradition of militarism as being both a probable and potentially powerful source of public support. The political demise of the fascists, ironically enough, was the result of the initial success and later failure of German fascism, which had been better able to absorb the militarist tradition. In order to keep the militarist tradition in Europe in its true perspective it is worth comparing the French and German cases with that of England. After these two major powers England was, with the exception of Russia (where the strange nature of political life makes comparison with most of the rest of Europe too difficult), the leading militarist power. Yet the gulf between the intellectual assumptions common in England and those of France and Germany was enormous, even in the early years of the twentieth century. In England the militarists formed an eccentric fringe and although some of them became more influential during the war of 1914-18 the reaction to the war and the peace soon produced a revulsion from these ideas. One of the major causes of Mosley's failure to create an army of the streets was a widespread belief that the wearing of uniforms was un-English, smacking of sinister or even comic foreign customs. Mosley was never able to overcome this unique blend of fear and contempt.

Yet there were Englishmen who tried to promote a militarist outlook on society. There were forms of jingoism and crude imperialism which could lend themselves very easily to militarism, but the non-European nature of the Empire convinced most people that there was comparatively little chance of conflict with a European power. The imperialists' sublime self-confidence that wars would have to be fought either at sea (where the Royal Navy was supreme) or on land only against ill-armed native forces remained virtually unchallenged. When these assumptions were shown to be erroneous, as in the cases of the Boer War and the naval rivalry with Germany, a reaction produced such evidence of militarism as may be found. On the whole the public never accepted for any lengthy period the argument that it was necessary for England to be armed to the teeth and to inculcate military virtues in all her able-bodied citizens.

The greatest enthusiast for the inculcation of military virtues was Lord Roberts, who worked through the National Service League, founded in 1901. It is worth noting at this stage that conscription had been a regular feature of life among all the major European powers for many years before there was a serious organization advocating its introduction in Britain. It was in 1904 that Roberts took up the campaign for conscription; within five years he had made great progress. Membership of the League stood at about 35,000 and it had the support of about half-a-dozen national newspapers or weekly journals. In 1912 he called for the raising of the school-leaving age so that there would be more time for instruction in 'order, obedience and discipline ... for social reform is a preliminary to any thorough system of national defence'.[45] Blatchford, who was a militarist himself, hit the nail on the head when he remarked in *The Clarion* '. . . the real danger . . . is that the masses of people are anti-patriotic and anti-militarist.'[46] This did not stop him campaigning for a powerful army in addition to the already strong navy. Blatchford also discerned, as a national socialist, one of the less endearing characteristics of the Left, already established as part of the English political tradition, observing, 'if we have soldiers and ships it will not be wise nor just to call those soldiers murderers, nor to wish for their defeat, nor to grudge them thanks for their gallantry'.[47] This was written at the time of the Boer War and had great public appeal.

There was also great public excitement at the time of the Dreadnought Crisis in 1908-9. Fears of Germany's steadily increasing naval power led to an upsurge of militarism and the development of a more extensive naval programme. Blatchford was not alone in his efforts to promote a change of attitude towards Germany, but he went far beyond the normal criticisms of governmental sloth and ineptitude. He called for the end of factionalism and 'purposeless party politics', advocating instead 'leadership by those who will be able to give the public what it really needs'.[48] Blatchford admired Germany for what it had achieved and wanted England to emulate this success by adopting similar measures: 'The German nation is an army. The British nation is a mob of antagonistic helpless atoms.'[49] Mackinder reinforced these views, calling for 'an organizer [who] regards society as so much man-power to be maintained in efficient condition . . . it matters little if he be militarist or capitalist provided that he be far sighted.'[50] The views of these men, demanding efficiency, leadership, imperialist goals and mass military participation were but one step removed from fascism.

If it can be seen retrospectively that militarism in England was based on an unsure foundation this was not always clear to her rivals. In France at the time of Fashoda there was much talk of Anglo-Saxon militarism and chauvinism. A decade later German writers had taken up the cry. Bernhardi wrote: 'We need not concern ourselves with any pacific protestations of English politicians, publicists, and Utopians, which, prompted by the exigencies of the moment, cannot alter the real basis of affairs.'[51] He also saw English militarism as of comparatively recent growth: 'The English have only considered the possibility of a German war since 1902. Before that year there was no idea of any such contingency, and it is therefore not unnatural that they are eager to make up for lost time. This fact does not alter the hostile character of the measures and the circumstance that the English preparations for war are exclusively directed against Germany.'[52] But the protestations of European critics of English militarism can be seen as natural reactions to measures taken in response to particular crises. The fact that Bernhardi stressed the comparatively recent nature of the change in policy is highly significant. It is hard to prove a permanent commitment to militarism from such evidence.

In view of the fact that the most ardent militarists in England saw the principal obstacle to achievement of their goal as the anti-militarist sentiment of the people it becomes clear why English fascism was unable to derive significant support from a militarist tradition. It hardly existed. The slaughter of the war of 1914–18 produced in England a widely-held wish to avoid war again. Movements which in other European countries enjoyed success had no real parallel in England. 'When I knew war I passionately loved it,' wrote La Tour du Pin, 'I shall not cease to love it, for all the splendour in which it has clad the most humble.'[53] He found no echo in England after the end of the war. Englishmen contributed their share towards making the ideology of fascism respectable, the militarists among them playing their part, but they did little to help fascism in their own country. Virtually every European country had writers, poets, statesmen, educationalists and industrialists who glorified militarism but in only two, Germany and France, had the inculcation of militarism so deeply penetrated public life that it made a direct contribution to the rise of fascism in that country.

8   The Fascist Interpretation of Economics

'Their whole way of looking at politics . . . appears to me to be entirely sordid and materialistic, not yet corrupt, but on the highroad to corruption.' Lord Robert Cecil on the Tariff Reformers, 25 January 1906

The background of economic theory which sustained the economic theories of fascism is readily divisible into two sections—the pre- and post-imperialist. Insofar as fascist economic theory was coherent it revolved around the central principle of economic autarky. The economic theory of imperialism with which it was connected was in a sense merely a refinement of this autarky, albeit very important. The imperialism and expansionism of the late nineteenth century brought the whole issue to the front of public life. The general public was made aware of the fact that economic imperialism was the subject of acute controversy regarding its potential or actual benefits for the imperial and the colonized country. This conflict of opinion was particularly significant in England where certain fundamental assumptions about Free Trade had been almost unchallenged for many decades. The conflict over the economic purposes of imperialism brought England into line with similar countries where similar disputes already raged. In Germany, France and the U.S.A. the concept of economic autarky was already well established. The prevailing opinion in favour of Free Trade in England, based of course on continued economic prosperity, delayed there the opening of this important debate and makes it possible to consider the development of the link between economics and fascism in two distinct periods. As it was only in the 1890s that many people in England began to realize that international trading competition was a reality it is at this point that the dividing line has been drawn.

The doctrine of economic autarky, or self-sufficiency, may be traced back as far as ancient times. Indeed the feudal system, mercantilism and the self-sufficiency of the *polis* may be regarded as examples of economic autarky in widely separated periods of time.

In the eighteenth century arose a formidable challenge to long-established traditions in the form of gradual acceptance of the argument that protective tariffs hindered trade and hence retarded the growth of prosperity. Among the leading figures supporting this thesis were the physiocrats, notably Quesnay,[1] and in England Adam Smith.[2] During the course of the next three-quarters of a century the concept of Free Trade gained ground steadily, especially in England, and by about 1850 the Manchester School had secured the almost total abandonment of tariffs. The weight of argument deployed by Cobden,[3] Bright,[4] Ricardo,[5] Mill[6] and Malthus[7] overwhelmed the feeble opposition offered to them by traditional farming and landed interests. Furthermore, the argument seemed justified by the remarkable advance in prosperity achieved by England during this period.

However, if opposition to Free Trade in England was weak it was strong elsewhere, notably in Germany, the U.S.A. and France. Many of those German nationalists who believed in the totality of the state also believed that the totality applied to economic life within the community as well as to the more obvious social and political aspects of existence as a citizen. Notable among these thinkers were Fichte, Herder and Müller. As Herder observed, 'every nation bears in itself the standard of its perfection, totally independent of all comparisons with that of others'.[8] Fichte took up this argument and turned it specifically towards detailed economic proposals in his *Der geschlossene Handelsstaat*. Fichte was totally hostile to the Adam Smith theory of economics, seeing the duty of the state as 'the removal of commercial anarchy in the same way as political anarchy is being suppressed, and the enclosure of the state as it has been enclosed legislatively'.[9] Fichte believed in the desirability of a planned economy, the strict regulation of external trade (which ought to be run down) and independence from the importation of essential goods. More striking still were his proposals to restrict the movement of citizens outside the state and to promote a policy of national expansion towards the natural boundaries of the state. Müller advocated a kind of state socialism to promote ultimate common ownership of property. He saw the state controlling all money, property, labour, investment and consumption.

These ideas were current at a time when the intellectual climate was not particularly favourable, during the era of the *Zollverein* and the adoption of outward-looking economic policies by many German states. However, these theories were favourably received in the U.S.A. where strong local and nationalist interests combined to produce much hostility to the doctrines of Free Trade. An anti-British tariff had been introduced in 1816 and during the next two decades economic autarky and the protection of native industries were advocated by Clay,[10] Niles[11] and Carey.[12] Under pressure from the South, however, tariffs were steadily reduced in the decade preceding the outbreak of the Civil War. Slightly later, the Australians also made a strong plea for economic self-sufficiency, Syme[13] writing in 1860 in the Melbourne *Age* that 'the doctrine of Free Trade is not science but cant, and cant of that kind which is meant to fill the pockets of its originators at the expense of its dupes . . . let us beware being bled to death . . . to fill the pockets of an oligarchy which treads down Englishmen as it does Irishmen when they stand in its way'.[14]

In 1847 Cobden returned from a long tour of Europe (during which he had sought to promote the cause of Free Trade) a disappointed and disillusioned man. While on his travels he had written to Bright to tell him that Free Trade would not be established for a long time in Europe and that there was little sympathy for the views of the Manchester School, which was not wholly surprising in view of the ignorance encountered 'even in the land of Adam Smith upon the question only a few years ago'.[15] The principal reason for Cobden's disappointment was the establishment of rival schools of economic thought, those of Sismondi,[16] Saint-Simon[17] and List. A material factor in the rejection of the doctrines of Adam Smith was continued poverty and the recurrence of economic crises. All these thinkers, and their followers, produced alternative theories more palatable to the French and Germans. Sismondi was hostile to the notion of competition, because of the social misery which it was capable of producing. He, therefore, advocated state intervention and the establishment of a patriarchal and benevolent rule—in fact a primitive form of state socialism. Saint-Simon demanded a rigorous control of production, envisaging the reduction of social discontent thereby. As a logical consequence he believed that 'politics must be transformed into a positive science of productive organization'.[18] While neither Saint-Simon nor Sismondi were complete believers in economic autarky the successful propagation of their views helped create an intellectual atmosphere favourable to the reception of much more startling concepts. Their followers and interpreters (sometimes erroneously) included Blanqui,[19] Fix[20] and Droz[21] in France alone.

It was List, however, who was the most important of all. He was important for two reasons: firstly, he was an industrial entrepreneur of some success, who thus commanded a willing audience, and secondly, he was a most persuasive writer, whose views remained influential, particularly in Germany, decades after his death. At first a promoter of railways and founder of the *Eisenbahnjournal* in 1835, List subsequently became the leading German economist of his day. In the 1840s, following the publication of *Das nationale System der politischen Ökonomie*, List's theories on national economics were widely read and admired. List believed in dynamism and potential, that the power of production was more important than wealth itself. He roundly denounced the doctrines of Adam Smith, declaring: 'Would not every sane person consider a government to be insane which, in consideration of the benefits and the reasonableness of a state of universal and perpetual peace, proposed to disband its armies, destroy its fleet, and demolish its fortresses? But such a government would be doing nothing different in principle from what the popular school requires from governments when, because of the advantages which would be derivable from general free trade, it urges that they should abandon the advantages derivable from protection.'[22]

List also believed in the acquisition of territory in order to promote the economic and political well-being of his country. 'The German nation', he wrote, 'will at once obtain what it is now in need of, namely, fisheries and naval power, maritime commerce and colonies.'[23] List's acceptance of the need for a planned economy led him to think of economics from a highly political point of view. He envisaged a huge economic system based on Germany, equipped with colonies and associated territories and including the incorporation (by force if necessary) of Holland, Belgium, Denmark and Switzerland. List's nationalism was the most consistent and most popular element in his writings and hence the most influential. He saw the essential requirement of the German people as national unity: 'From day to day it is necessary that the governments and peoples of Germany should be more convinced that national unity is the rock on which the edifice of their welfare, their honour, their power, their present security and existence, and their future greatness must be founded.'[24] The emphasis on nationalism, power, expansion, ambitious colonial and trading policies was to be reflected in the Nazi economic control of Europe between 1940–45. As has been justly observed, 'List may be considered one of the precursors of that economic imperialism which led William II's Empire into the First World War and, later, transformed into the doctrine of "living space", inspired National Socialism.'[25]

The opinions of List were taken up and developed by a whole school of economists in Germany, known as the Historical Economists. The leading figures in this group were Roscher,[26] Knies,[27] Hildebrand[28] and, later, Schmoller.[29] As all of these men held important academic posts their teachings were of great influence. All emphasized the importance of national economics and Hildebrand, who founded the *Yearbook for National Economy and Statistics* in 1862, held views which were later eagerly adopted by Nazi theorists in the 1920s. Hildebrand went further than List, suggesting that 'List seems to think that the entire subordination of private interest to public utility is dictated by custom, and even by private interest when properly understood, but he never regards it as a public duty rising out of the very nature of society itself.'[30] Members of this school differed from one another over a whole range of issues but the general line of their argument was clear and consistent. It pointed in the direction of militant expansion in order to achieve economic autarky.

The views of the protectionists were given further reinforcement by economic developments after 1873. In that year the international boom collapsed and a period of depression ensued which was to last until about the end of the century. In Germany the continued economic expansion of this period confirmed popular belief in the efficacy of protective measures while the slow decline of England's economic position led to the growth of an anti-Free Trade party. One of the earliest broadsides against Free Trade launched by an Englishman was that of Leslie[31] in his *Essays on Political and Moral Philosophy*, published in 1879. Leslie, who became steadily more protectionist the longer he lived already advocated some ideas which were to gain ground in the 1890s with great rapidity. He was concerned about the loss of economic self-sufficiency in an era of increasing agricultural depression. His solution was strongly influenced by the theories of the German historical school. In France there had been an earlier reaction against Free Trade, which was never as popular there as in England. In that country the debate took place upon politico-economic lines, as in Germany. Economic autarky was seen as an extension of state power and the debate over economic development was on the whole subsumed in the larger issue. Bastiat[32] put forward a classic definition of the dangers of state intervention when he wrote: 'The distinctive character of the State merely consists in this necessity to have recourse to force, which also helps to indicate the extent and the proper limits of its action. Government is only possible through the intervention of force, and its action is only legitimate when the intervention of force can be shown to be justifiable.'[33] These views were, however, effectively challenged by a number of other intellectuals, the most prominent of whom was Dupont-White[34] who, in his *L'individu et l'état*, published in 1856, exalted the state and the growth of its power. The question of economic autarky became for these French economists part of the problem of defining the legitimate sphere of state action. The attempts of Napoleon III to intervene actively in French economic life made little difference to the fashion in which these arguments were conducted in the period up to 1870.

As well as the school of Historical Economists (usually known as the *Katheder Sozialisten*) in Germany, there also existed a more vigorous form of national socialist economic doctrine. These theories were largely the creation of Rodbertus and Lassalle, who corresponded closely from 1862–4, when Lassalle died. Many of the notions of Rodbertus had been formed long before they gained popularity; indeed, his *Forderungen*, which dates from 1837, contains most of his original contributions to economic thought. Rodbertus was deeply indebted to Sismondi and Saint-Simon, though he took their arguments much further. In fact, he may be described as the father of the theory of state socialism. He advocated a controlled economy, the regulation of wages according to productivity and the total absorption of economic functions by the state in the interests of the citizens. His views were much stronger than those of the *Katheder Sozialisten*, whom he contemptuously described as 'sweetened water thinkers'.[35] Roscher, who believed that each nation ought to have an economic system peculiar to itself, found himself swept aside by Rodbertus' urgent avowal of the organic state. Writing of the economic institutions of the state, Rodbertus put forward the opinion that 'The organs of the State do not grow up spontaneously. They must be fostered, strengthened, and controlled by the State.'[36] In rebuttal of his opponents he asserted that 'The State in its passage from one evolutionary stage to another presents us not merely with a greater degree of complexity, each function being to a greater and greater extent discharged by some special organs, but also with an increasing degree of harmony. The social organisms, despite their ever-increasing variation, are placed in growing dependence upon one another by being linked to some central organ. In other words, the particular grade that a social organism occupies in the organic hierarchy depends upon the degree to which division of labour and centralization have been carried out.'[37] Rodbertus thus put forward a coherent theory embracing political and economic factors and assigning Darwinian ideas of evolution to the state. The organic state which would thus have been created could realistically have been described as fascist.

The influence of Rodbertus was strengthened by the oratorical power of Lassalle, who was bitterly hostile to the Manchester School. In an almost mystical fashion he saw the state as the destiny of mankind, believing that there existed a moral unity between all members of the same nation, irrespective of class or creed. Lassalle strongly urged the protection of the national economic interest of the nation by the state. In 1863 at a public meeting in Frankfurt he declared that 'State intervention is the one question of principle involved in this campaign. That is the consideration which has weighed with me, and there lies the whole issue of the battle which I am about to wage.'[38] The banner of an increase in state power for economic benefit was taken up by Dühring, particularly in his *Kritische Geschichte der National-ökonomie und des Socialismus*. It was Dühring's work which provided the best example of a blend of conservative and socialist views of economics and the state in pre-Nazi times. In addition, owing to Dühring's anti-Semitism, there was present the belief that Free Trade was part of a Jewish world conspiracy to undermine national economic autarky. Dühring's publications helped the protectionist cause in Germany in the 1870s, when in 1876 the Central Union of German Industry was founded, followed in 1879 by the agricultural tariffs. Dühring suggested that 'Every nation which is large enough to form a state that is suitably equipped in the various essential respects, and which includes besides within its scope the preconditions of an all-round economic development, must also become the basis of an economy that is to a certain degree self-sufficient. Over against other nations it must regard itself in an economic sense as a solidary community whose interests centre independently in itself and are to be distinguished from those of the other national economic bodies.'[39] To this advocacy of an intensely national economic autarky he added anti-Semitism: 'The doctrines of egalitarian free economics and of corresponding human rights in economics, as they were formulated in a humanely well-meaning way by the Scotsmen Hume and Smith, were used by the Jews in order to derive thence their own monopoly ... Essentially they want to be able to make of freedom a Jewish freedom; i.e. a Jewish monopoly.'[40]

The behaviour of other countries in relation to the worsening economic position of England began to have some influence upon economic and intellectual thought in England in the 1890s. The major trading partners of England began to revive protectionist tariffs and such actions produced demands for reciprocal retaliation. As early as 1861 a substantial tariff had been introduced by the U.S.A. In the 1890s a spate of protectionist legislation followed. In France the Méline tariff was passed in 1892, in the U.S.A. the McKinley tariff of 1890 and the Dingley Act of 1897 raised rates ultimately to 57 per cent. Germany had adopted protectionist policies ever since 1879 and Italy, Russia, Spain and Austria-Hungary followed the same course in the next decade or so. Still more significant was the adoption of protection by several of the major territories of the Empire simultaneous with their acceptance of state socialism. Canada, Australia, New Zealand and, later, South Africa followed the European lead. By the early 1900s in Australia the policy of New Protection was firmly established. Throughout all this, and indeed until 1914, England remained the home of Free Trade. In so doing she probably rendered a major service to inter-national economic development, but it was at the cost of ever-slowing rates of expansion and increasing reliance upon services to balance the growing import/export deficit.

Although the doctrine of Free Trade (in association with the cheap loaf) was apparently triumphantly vindicated in the election of 1906, it was in England that the theoretical battles about economic autarky were most fiercely contested. Perhaps the reason for this was that the declining prosperity of England in relation to her fellow European competitors and the apogee of imperialist sentiment were more or less coincidently visible events. It became possible for English intellectuals to argue a coherent case for economic autarky, based upon imperialist expansion, imperial preference and a global self-sufficiency. By the time this major economic and political issue was seriously debated in England most other nations had already accepted the validity of this new form of economic autarky and the extension of state power which it involved. In Germany, for example, under pressure from Schmoller and his allies an attempt had been made to build up a colonial empire in the 1880s. In the following decade Wilhelm II embarked upon the fatal policy of constructing a great navy. These were essential parts of schemes for economic autarky which had been advocated by List and Rodbertus.

Resistance to a policy of state socialism was strong in England and, in terms of its history before 1914, successful. Liberals and Conservatives alike resisted pressure for the introduction of *dirigisme*. They correctly judged that it would be easier to erect an apparatus of state control than to demolish it once it had been created. On the other hand a policy of expansion would be much easier to complete successfully if it were under government control. This had already been appreciated by the colonial parties in France and Germany and was to be recognized by Chamberlain in the late 1890s. The almost casual acquisition of territory that had marked earlier English expansion was replaced by continued state intervention—in West Africa, Egypt, the Sudan and South Africa. By the early years of the twentieth century a form of economic national socialism had secured a firm grip on a large section of the intellectual community and in some cases had even caught the imagination of the general public.

The two principal economists in England who advocated state socialism and economic autarky were Cunningham[41] and Ashley.[42] Cunningham had studied in Germany and his stay in Tübingen perhaps had great significance in moulding his later beliefs. At first a Free Trader he gradually veered round to a totally nationalist view of economics: his conversion may be dated at about 1900. Yet even before that date Cunningham had started to display the xenophobia which was so characteristic of those who supported nationalist economics. In 1897, for example, he wrote that the English 'have not much to gain from imitating the institutions of the Polish Jews'.[43] Cunningham consistently attacked Free Trade institutions in England and almost inevitably began to make the same assumptions about the future destiny of his country as Germans were making about theirs. Cunningham believed that 'It should be our ideal to render the rising generation, in all classes of our population, fit for work and for responsibility, in some part of the Empire overseas.'[44] He was not afraid of being called a chauvinist, militarist or rabid nationalist, declaring that his aim was to 'develop the nation's resources . . . so as to sustain and prolong our national life'.[45] He also accepted the need for the state to pay close attention to the activities of its citizens: 'The question of the effectiveness of our population for industrial or military pursuits', he wrote approvingly, 'is once more attracting the attention it deserves.'[46]

As well as being an ardent supporter of Chamberlain's Tariff Reform movement Cunningham also worked closely with Ashley after 1899. Ashley has been described by Schumpeter as more similar 'than any other English economist to the German professional type of that time'.[47] Ashley corresponded regularly with Schmoller and other members of the German school, so it is hardly surprising to find in him an enthusiastic supporter of the theory that history could serve as a useful guide in the determination of state policy. Ashley was also strongly influenced by the years he spent in the U.S.A. after 1892, deriving from American industrial practice his toleration of the development of trusts and cartels (which were in the future to be closely associated with fascist economic doctrine). Ashley regarded trusts as merely 'an attempt to lessen and, it may be, avert altogether the disastrous and harassing effects of cut-throat competition'.[48] Ashley saw the development of these huge and powerful organizations as necessary for the protection of the national economic interest. Ashley also argued the case for Tariff Reform, pointing out that England should copy the example of Germany, where it was realized that 'for a State to shirk a duty because it is difficult and can only be imperfectly performed, would be to abdicate its essential function'.[49] Ashley also associated, again in a characteristically German way, social reform and the introduction of protection. The society that he envisaged was definitely corporative, that is to say a combination of nationalism and socialism.

While the battle for Tariff Reform was being fought and lost in England, despite the support given to it by Chamberlain, Ashley, Cunningham, Mackinder, Shaw, Amery and Maxse, elsewhere the doctrines of economic autarky continued their advance. In Italy large industrial combines were set up under governmental direction and cartels and trusts not only became common but were regarded with favour by the government. In France the followers of Le Play[50] had attempted to limit the involvement of the state in economic affairs, but they had been conquered by the advocates of 'solidarism', which was a characteristically French version of state socialism. Solidarism showed more respect for individual freedom than its German equivalent, but still laid great stress upon the importance of state control. Its leading theoretician, and practical politician, was Bourgeois.[51]

In Germany the doctrine of economic autarky was pushed forward still more insistently by Lamprecht, Naumann, Bernhardi and Skarzynski. It was during the two decades preceding the outbreak of war in 1914 that the most violent concepts were incorporated into the mainstream of German economic thought. The will to power, militarism, imperialism, state socialism and racialism may all be detected in the writings of these men. Lamprecht asserted that economics should be exploited in the overriding interest of national power; '... to this end internal unity of economic life is above all necessary: in external affairs, in tariff and commercial policy as in other cases, it must be possible readily to employ the economic forms as a whole, like an army. Yes, just like the army and the navy: for in this connection these (instruments of policy) directly approximate to the national economy as being other forms and instruments of the expansion of the national existence.'[52] This revulsion from the concept of free trade was seconded by Skarzynski, who wrote in 1894 that 'it is absolutely clear to us that the destiny of Europe, Russia excepted, was decided when its nations failed to see how to free themselves from the blight of English economic theory as represented by Adam Smith, Ricardo, Malthus, Stuart Mill and Cobden. Under Bismarck, it is true, Germany attempted to free herself in 1879 and again in 1887, but our nation failed to accept the theories of List, Carey and Dühring in their totality.'[53]

How closely the doctrines of these men compared with those of the Nazis is illustrated by a brief examination of assertions made by Banse and Bernhardi. In his *Raum und Volk im Weltkriege* Banse observed that the wars of the future would be total, they would be fought not 'with bayonets alone, but with corn and meat, oils and fats, iron, nickel, wool and cotton, railways and lorries ... characters and souls'.[54] Bernhardi wrote that 'We are absolutely dependent on foreign countries for the import of raw materials ... we shall very soon see ourselves compelled to find for our growing population means of life other than industrial employment ... what we now wish to attain must be fought for, and won, against a superior force of hostile interests and powers.'[55] The concept of economic autarky is most strikingly expressed by Bernhardi: 'A vigorous colonial policy, too, will certainly improve the national prosperity if directed, on the one hand, to producing in our own colonies the raw materials which our industries derive in immense quantities from foreign countries, and so making us gradually independent of foreign countries; and, on the other hand, to transforming our colonies into an assured market for our goods by effecting promotion of settlements, railroads, and cultivation. The less we are tributaries of foreign countries, to whom we pay many milliards the more our national wealth and the financial capabilities of the State will improve.'[56] Once Hitler had conquered most of the mainland of Europe he tried to turn Eastern Europe into client states or *Ergänzungsgebiete* (a term coined appropriately enough by List) whose resources were to be used for the fulfilment of German economic autarky. The link and the derivation of these economic concepts is continuous and clear.

The importance of these writers and thinkers was obvious, but it was as nothing compared with the immense influence wielded by Naumann. His blend of nationalism, economic autarky and imperialism in a geopolitical framework proved irresistibly attractive to his contemporaries and to Germans in the inter-war years. It was Naumann who asserted: 'Another twenty years and we shall have before us the most comprehensive distribution of labour and plans for domestic economy. The regulation of production is on the march. What appeared forty years ago to be the ideologies of socialist and state-socialistic dreamers, remote from reality, now appears with incredible certainty as a form of reality that has become an accomplished fact in the meantime. Germany is on the way to becoming not only an industrial state but especially an organizational state.'[57] It was Naumann who discerned that Germany had become different from other European states because of its successes and failures in 1914–18. It was his belief that after the war 'only we central Europeans will have learnt and experienced something positive, something particular . . . for we have experienced the "closed commercial state", the bold dream of the German philosopher Fichte, which, thanks to fate and folk-tendency, realized itself with us in war. The enemy thought to do us evil, but God, the God which Fichte believed in and taught, thought to do us good.'[58] Naumann later realized the bitterness of defeat, made all the more galling by the apparent triumph of economic autarky at Brest-

Litovsk. It was Hitler's dream too to acquire the granaries of the Ukraine and the oilfields of Baku.

More prescient than the bulk of political observers, Naumann realized that economic necessity would lead to a fascist state. He represented the case for a combination of conservative and socialist measures with the greatest plausibility. He advocated a strictly regulated and planned economy, which would be acceptable to industrialists and workers. If resistance took shape it should be crushed by the state, for the future of Germany had been dictated by a process of historical necessity: 'Everywhere in Germany national socialism is on the increase; the planned economy waxes large. The spirits of Fichte and Hegel have given their assent; for the first time after the war the German citizen will become body and soul an integral part of the economic state; his ideal is and shall be the organism, not individual liberty. . . . In this way we shall most certainly fulfil our historic destiny.'[59]

Acceptance of state direction and the need for living space became the most obvious characteristics of fascist economic thought. Mussolini and Hitler venerated the concept of national regeneration through self-sufficiency. They wished to incorporate all Italians and all Germans into their empires, for only then would the nations fulfil their destiny. Their views were a compound of pragmatism and mysticism, the urging of popular forces seeking economic benefit at the expense of other nations combined with a belief that in attempting the promotion of this goal some inexorable law of history was being worked out. The combination of mysticism and reality enabled explanations for political actions to be given which would have been unsatisfactory had they been proffered in conventional form. The two main contributory streams of fascist economic thought have been well illustrated by the observations of Hasse and Spengler. Hasse, the conventional imperialist supporter of an autarkic economic unit, wrote: 'We need land . . . even when it is inhabited by foreign peoples, in order to be able to shape the future of those peoples according to our needs . . . elbow-room, expansion, land.'[60] Spengler's view was as important in the fascist approach, but on a different plane. He asserted that 'All economic life is the expression of a soul-life. Economics and politics are sides of the one livingly flowing current of being, and not of the waking-consciousness, the intellect. In each of them is manifested the pulse of the cosmic flowings that are occluded in the sequent generations of individual existences. They may be said, not to have history, but to be history. Irreversible Time, the When, rules in them. They belong, both of them, to race and not, as religion and science belong, to language with its spatial-causal tensions; they regard facts not truths. There are economic Destinies as there are political, whereas in scientific doctrines, as in religions, there is timeless connexion of cause and effect.'[61]

There was, of course, resistance to those economic doctrines which proved to be a basis for fascist ideas, even in German-speaking areas. In the late nineteenth century Menger[62] fought a long battle with Schmoller and his followers, although his views may be seen as tending towards economic autarky but without many of the more chauvinistic features of the main line of thought. In Italy Pareto and his followers, notably Barone,[63] conclusively demonstrated to those of their contemporaries who were willing to look that tariffs diminished the revenue of the country which imposed them, thus undermining the theory of economic autarky. However, the autarkic ideal was too strong, it had a firm base in popular writings of the past, it was endorsed by popular politicians of both the past and the present. Acceptance of the doctrines of economic autarky meant that each national economy was obliged either to become a timid self-sufficiency or to undertake a policy of possibly unlimited expansion. Either a country which did not possess oil had to be ready to do without oil, or it had to be prepared to seize the oil from some other nation, possibly absorbing that nation's territories in order to ensure total control of the vital supply. The fascists and, indeed, the bulk of Western opinion, were in no doubt as to which course to adopt.

In this sense fascist economic theory owed much to an international political tradition. Elements of the thought which may be deemed characteristic of inter-war fascism may be detected in the history of England, Germany, France, Italy and the United States, as well as in many smaller and less important powers. In some respects the antecedents of fascist economic theory were also those of imperialist economic theory. National socialist economics was, after all, only one step further along the road to economic autarky than imperialist and colonialist economics. If imperialism proved to be an intellectual breeding ground for fascist economic doctrine among the great powers in the West it had little influence upon the many European nations without colonies. Yet these countries frequently adopted economic and political measures during the inter-war years which may fairly be described as fascist. In part the influence of German thought was strong, but this was not the sole explanation. In two countries, Austria and Romania, not only were fascist movements powerful but they also found inspiration in a national socialist economic tradition. In Austria, Schüller,[64] who played an important part in tariff negotiations after 1918, formulated a whole series of rules justifying an elaborate system of protection designed to encourage autarky. The Romanian, Manoilesco, in his *Théorie du protectionnisme et de l'échange international* similarly wished to promote the growth of an industrial society by protectionist tariffs. He allied to this a conviction that only through the exercise of state control in the economic field could the proper destiny of his nation unfold. The influence of these men in a European context was slight, but in their own countries they made significant contributions to the development of an indigeneous corpus of fascist theory.

If much emphasis has been placed upon the contribution of German writers to the doctrine of economic autarky and the intimate relationship between this doctrine and fascist economics it must not be thought that German economics were just an unhappy exception to the rule. Outside England, Belgium and Holland the enthusiasm for non-autarkic principles was always weak. The German economists merely represented the most articulate and coherent section of an international intellectual movement, to which all major Western powers, including England and the United States, made a significant contribution. The peculiar characteristic of the Germans was that they pursued the remorseless logic of their own theories to the bitter end. In Germany aggressive economic autarky fitted in best with the political and intellectual spirit of the time. The catastrophes of the years after 1918 did nothing to alter this state of affairs and so it was in Germany that the process of transition from theory to practice was most smoothly accomplished.

The intimate connection between the doctrine of economic autarky and the aggressive German and Italian fascist solutions to economic problems has tended to obscure the existence of what may be termed a defensive belief in autarky. While in the cases of Germany and Italy autarky was related to expansion of the state, it was not necessarily intended to be so by all those who wrote in its favour. Critics of the doctrines of free trade are not necessarily fascists by implication. List, for example, would in all probability have been horrified at the bastardized version of his theories produced by the Nazis. Defensive autarky has a respectable intellectual background, untainted by fascism, and has many exponents among those who advocate closed economies in under-developed areas of the world. Aggressive autarky is more likely to be a feature of an industrialized and developed society. Economic nationalism and autarky can thus take on a virulent and aggressive form (fascist or neo-fascist) or a mild, essentially defensive form (frequently for defence against exploitation by stronger economic units).

The importance of this distinction can be seen in any inspection of economic developments in modern Africa, Asia, Latin America and the Middle East. Autarkic measures taken in these areas may be inspired by a form of neo-fascism but are not necessarily so. Similarly some countries which have 'open' or 'partially open' economic systems, such as Spain and Portugal, have not ceased to be described as fascist by the bulk of political commentators. It is thus quite clear that autarky may be part of a fascist background (and in Germany it certainly was) but that there are variant forms and no hard and fast rule dividing protectionists of all kinds into fascists and free-traders of all kinds into non-fascists can possibly be made. That this was the case even in the nineteenth century has been made clear by the writings of Gallagher and Robinson, who noted the connection between imperialist expansion and advocacy of free trade. They rightly saw that imperialist autarky as described by Lenin did not make sense in the context of British imperial expansion in the period before 1880. Writing in 1953, they asserted: 'Whether imperialist phenomena show themselves or not, is determined not only by the factors of economic expansion, but equally by the political and social organization of the regions brought into the orbit of the expansive society, and also by the world situation in general.'[65] This comment is even more relevant to the history of the twentieth century and in particular to the history of fascist growth. A firm line distinguishing fascists and believers in economic autarky from the free-traders cannot be drawn. All that can be said is that autarkic doctrines made a major contribution to the development of fascist theory and in the German state aggressive autarky reached a new peak. Elsewhere in the world doctrines of economic autarky must be examined in the context of their social, historical, geographical and cultural background, and not be assumed to be fascist or proto-fascist.

Aggressive autarky was, however, in both Germany and Italy closely related to the concepts of corporativism and the corporative state. Just as economic autarky demanded a total commitment to the promotion of the economic well-being of the state so did the doctrine of corporativism extend the principle to the whole working of the state. Fascism, through corporativism, sought to concentrate all power and direction in the hands of the state. Corporativism sought to crush such movements which could retain power outside the approved structure of the state—the church, the army, the trade unions. Corporativism was thus an essentially radical doctrine and also closely connected with that view of the state which held the state to be a living organism. The theory behind corporativism was that through state organization (a halfway-house between syndicalism and totalitarianism) individuals could contribute in greater measure to their own and the public welfare. The essence of the doctrine was well expressed in *The Times* in 1927; 'The Corporative State offers greater opportunities than the Liberal State.'[66] If the doctrine of corporativism in its origins owed a great deal to believers in co-operative movements, socialism and syndicalism, in its development it owed more to aggressive economic autarky. If the autarkic system were ever to work control was necessary and corporativism provided the theoretical justification for the organization of society towards aggressive ends. Those who advocated economic expansion were obliged to fall back upon the means of control that could be supplied through the acceptance of corporativism. The two doctrines supported, reinvigorated and reinforced each other and in German fascism came closest to complete identification. Corporativism, which had originally implied some consideration of welfare, became a doctrine of absolutism, the repression of dissent, the abolition of bargaining power and of aggressive economic expansion (as a compensation for the other restrictions on freedom). The connection between economic theory and fascist economic practice thus lies in aggressive autarky and corporativism. Well-established and respectable economic doctrines were made to serve the needs of the fascist state and in so doing were conceptually distorted, frequently almost beyond recognition.

9 The Concepts of Morality and Might in International Affairs

'Law is what Aryans deem to be right.' Alfred Rosenberg, *Der Mythus des 20 Jahrhunderts*, pp. 571–2

A close examination of the speeches and writings of many of those politicians and authors mentioned in previous sections makes it clear that the ordinary concepts of law, natural right and morality could not apply within the organic state. The frenzied search for the heroic leader, militarist glory and economic autarky left no place for individual rights or free will. It was a fundamental supposition of fascist régimes that the state could do no wrong. Furthermore, it was this supposition which was most readily recognized by observers of the fascist phenomenon. It is, therefore, taken for granted that all are agreed as to the nature of the fascist state in its relationship to rights within the state. What is of greater interest, perhaps because it is more hotly contested, is the extent to which the fascist state applied different standards in dealing with other states and the extent to which such actions were inspired by a literary and intellectual tradition.

It has long been a maxim of international relations that 'might is right', for it is a doctrine more easily justifiable in an international than in a domestic context. The concept of the national interest has frequently been used to disguise actions in foreign policy which would not have been tolerated at home. Political practice was based upon this assumption for centuries, though few political philosophers seem to have considered the matter worth writing about. Machiavelli was an exception to this rule. Writing in 1513 he declared: 'You must know that there are two ways of contesting, the one by the law, the other by force; the first method is proper to men, the second to beasts; but because the first is frequently not sufficient, it is necessary to have recourse to the second . . . a prince ought to take care that he never lets anything slip from his lips that is not replete with the above-named five qualities, that he may appear to him who sees and hears him altogether merciful, faithful, humane, upright and religious. There is nothing more necessary to appear to have than this last quality, inasmuch as men judge generally more by the eye than by the hand, because it belongs to everybody to see you, to few to come in touch with you. Every one sees what you appear to be, few really know what you are, and those few dare not oppose themselves to the opinion of the many, who have the majesty of the state to defend them; and in the actions of all men, and especially of princes, which it is not prudent to challenge, one judges by the result.'[1] Machiavelli thus perceived the essential requirements for international action; a sound basis of popular support at home, ability to confuse and deceive one's opponents and judgement by results. In a more advanced and refined form these were to become the principles of action in foreign affairs for fascists.

If Machiavelli wrote about an idealized practice there were those who sought to put right in the place of might as the determining factor in the conduct of international affairs. The first modern writer to advocate the necessity of moral conduct in foreign relations and, indeed, to construct a scheme of international law was Grotius.[2] It is in the Prolegomena to his *De Jure Belli ac Pacis* that some extremely influential ideas were first put forward. Grotius observed that 'amongst all or most states, there might be, and in fact there are, some laws agreed on by common consent, which represent the advantage of all in general . . . if those laws be observed all nations will benefit, and aggressors who violate the laws of nature and nations break down the bulwarks of their future happiness and tranquillity . . . for the moment we recede from Right we can depend on nothing'.[3] It was he also who first examined in critical detail the concept of the just war. While his theories did little in practice to halt the almost incessant wars between the emerging nation states they contributed substantially to the evolution of international customs involving trade and diplomacy.

However, there were those who contested the validity of the assertions of Grotius, while accepting the benefits which might accrue from observing his laws when vital interests were not at stake. The desire for security could only be fulfilled through strength, argued Hobbes: ' . . . there is no way for any man to secure himselfe, so reasonable, as Anticipation; that is, by force, or wiles, to master the persons of all men he can, so long, till he see no other power great enough to endanger him: And this is no more than his conservation requireth, and is generally allowed. Also because there be some, that taking pleasure in contemplating their own power in the acts of conquest, which they pursue farther than their security requires; if others, that otherwise would be glad to be at ease within modest bounds, should not by invasion increase their power, they would not be able, long time, by standing only on their defence, to subsist. And by consequence, such augmentation of dominion over men, being necessary to a mans conservation, it ought to be allowed him.'[4] Hobbes' views were, on the whole, those of statesmen in the succeeding centuries. Few were as outspoken as Frederick the Great, who told his nephew: 'Policy and villainy are almost synonymous terms . . . it is good policy to be always attempting something and to be perfectly persuaded that we have a right to everything that suits us . . . I mean by the word policy that we must always try to dupe other people . . . Do not be ashamed of making interested alliances from which only you yourself can derive the whole advantage. Do not make the mistake of not breaking them when you believe that your interest requires. Uphold the maxim that to despoil your neighbours is to deprive them of the means of injuring you.'[5] Frederick, in word and deed, was the forerunner of the *Machtpolitik* of the twentieth century.

It is hardly surprising that in the nineteenth century the division between those who believed in the international rule of law and those who believed in the international law of might corresponded very closely to the supporters and opponents of Free Trade. List drew attention to the fact that internationalism would never be able to supply German wants. Cobden, the international man, on the other hand, wished to deprive governments of the resources to make war. Cobden even went so far as to denounce the concept of the just war, so opposed was he to the exercise of power: 'Some people will say, do you intend to leave these evils without a remedy ? Well, I have faith in God, and I think there is a Divine Providence which will obviate this difficulty, and I don't think Providence has given it into our hands to execute His behests in this world. I think, when injustice is done, whether in Poland or elsewhere, the very process of injustice is calculated, if left to itself, to promote its own cure; because injustice produces weakness—injustice produces injury to the parties who commit it.'[6] Internationalism was widely advocated during this period, but, like its economic counterpart, it began to collapse before the more persuasive arguments of the nationalists.

The major figures who advocated the use of power rather than

right in the conduct of international affairs were, perhaps predictably, Bernhardi, Spengler, Chamberlain, Novalis, Haller,[7] Gobineau, Nietzsche, D'Annunzio, Treitschke and Pearson. This list is, of
course, not exclusive, but it does give some idea of the range and
power of support for the concept of 'might is right'. These writers,
virtually all of them ferociously nationalistic in outlook, belonged to
an intellectual movement which gathered strength as the First World
War approached; a movement, moreover, which was not bounded by
frontiers.

These thinkers' concept of power in international affairs was
closely related to their view of the role of the individual in relation to
the state. Assigning life to the state they naturally attributed to the
state all the characteristics of a corporate personality. It was clear
from a very early stage where this was leading: ' . . . all men are by
nature only relatively equal, which in fact is the old inequality,'
wrote Novalis, 'the stronger has also the stronger right.'[8] How much
more significant this was when it was applied to the state. It was
possible for the individual to be wrong, even to be unjust—it was
extremely unlikely that the state would suffer from such defects. The
principle of sheer, self-justifying power was soon widely advocated.
As Haller observed: ' . . . it is clear that it is the eternal and immutable
law of God that the more powerful should rule, must rule and will
rule always.'[9] Any action in international politics could be justified in
these terms, from annexation to assassination. The doctrine of the
national interest set might above legality, as Treitschke showed in
1865: ' . . . in the matter of Schleswig-Holstein positive law is
irreconcilable with the vital interests of our country. We must set
aside positive law and compensate those who may be injured in
consequence. This view may be erroneous; it is not immoral. Every
step in historical progress is thus achieved . . . Positive law when
injurious to the common good must be swept away.'[10]

It is a matter of interest that as the nineteenth century advanced so
did the theories relating to the conduct of foreign relations increasingly become subject to the concept of national necessity. Those, like
Spengler, who had been educated in an atmosphere extremely
favourable to conquest, domination and spoliation were almost
inevitably bound to carry widely-held beliefs to their logical conclusions. National necessity came to mean not only the right to
ignore the ambitions of other nations but also the total dispensability
of nations and individuals. The fascists put this theory into practice

with energy and enthusiasm, for it involved them in minimal political repercussions on the domestic front.

It is then, perhaps, useful to follow chronologically the development of this line of thought in the nineteenth and early twentieth centuries. Some mention has already been made of the views of Haller and Novalis, List and Müller. However, the concept of power received a new stimulus in the racial teachings of Gobineau. The continual stress that he laid on desirable and undesirable racial characteristics demonstrated clearly that certain persons and nations were not merely unnecessary but an actual hindrance to the proper evolution of mankind. This concept became deeply embedded in nationalist thinking. If no other reason could be found for national desires then it was easy to say that nations which opposed the interests of another were effete or corrupt, that they should be destroyed in the interests of mankind. After all, was this not an extension of the principle of survival through ability to adapt to environmental problems ? So reasoned many of the nationalists and totalitarians, so reasoned Hitler and the anti-Semites. The contribution of Gobineau and Darwin (inadvertently) to the concept of might was considerable. Quite apart from the subsequent misinterpretation of their writings they consciously helped to undermine the well-established belief that Christian states would be moral in their actions towards each other. Gobineau just rejected the whole argument. Darwin, operating in a completely different field, successfully challenged the traditional image of man and in so doing facilitated the attack upon the rule of humanitarianism and natural right which was to gain in vehemence during the rest of the century.

The writings of Gobineau and Darwin, although important in marking a stage in the development of sociological thought, were insignificant in comparison with the direct contribution made by other thinkers. It is worth paying particular attention to the ideas of Treitschke and Nietzsche. Treitschke was one of the key figures in the development of state power, both internally and externally, from a theoretical and a practical point of view. His ideas were sometimes novel but always argued articulately, and they influenced a whole generation of German students. Treitschke was not unaware of the dangerously inflammable nature of the doctrines he preached. He wrote approvingly of Machiavelli, who 'sacrifices right and virtue to a great idea, the might and unity of his people . . . the underlying thought of the book, its glowing patriotism, and the conviction that the most oppressive despotism must be welcome if it ensures might and unity for his mother country—these are ideas which have reconciled men to the numerous reprehensible and lawless theories of the great Florentine'.[11] By implication Treitschke was not only one of those who approved of Machiavelli's teachings but was also very well aware that they were in conflict with the concept of law.

Where Treitschke's influence was so important was in convincing his readers that power could be equated with morality. Power and its use had a moral quality of its own, although Treitschke recognized that this doctrine allowed no room for failures or second chances: '. . . the theory of power, in which the first and highest obligation is to push forward with one's purpose completely and unconditionally, is a hard one'.[12] Hitler too favoured only the strong and the successful. In *Mein Kampf* he made a number of observations to this effect: '. . . right abides in strength alone' and '. . . the sole earthly criterion of whether an enterprise is right or wrong is its success'.[13] Indeed, Hitler, who was no lover of democratic rights, felt so strongly about these points that he even admitted that 'if a government uses the instruments of power in its hands for the purpose of leading a people to ruin, then rebellion is not only the right but also the duty of every individual citizen'.[14] The road from Treitschke ran straight and true towards the fascists.

Just as force fascinated Spengler and his followers so too was it a subject of great interest to Treitschke. He argued cogently from the political practice of his day, declaring that 'physical force is especially important in times like ours'.[15] In this belief he was strongly supported by a long intellectual tradition, formed in times of uncertainty and including Hobbes and Machiavelli among its disciples. In more recent times it had acquired peculiar significance in Germany from the writings of von Rochau,[16] whose *Grundzüge der Realpolitik* had considerable influence. Von Rochau believed, for example, that 'we cannot wait for an abstract justice to unfold its decision, our destiny is marked out by our strength and will; the morality of state relations is that of power . . . as Germany has discovered to her cost so often in the past'.[17] Treitschke also accepted the validity of this theory, writing that 'When a state realizes that existing treaties no longer express the actual relations between the powers, then, if it cannot bring the other contracting state to acquiescence by friendly negotiations, there is nothing for it but the international lawsuit—War . . . the justice of war depends simply on the consciousness of a moral necessity.'[18] The theme of the morality of power is thus emphasized once again—it was Hitler who perceived its utility: 'Forget all you have learned hitherto,' he instructed a meeting of young Nazis in 1934, 'we do not seek equality but mastery. We shall not waste time over minority rights and other such ideological abortions of sterile democracy. When Germany is great and victorious no one will dare to give any of you the cold shoulder.'[19]

The contribution of Nietzsche was as great. In a way his wild and impassioned pleadings had even more influence than the cold-hearted and sinister logic of Treitschke. The romantic and inhuman fervour of Nietzsche struck a chord in the hearts of the fascists. Sacrifice, the will to power, the rule of the strong, were the fundamental elements of Nietzsche. These ideas proved to be attractive to the fascists of all nations for they implied that civilization was tired and anaemic, that it needed regeneration. Power became a moral thing in itself, for only through its exercise could civilization be saved and, later, guided towards new triumphs. The justification of terror and all other means of compulsion could be found in Nietzsche's writings. It was impossible for him to believe in right or morality, for it was his contention that 'Evil is man's best power. Man must become better and more wicked—thus I teach.'[20] Nietzsche's superman could brook no rival, for the 'right of others is the concession of our feeling of power to their feeling of power. When our power is obviously broken down and quite impaired, our rights cease; on the other hand, when our power has greatly increased, the rights of others, as we have hitherto conceded them, are no longer binding on us.'[21]

Nietzsche was no lover of the state although he helped create an atmosphere in which the state could become all powerful. He referred to the state as the new idol—clearly one that he did not worship. 'The State is the coldest of all cold monsters. Coldly it uttereth its lies; and this is the lie that creepeth out of its mouth: "I, the State, am the people" . . . Where the State ceaseth—I pray you look there, my brethren! Do you not see it, the rainbow, the bridge to the Superman?'[22] Yet the will to power stood out as the most significant intellectual item in Nietzsche's works. It was this above all else which made his writings gospel to the fascists. In *Ecce Homo* he asserted that 'Life itself is essentially appropriation, infringement, the overpowering of the alien and the weaker, oppression, hardness, imposition of one's own form, assimilation and, at the least and the mildest, exploitation.'[23] Nietzsche saw, too, where this logic led him and gloried in his conclusions: 'The criterion of truth lies in the enhancement of the feeling of power . . . All values are results of particular perspectives of utility in respect to the preservation and intensification of human organizations of power.'[24] Small wonder then that Rosenberg saw him as one of the great inspiring fathers of fascism.[25]

The spiritual heirs of Nietzsche were Spengler, Chamberlain, Bernhardi and D'Annunzio. However, they were also greatly influenced by the school of Pearson. Pearson elevated the state to a position of new dignity in his writings, its all-embracing power had acquired its own morality: 'If the welfare of society be the touchstone of moral action, then respect for the State—the State as *res publica*, as commonweal—ought to be the most sacred principle . . .'.[26] Pearson advocated that if there was need it should be satisfied, albeit at the expense of other nations and at the risk of war. In fact the exercise of might became a moral duty, for when wars ceased, then 'there will be nothing to check the fertility of inferior stock; the relentless law of heredity will not be controlled and guided by natural selection'.[27] The lesson was clear—the state should end 'internal struggle, that the nation may be strong externally'.[28]

Pearson's mixture of racism, eugenics, imperialism and the gospel of power was added to by Bernhardi and Chamberlain. Bernhardi placed the concept of *Machtpolitik* in a context which was bound to be extremely popular among German nationalists. By a simple process of substitution the arguments he advanced in relation to the future of Germany in great power politics could, of course, be adopted by the nationals of other countries. Even critics of Bernhardi, such as Cramb, could write that 'War remains as the supreme act of the State, unchanged in essence, though varying in mode. In Europe, which really governs the planet, every advance in politics or religion has been attended by war.'[29] Bernhardi's arguments, however, unlike those of many of his critics and imitators had a tight, clear logic of their own. It was he who declared that 'might gives the right to occupy or to conquer. Might is at once the supreme right, and the dispute as to what is right is decided by the arbitrament of war. War gives a biologically just decision, since its decisions rest on the very nature of things.'[30]

Bernhardi was totally contemptuous of the concept of human rights in any international sense. He saw only the rights of nations, the rights of the strong and the determined, those who had the will to power. 'Each nation evolves its own conception of right,' he insisted, 'each has its particular ideals and aims, which spring with a certain inevitableness from its character and historical life. These various views bear in themselves their living justification, and may well be diametrically opposed to those of other nations, and none can say that one nation has a better right than the other. There never have been, and never will be, universal rights of men. Here and there particular relations can be brought under definite international laws, but the bulk of national life is absolutely outside codification. Even were some such attempt made, even if a comprehensive international code were drawn up, no self-respecting nation would sacrifice its own conception of right to it. By so doing it would renounce its highest ideals; it would allow its own sense of justice to be violated by an injustice, and thus dishonour itself.'[31] It is difficult to conceive of a more perfect exposition of the principles of direction and action of the fascists in their conduct of international affairs. No wonder, then, that both Hitler and Mussolini heartily approved of the writings of Bernhardi and the military tradition which his books helped develop.

Bernhardi even extended the concept of *Machtpolitik* to cover the development of relative international standing. He saw it in Darwinian terms, survival of the fittest, the victory of those who were well-equipped both in terms of heredity and adaptability to environment. He could not accept the working of any laws other than his organic law of nature. He wrote with hatred and loathing of the proposal 'to obviate the great quarrels between nations and States by Courts of Arbitration—that is, by arrangements. A one-sided, restricted, formal law is to be established in the place of the decisions of history. The weak nation is to have the same right to live as the powerful and vigorous nation. The whole idea represents a presumptuous encroachment on the natural laws of development, which can only lead to the most disastrous consequences for humanity generally.'[32] Later in his book Bernhardi discussed this topic in still more precise terms: '. . . no-one stands above the State; it is sovereign, and must itself decide whether the internal conditions or measures of another State menace its own existence or interests. In no case, therefore, may a sovereign State renounce the right of interfering in the affairs of other States, should circumstances demand. Cases may occur at any time, when the party disputes or the preparations of the neighbouring country become a threat to the existence of a State . . . it must be remembered that the dangers which may arise from non-intervention are occasionally still graver, and that the whole discussion turns, not on an international right, but simply and solely on power and expediency.'[33]

Chamberlain, in a rather incoherent and less precise fashion, also sought to promote ideas akin to those of Bernhardi. Justifying the superiority of Germany in racial terms, he wrote that 'the power of might is the destiny of the selected races . . . it is their duty to conquer and to destroy the impure and the inferior . . . they cannot be restricted by a morality of rights designed to protect the weak from the strong'.[34] The teachings of Bernhardi and Chamberlain in Germany were to find an Italian parallel in those of D'Annunzio. The leading intellectual figure in Italy for many years was a firm believer in the use of force. It was D'Annunzio who advocated Italian involvement in the war of 1914–18, it was he who occupied Fiume in the days of Italian dissatisfaction immediately after the end of that war. Always he was a believer in might, the racial destiny of the Italians and their right to ignore obligations if benefit could be secured by such action. In 1937, hearing that Mussolini had withdrawn Italy from the League of Nations, he wrote to him glorifying the decision: '. . . you know how I have been waiting for the last five years for the courageous and incomparable gesture you have made. Many people are undoubedly amazed and intoxicated by it. But no one has been as moved by it as I am, to my very depths—as by a kind of supernatural revelation. Not infrequently, I have understood you, and represented your myth with mystical purity. You have no more to fear! You have no more to fear! Never has there been such a complete victory! I remain proud at having foreseen it, at having announced it.'[35] D'Annunzio rejoiced in the defeat of the League of Nations, which he had always seen as an attempt to thwart the destiny of his country, an organization to protect international rights against national vigour.

Spengler too played an important part in the further development of the ideology of *Machtpolitik*. It was his view that 'We do not need any more ideologists, or any talk about the culture and cosmopolitanism and spiritual mission of the Germans. We need hardness, we need brave scepticism, we need a class of socialist master-natures. Once more: socialism means might, might, might again and again. Plans and ideas are nothing without might.'[36] It was this philosophy that proved extremely attractive in the inter-war years. Spengler himself was bitterly critical of the false values that had been instrumental in shaping the Treaty of Versailles, so it is hardly surprising that his views struck an answering response among fascists everywhere. He looked forward to the rule of the Caesars, when politics would be directed by those who had the will to power: 'The dreary train of world-improvers has now come to an end of its amble through these centuries, leaving behind it, as sole monument of its existence, mountains of printed paper. The Caesars will now take its place. High policy, the art of the possible, will again enter upon its eternal heritage, free from all systems and theories, itself the judge of the facts by which it rules, and gripping the world between its knees like a good horseman.'[37] Spengler also looked with contempt upon the notion of rights, both within and outside the state: 'Equal rights are contrary to nature, are an indication of the departure from type of ageing societies, are the beginning of their irrevocable decline. It is a piece of intellectual stupidity to want to substitute something else for the social structure that has grown up through the centuries and is fortified by tradition. There is no substituting anything else for Life. After Life there is only Death.'[38]

The views of Spengler were eagerly assimilated by the fascists, particularly when he postulated a world order that fitted in well with the racial and political fantasies which formed the basis of their ideology. It was Spengler who deified the notions of strength and success: 'To the priestly and idealistic moral of good and evil belongs the moral distinction of right and wrong, but in the race-moral of good and bad the distinction is between those who give and those who receive the law. An abstract idea of justice pervades the minds and writings of all whose spirit is noble and strong and whose blood is weak, pervades all religions and all philosophies—but in the fact-world of history knows only the success which turns the law of the stronger into the law of all. Over ideals it marches without pity, and if ever a man or a people renounce its power of the moment in order to remain righteous—then, certainly, his or its theoretical fame is assured in the second world of thought and truth, but assured also is the coming of a moment in which it will succumb to another life-power that has better understood realities.'[39] The invitation to reject the values of civilization and to take up the sword is most clearly expressed. The debt of the fascists to this style and form of argument was enormous. Goebbels, speaking in 1938, put the views of Spengler in language his own followers could clearly comprehend when he announced that 'Germany is marching with *Mein Kampf* in one hand and in the other the sword, for her advance as the new world power'.[40]

It was Spengler's deification of Caesarism that also appealed to the Nazi mentality. The concept of the heroic leader, shorn of moral obligations (except for preservation of the race) and fallibility, was deeply embedded in fascism. Spengler contributed to the barren philosophy of fascism the belief in the inexorable purpose of the historical figure, so clearly foreseen in the writings of Hegel. As an observer of Germany in the inter-war years has commented: 'With Spengler, however, the mists have lifted: the spiritual bankruptcy itself is our history, our Absolute, our guiding principle. If Spengler is, after all, not quite out of date, this is because he has reduced to a wicked kind of absurdity a tendency of the mind which is certainly not unfashionable yet: the habit of applying to historical necessity for the marching orders of the spirit.'[41] It was this intellectual tradition of reverence for the leader which found its expression in Göring's view that the law and the will of Adolf Hitler were one and the same. Dr Frank[42] put this belief in even more startling form: 'We are under great obligation, then, of recognizing as a holy work of the spirit of our *Volk*, the laws signed with Adolf Hitler's name. Hitler has received his authority from God. Therefore he is the champion, sent by God, of German right in the world.'[43] In view of these attitudes towards the leader of fascism in Germany it is clear that the concept of absolute right in international affairs was opposed to the strongly preferred German right. It was the hatred of traditional concepts of morality and human rights which inspired Rosenberg's theory that 'The sign of our times is departure from the infinite absolute.'[44]

The notion of might being superior to right in dealings at an international level was thus a central part of the European intellectual tradition, as were so many other of the constituent parts of fascist theory. The assumptions made by statesmen and thinkers were similar in many lands and many periods of time. The continuity is clear, from Frederick the Great, who saw international relations as an aspect of war, which was in turn 'a trade, in which any the least scruple would spoil everything . . . Do not suffer yourself, dear Nephew, to be dazzled by the word "Justice" . . . I should never have done anything if I had been hampered by it,'[45] to Hitler, who saw that 'no one will willingly cede us the space we want . . . what is not voluntarily given to us the fist must simply take'.[46] The thinkers hardly discouraged the assumptions behind these statements of practice, accepting a form of mysticism as justification of the most ruthless actions. The historical process of the fulfilment of destiny was held to validate the most extraordinary violations of human rights. Significance was read into symbols and birthplaces, there was a revival of astrology and necromancy, discredited since the dawning of the 'Age of Reason'. Von Leers, for example, spoke of 'rising again under the sign which never yet failed us, the cross of the Great Stone Age: the ancient and most sacred Swastika . . . the symbol of our racial right and destiny'.[47] Anything could be justified by signs and portents which pointed in the direction of the fulfilment of destiny. No aggression, no maltreatment, no misrepresentation was invalid if it advanced the cause of force and might.

Perhaps the last word should be left with Spengler, whose view of the historical process was so important in producing an intellectual justification of the fascist attitude that history would judge only success or failure and not intentions. 'In the historical world there are no ideals, but only facts', he wrote, 'no truths, but only facts. There is no reason, no honesty, no equity, no final aim, but only facts, and anyone who does not realize this should write books on politics—let him not try to make politics.'[48] The fascists tried to make politics according to Spengler's recipe. The results were catastrophic for European civilization.

10 A Postscript

Much attention, perhaps too much, has been paid in the above analysis of the principal trends in the intellectual background of fascism to the German tradition. It should be stressed, therefore, that although Germany provided an intellectual tradition conducive to the rise of fascism in that country, it was not an intellectual tradition totally different or cut off from the rest of Europe. I do not agree with Butler's view that the German outlook on society represents a type of national *Doppelgänger*—'the triumph of the night-side of the German soul'.[1] It is too easy to explain fascism almost totally in terms of Germanity and to ignore the contributions made to its theory by the rest of Europe. It is too easy to see fascism as a German phenomenon and not as a circumstance of European history. That nineteenth- and early twentieth-century Germany provided a suitable historical background for the flowering of fascism in its most powerful form is undeniable, but mutations existed almost everywhere in Europe, and, in some cases, outside.

Fascism was a bizarre and horrendous combination of constructive and destructive forces in society. It incorporated socialism, nationalism, militarism, racialism, élitism, absolutism, the worship of force and mysticism among many other forms of belief. It developed more strongly where there were the writers and politicians most suitably equipped to take advantage of chaos and national disintegration. It was founded upon the rule of the strong over the weak and upon the elimination of hostile sections of society. It was an attempt to provide an answer to the apparently insoluble problems of the inter-war years (although its ideological background stretched much further back into history). As such it was a failure and hence discredited, like most unsuccessful social experiments. But the ultimate irony is that fascism has been so often regarded as a purely political phenomenon, as if politics could be divorced from the social environment in which they are practised. In the case of the self-designated organic state this mistaken identification of fascism as a political but not a social phenomenon is both wrong and dangerously wrong.

PART II

The Political Development and Practise
of Fascism in Germany and Italy

11   The Nazi Appeal to Germany

'The Kingdome of Darkness is nothing else but a Confederacy
of Deceivers, that to obtain dominion over men in this present
world, endeavour by dark, and erroneous Doctrines to extinguish
in them the Light . . . ' Thomas Hobbes, *Leviathan*

The purpose of the first part of this book has been to set fascist
ideas in the context of a European historical and literary tradition.
It is not enough, however, merely to perform this operation without
further consideration of how appropriate such ideas were in the
practical development of fascism. Yet in order to make any useful
assessment it becomes necessary to ask further questions. It is
essential to know who the fascists were, to which classes in society
fascism appealed, whether fascist practise was anywhere grounded
upon fascist principle and to what extent fascism was an international
movement rather than a series of occurrences hopelessly fragmented
by the rival constituent forces of aggressive nationalism.

It would clearly be impossible to answer all these questions in
relation to all the countries in which fascist movements have been
deemed to exist. Indeed, within the scope of this book it would be
impossible to give a definitive answer for one important fascist
country. Justice could not be done to the numerous views and
differing interpretations of either German or Italian history. What
follows, then, is a synthesis—an assemblage of facts and opinions
which makes no claim to provide a definitive view. What is hoped is
that by examining a number of major developments in Italian and
German fascism an overall picture will emerge which will not be too
misleading. Where scholars have opinions that differ significantly
these are stated, but the reader is advised to refer in detail to these
scholarly works in order to ensure that he has a firm grasp of the
issues in dispute.

It seems to me that the most important question to try to answer
is not how or why fascism occurred but how it affected contemporary
society. It is a problem that has significance not only in the historical
context but also in modern political life, for fear of a recurrence of

fascism has been prevalent even in the post-1945 world. Even a casual look at the kind of societies in which fascism became estab-lished reveals that there is no truly consistent pattern. Fascism was not just a phenomenon of the developed world, as many Marxists insisted. To see it as a last desperate throw of the propertied and moneyed classes in the face of the irresistible advance of the pro-letarian revolution is nonsensical. Not only has economic advance in, for example, West Germany since 1945 provided a more plausible defensive socio-economic system against the assault of communism than anything fascism was able to create, but also fascism has clearly managed to exist in some countries that are so under-developed in economic terms that the equation fascism = privileged desperation can be ruled out of the reckoning from the very start. As Organski rightly observed: 'The term fascist has been applied to national socialist Germany (already a fully developed nation), to Mussolini's Italy (midway in the development continuum) and to the dictator-ship of Duvalier in Haiti (a very backward system and nation). As might be expected, these systems are very different.'[1] Nor is it sufficient explanation to assert that in using the term fascist to describe Duvalier's Haiti a serious terminological inexactitude has been committed. In many respects fascism is the only meaningful description for that particular form of the organization of society. Certainly it is not one which Marxists such as Castro have hesitated to use.

Since hope of financial gain has frequently proved to be a main-spring of political action it seems worthwhile to look first at fascism in terms of its economic relationship to society. The starting point must necessarily be that fascism can have very different economic effects in different countries. Is it possible to discern any common factor? According to Woolf, 'One can legitimately doubt whether it is appropriate to use so distinctive a term as "system" when discuss-ing fascist economics . . . were fascist economics, consequently, anything more than a series of improvisations, of responses to particular and immediate problems?'[2] However, Woolf in his discussion of this problem subsequently modified his viewpoint and recognized a definable form of fascist economic life common at least to Germany, Italy and Japan, despite his earlier insistence that 'in the economic field fascism' could not 'lay claim to any serious theoretical basis'.[3]

It seems to me that certain general propositions may be advanced in relation to fascist economic life and that these have some relevance to the form of society that evolved. The fascist basis in a developed state or a state well advanced on the road to development is that of the closed commercial state, as originally envisaged by Fichte (incidentally at a time when Germany was not a developed state). The fascist basis in an under-developed state is a form of economic nationalism which effectively restricts development with the intention, not always successful, of thereby reducing dependence on external powers or bodies. While it must be remembered that these forms of economic management are not sufficient in themselves to warrant the description of a state as fascist, taken in conjunction with certain political forms within that state, they provide generally reliable pointers. It is no accident of history that Bernhardi declared: '. . . there must be a sort of mobilization in the sphere of commercial politics in order to insure under all eventualities the supply of the goods necessary for the material and industrial needs of the country'.[4] If Bernhardi spoke for the developed nations, in 1963 the organ of the African Development Bank put forward a similar case for the underdeveloped states: '. . . political direction is needed if the African Development Bank is to become a lever for promoting the economic independence of African states. To leave it either without political direction or with a conflict of political objectives will quite conceivably convert the bank into an instrument for the penetration and further enslavement of Africa by international financial oligarchies.'[5] The fascist characteristic—the desire to attain total control over economic destiny—has thus been present in widely different forms of society. Both concepts, although originating from different starting points, are the antithesis of the doctrine of free trade.

One assumption may therefore be made about the fascist approach to economics—that fascism is most likely to flourish in societies where there is a process of attempted economic change. Economic policy is, of course, more likely to vary over short periods of time when the traditional basis of national prosperity has been undermined. Fascist economic theory sought to provide definitive answers to these problems and in so doing drew heavily on the tradition of economic autarky. Quite apart from all the other factors that militated against the fascists in Britain, their political attractiveness was greatly inhibited by the widespread failure of both the British politicians and public to recognize the need for new solutions to long-standing economic grievances. British politicians believed that traditional remedies would, eventually, cure unemployment and the other serious problems that afflicted Britain in the 1930s. In Germany, on the other hand, politicians of the centre as well as of the extreme Left and Right advocated drastic cures. It was Stresemann who introduced the *Rentenmark* in 1923 in an attempt to reduce inflation and stabilize the economy. By comparison, the British Labour Party had no answer at all in 1931 while the other parties took refuge under the umbrella of traditional economic wisdom. What is particularly revealed by the comparison is that the implementation of radical measures produced a political taste for experimentation while dull conservatism resulted in political apathy and not a violent revulsion from traditional political styles.

The attractiveness of fascism in economic terms was that it provided an answer to contemporary problems, although it is clear that the solution varied according to the nature of the society. In Germany fascism was inevitably connected with industrial reorganization and development, as befitted a highly industrialized country. In Romania fascism became linked with agrarian areas and hence with more conservative forces in society. The important feature common to both societies, however, was acute political consciousness born of a desire for economic change. Conventional parties were on the whole unable to beat off both the fascist and the communist challenges. In Europe economic change was generally linked with the process of industrialization—conflicts arose between traditional and modern groups within society of which fascism first sought to take advantage in order to arrive in power, and later to assuage in the name of national unity and the common good. The fascist economic appeal was closely linked with nationalism, for the policies advocated by Hitler and Mussolini required sacrifices, particularly of consumption. The restrictions on demand that were enforced could only be justified in political terms by promises that the goals that were being pursued would be attainable within the immediate future. Much of Hitler's popularity must have stemmed from success at reducing the level of unemployment, which in turn increased the credibility of the rest of his economic programme.

In order to obtain any clear view of the attractiveness of fascist economic doctrine it is essential to examine some of the fascist proposals. On a propaganda level one of the most common assertions was that the nation was at the mercy of international capitalist oligarchies or some similarly nebulous bodies (these assertions bear close similarity to those made by some under-developed countries of the present, notably Nkrumah's Ghana and Sekou Touré's Guinea). Goebbels on one occasion even went so far as to suggest: 'We shall be the mercenaries against Russia on the battlefields of capitalism. Turn and twist as much as you will. We have been sold. And in the last analysis better go down with Bolshevism than live in eternal capitalist servitude.'[6] The concept of an international capitalist conspiracy was bound to be popular in Germany if for no other reason than that it satisfactorily explained not only defeat in the war of 1914–18 but also the strange and untoward economic developments in Germany in the 1920s. In fact, the notion of conspiracy was given a still more potent appeal by the involvement of the capitalists with the Jews. The fascists in Germany and in much of Eastern Europe insisted that plutocracy was the major characteristic of modern democracy and that Jewish financiers, most notably the Rothschilds, were the most enthusiastic backers of this evil social system. If in a modern context Latin America is substituted for Germany and the Americans for the Jews much of the propaganda has a familiar ring.

The conspiracy theory attracted many adherents outside Germany. Quisling spoke of 'a gigantic international plot by the Jews and moneylenders to destroy nationalism',[7] and his views were by no means unique. The addition of anti-Jewish sentiment to the already powerful mixture opened the way for new recruits. Exactly how much the Nazis believed in the economic role of the Jews is debatable. As far back as 1890 Barrès had asserted that the term 'Jew' merely indicated a usurer, monopolist and plutocrat rather than a racial identity. Barrès wished the Jews to be deprived of political rights for economic reasons, as did so many of the Frenchmen who succeeded to his fascist inheritance. Maurras, like Barrès, saw the Jews as a politico-economic force rather than as racially decadent. On hearing his sentence in 1945, he bellowed 'It is the revenge of Dreyfus!'[8] Conventional anti-Semitism, already widely spread in Europe, could thus be harnessed in support of fascist economic dogma.

If, superficially, fascist economics pointed in the direction of unity and the total state, in practice the fascists frequently behaved differently. In 1938 Keitel described the economic system as 'a war of all against all'[9] from which not even the overlordship of Speer could rescue Germany. When Speer took over direction of the armaments industry he found that although pressure and coercion maintained production the result of rivalries was a number of small empires. On 21 March 1942 a declaration was even made to the effect that industry was not 'knowingly lying to us, stealing from us, or otherwise trying to damage our war economy'.[10] Even in wartime, then, the concept of the total state in which all citizens worked together for the benefit of the nation was not attained. The appeal for unity was frequently made but the target was seldom reached.

Fascist economic theory thus sought to attract different types of people into the party. In Germany appeals were made to traditional conservative interests (protection of the middle class), to expansionists (the closed commercial state), to the working class (abolition of unemployment and the introduction of certain benefits), to the prejudiced and the dispossessed (the connection with anti-Semitism) and to the rabid nationalists (international financial conspiracy). Obviously not all these promises were fulfilled either as a whole or in part, but they provided powerful attractions for the German people. Similar types of promises were made to Italians, Dutch, French and other populations where fascism came to be established. What, then, were the effects of these usually inconsistent proposals upon the societies within which their inventors moved?

The most pressing problem that faced several of the societies in which fascism became firmly established was unemployment. In Germany unemployment figures exceeded 6 million in 1932 and 1933. In the same years there were over a million out of work in Italy. The slump in these two countries was of particular significance owing to heavy dependence on foreign trade. It made any solution essentially an internal one, owing to the collapse of international collaboration in economic affairs in the early 1930s. Yet at the same time the slump gave greater plausibility to attacks on foreign capital, as exemplified by the interests of the Rothschilds or plans such as those of Dawes and Young. Despite the lack of foreign aid, the German government was able to bring about a dramatic drop in unemployment, for by 1938 the number of unemployed had decreased to less than half a million. The basis of this achievement was the economic genius of Schacht rather than the existence of a detailed plan based upon fascist theory. In his memoirs Schacht asserted that 'Hitler never interfered with my work. He never attempted to give me any instructions, but let me carry out my own ideas in my own way and without criticism . . .'.[11] Schacht, of course, managed to blend together successfully the ideas which Hitler held—the expansionism of Bernhardi, the autarky of Fichte and the national socialism of List and Dühring. As long as he continued to operate the economy on lines of which Hitler generally approved he was left alone, but as soon as he began to develop policies suggested by his own immense economic genius he was removed from office.

However, no matter who selected the policies, those adopted by the Nazis in the mid-1930s enjoyed considerable success. The basis of success was very high government expenditure. Initially credit was extended to industry in order to facilitate employment of a larger labour force (this was a policy first introduced by von Papen), later there was an extensive programme of public works, especially roads. It was only later that rearmament began to play a major part in the German economy, probably not until 1936–7. During the first six years of Nazi rule the expenditure on rearmament was only 40,000 million marks.[12] This figure conceals a very wide variation over the whole period, but makes nonsense of Churchill's claims regarding arms expenditure in 1936. However, the long-term consequences of rearmament proved much less attractive.

The chief defect of the intensive rearmament programme was the pressure of inflation which resulted. Control of prices and wages partly eased these effects, but it is obvious that by 1939 the economy was seriously strained. There were serious shortages of labour in both industry and agriculture and in 1938 the balance of payments moved into deficit. As Germany had not yet attained a position of economic autarky such a position was not only dangerous in itself but also implied the failure of the theory. One of the central problems was political rather than economic in nature—the fact that in political terms Germany was pursuing aims likely to lead to war while the economy was geared to rearmament rather than total war. As is well known the German economy attained maximum production only in 1944, so the gulf between economic and political actions was particularly wide given that the years of maximum political activity were 1938–41.

If the most important source of support for the Nazis initially lay among the unemployed there must have been much satisfaction with the régime of 1935. However, there were other strings to the fascist economic bow. Dwarfed only by the spectre of unemployment was the agony of German agriculture. The agrarian depression played a central part in the rise of the Nazis to power. By 1932 agricultural products on average sold for only 65 per cent of what they had fetched in 1928. The Nazis cashed in on this discontent to great effect. In the July election of 1932 the half-dozen areas in which the percentage of Nazi votes was highest all contained a well above-average number of people dependent on agriculture.[13] The Nazis also profited from the agricultural depression which drove farm labourers into the towns where they joined the armies of the streets and graduated by this route to become members of the party. Fascist policy in relation to agriculture convinced many peasants that they had at last discovered a party that would protect their interests. The Nazi economic programme was particularly attractive in terms of both specific measures and general sentiment. The Nazis proposed a reduction in the capital value of agrarian debts and a cut in the rate of interest to about 2 per cent. In addition, higher tariffs and lower taxation were envisaged as well as recognition of the farm labourer's right to work. The man who made all these proposals was Darré,[14] who was appointed Minister of Agriculture as soon as Hitler came to power. In practice, however, Darré's influence was confined to the period 1928–33 when Hitler was still seeking power, for nothing more was heard of the more radical proposals he made after the summer of 1933. Yet the fascist appeal to the peasants hardly diminished, for there were important benefits from Nazi rule. Industrial policy led to the payment of prices for food which were well above the world average, and this applied not only to foodstuffs purchased from Eastern Europe and Latin America but also internally. The increasing purchasing power of the German industrial worker, together with a more favourable pricing system (and the desire for self-sufficiency), combined to revive memories of the privileged position enjoyed by agriculture in Imperial days.

One of the most curious aspects of fascist doctrine is, however, that it contrived simultaneously to appeal to radical and conservative economic forces. While this process was all very well during a period of opposition (assuming that opponents were not able to expose the inevitable contradictions), once in office it could hardly be maintained. Fascist doctrine in Germany contained a number of radical economic proposals; Feder believed that there should be the abolition of profit for individuals at the expense of the community, the abolition of unearned income, the removal of the power of interest and the introduction of nationalization on a large scale. There were thus considerable elements in the programme likely to appeal to the working class, though with the downfall of the Strassers and the retirement of Feder into obscurity there was left no obvious leader of the radical section of the party. Significantly, Hitler declared in a speech of 13 July 1933 to his assembled Gauleiters, 'political power we had to conquer rapidly and with one blow; in the economic sphere other principles of development must determine our action'.[15] What these principles were could be seen not only in a speech made just a week before when the Führer had revealed that 'the revolution is not a permanent state of affairs, and it must not be allowed to develop into such a state. The stream of revolution released must be guided into the safe channel of evolution.'[16] In the summer of 1933 Hitler matched his words with action. Schacht found that the major figures with whom he had to co-operate were not the radicals (though Darré retained his post) but conservatives, such as Schmitt,[17] Krupp and Thyssen.

The power of the radicals was quickly broken, though they had played an important part in Hitler's rise to power. The party's Economic Section had been headed by Wagener who had tried to dominate the Employers' Association and had been an active campaigner against international capitalism. Wagener had been strongly supported by von Renteln, representative of the small shopkeepers who were terrified by competition from multiple stores. In 1932, when votes were needed, the party had been glad to call upon the services of these men, but on 7 July 1933 Hess[18] issued an edict prohibiting action against multiple stores and later he let it be known that disciplinary measures would be taken against members of the party who failed to follow the Führer's evolutionary path. The purge of Röhm and his associates in 1934 ended all prospect of a radical revival.

Fascist economic doctrine as practised in Germany should not be seen as a mere surrender to conservative capitalist forces. If it was true that there was 'little desire to nationalize industries, for ideological as well as political reasons'[19] it was also true that 'both the domestic and the foreign policy of the National Socialist government became, from 1936 onwards, increasingly independent of the influence of the economic ruling classes and in some respects ran contrary to their interests'.[20] There was a far greater weight of bureaucratic machinery than would have been the case in a normal capitalist economy. This was perceived by Speer for whom the problem was of particular importance. Referring to the wartime situation, he wrote: '. . . among the causes for this backwardness I always reckoned excessive bureaucratization, which I fought in vain . . . the longer I fought the typically German bureaucracy, whose tendencies were aggravated by the authoritarian system, the more my criticism assumed a political cast . . . the war was a contest between two systems of organization, the "struggle of our system of overbred organization against the art of improvisation on the opposing side" '.[21]

As it is quite clear from a study of Hitler's rise to power that he was ready to collaborate with conservative forces (at least until his most important goals had been achieved) in politics, it should not be a cause of surprise that this affected his attitude towards economic development. The demands of fascist policy only gradually ate away the resistance of conservative forces, thus introducing change, albeit hardly radical change. Ever since the Bismarckian era heavy industry had dominated German economic life and on the occasions when its supremacy had been threatened its leaders had drawn together in cartels or similar associations. Concentration of industrial power continued under the Nazis, though this accorded ill with opposition to capitalist enslavement. The extremely important chemical industry was dominated by I. G. Farben and the growing electrical industry by Siemens. A new combination, the Reichswerke Hermann Göring, led the way in iron and steel production. The fact of the matter was that the industrialists surrendered to the fascists long before the army and the Foreign Office. Their hope that this surrender of power would prove to be temporary was illusory. Every error of judgement led to a reduction of power. When private industry would not risk money to expand the metallurgical industry the extension of government credit enabled Göring's combine to come into existence in the summer of 1937. The industrialists' lack of real power was recognized in the form of industrial consultation adopted—Schacht's creation, the *Reichswirtschaftskammer*, founded in 1936, proved to be little else but a sounding board for first his, and later Göring's, ideas. If the great industrial magnates gave help to the fascists in the belief that they would thereby preserve their monopolistic power, as they did, they must have been sadly disappointed.

If the emphasis of industry changed, so too did its appearance. After a few years in power the fascists had seriously undermined the position of both industrialists and workers, although this had, almost inevitably, led to a stronger grip by the bureaucracy on the economic levers. The drive towards economic autarky was hardly consistent, nationalization was not carried out on a large scale, cartels were attacked but not destroyed. Nonetheless the fascist approach to economics had some dramatic effects, not only upon unemployment figures, as has already been mentioned, but on industrial society as a whole. After 1936 there were serious shortages of both labour and raw materials which led to ruthless competition between firms for these basic factors of production. The increase in the strength of the armed forces hardly eased this desperate situation. Even under the uninspiring leadership of Ley[22] the power of the Labour Front grew. The Charter of Labour, dating from 1934, attempted to regulate wages, taxes, holidays, hours, insurance and other factors affecting the labour force, but in practice there were still strikes and wage increases. In 1938 serious attempts were made to allocate priorities but the division of national economic life into a number of jarring and competing empires was already far advanced. Workers were being paid secretly in the form of bonus systems or extra privileges in order to retain their loyalty and it was not until the introduction of a sensible scheme of labour deployment, after war had broken out, that this problem was solved. Many members of the working class thus enjoyed a good economic position under Nazi rule, not least because the concept of the national economy was not carried through. If economic autarky had been seriously implemented then the drift of labour away from the farms and mines would have been prevented on political as well as economic grounds. An element of labour mobility at a time of labour shortage gave workers more strength in bargaining than has usually been realized.

In economic terms, then, Nazi Germany failed to pursue an ideologically unified policy. Yet Nazi economic policy had a great impact on German society. One of the major causes of Hitler's rise to power was the adverse economic position of Germany between 1929 and 1933. In those years Nazi appeals to the public extended over a whole range of interests—from promises to protect the interests of capital to radical declarations of support for the notion of reconstituting economic patterns in the interests of ordinary Germans. In theory the policy statements could absorb such contradictions by reference to the notion of the autarkic state, but in practice the inconsistencies were exposed. After the acquisition of power in 1933 the success of Nazi economic policy stemmed from political agility which enabled Hitler to play off all important sections of the community against each other by promising a vast increase in national wealth (from which all would benefit) once his policy had come to fruition. If his goal of domination in Eastern Europe and use of its resources had been attained there can hardly be any doubt that his prophecy would have come true. The appeal to the general public of Nazi economic policy, its effects on industry and society, and its place in fascist ideology must, therefore, be seen in the larger context of Hitler's commitment to expansionism. Unless this is recognized the contradictions between theory and practice become almost incomprehensible.

12 Mussolini and the
Fascist Prototype

'I declare here before this assembly, before all the Italian people, that I assume, I alone, the political, moral, historical responsibility for everything that has happened.' Benito Mussolini, *Autobiography*, p. 231

It is of interest to compare the fascist experience in Italy with that of Germany. It is an instructive process not only because these were the two principal countries in which it is most meaningful to speak of a fascist impact upon society but also because in Italy the fascists had much more time in which to make their mark. Germany had a mere five years or so (1933–8) before her economy was placed on a war footing; in Italy the period was three times as long (1922–39). Furthermore, the experiences of Italy acted in some cases as a model, in others a warning, to innovators in other countries.

Just as in Germany the rise of the fascists to power in Italy was greatly assisted by economic chaos. Mention has already been made of the disruptive forces at work in Italian society. These were intensified by the primacy in politics of economic issues. Ever since the close of the nineteenth century the economy had grown in an unbalanced fashion, speculation and a prolonged period of inflation being two prominent characteristics. Governmental attempts to hold down wages enjoyed little success and industrial unrest grew markedly in the period immediately after the end of the war. In July 1919 there were widespread riots against the increase in the cost of living; in 1919–20 many peasants seized land, an action which the government was forced to recognize retrospectively. Membership of the Socialist Confederation of Labour rose from about 350,000 in 1913 to 2.2 million in 1921. Militancy was the order of the day, both among the workers and the industrialists. Italian industry was already inclining towards the creation of cartels, for, as Lombardini has pointed out: 'Entrepreneurial activities were not fostered by the cultural environment; the survival of a feudalistic culture and the generally accepted conception of the state as a patron which can

grant privileges or threaten safety did not encourage free enterprise.'[1] The fascists were thus able to put forward an economic
programme which contained elements that appealed strongly to
many sections of society. As in Germany a decade later, working
class, middle class and industrial barons were all able to see the
fascists as potential protectors of their interests.

In considering the social and economic significance of fascist
policies in Italy it is worth bearing in mind the charge that fascism
just responded to situations as they arose, rather than having a
coherent doctrine upon which to base action. Times change and
circumstances alter cases. It is now usually regarded as a vice if
governments fail to respond to challenges by adhering too formally
to their programmes. Indeed, writing of the Labour government of
1929–31, Skidelsky observed: 'Inexperience may well excuse administrative failure, but it does not entirely explain the want of courage,
the intellectual paralysis that gripped the Labour Government.'[2]
There is a clear implication that flexibility and responsiveness were
two of the qualities which were missing. Why, then, should the
fascists be condemned for their possession of these qualities? The
answer, perhaps, lies in the fact that observers constantly found
themselves baffled by the twists and turns of fascist policy and found
it easier to offer inconsistency as an explanation than the existence of
a flexible plan. It ought not to be forgotten that if strict adherence to
party dogma (defined perhaps many years before) be taken as a test
of opportunism then Stalin emerges as the greatest opportunist of
the 1930s rather than Hitler or Mussolini. As Welk stated, as long
ago as 1938: 'While critics of the Fascist régime are inclined to
regard, not without some justification, such shifts and changes in
policy as sheer opportunism, Fascists call this apparent lack of
consistency "a courageous steering of their ship on troubled economic seas". Storms, they point out, are not rational and must be
fought as best they can when they arise.'[3]

Certain clear suppositions were made by the fascists in Italy. On
the whole they preferred non-interference by the state in economic
processes, save in the national interest. They also recognized the
right to private property, individual initiative and the desirability of
freedom of competition. As the fascists grew accustomed to power
these notions were subtly modified. Intervention on the grounds of
raison d'état became increasingly frequent; the fascists discovered
that pure politics could not be practised without some close control

over the economy. In the second place they came to see economic liberty as 'an expedient method, a concession made to the individual by society in the interest of the social group as a whole, a concession which may, whenever necessary, be revoked'.[4] The implications of these modifications are clear. Italian fascism regarded economic life as primarily a social interest; society was seen as having 'a direct and superior concern in all phases of the nation's economic life'.[5] This is a direct contradiction to Organski's assertion that 'fascism is part of the process of transition from a limited participation to a mass system, and fascism is a last-ditch stand by the élites, both modern and traditional, to prevent the expansion of the system over which they exercise hegemony'.[6]

In the first few years of rule the Minister for Economic Affairs, De Stefani,[7] reformed the tax system and balanced the budget. A number of state enterprises were returned to private ownership, but this was not a general pattern. Serious attempts were made to stimulate both agriculture and industry; there was a liberal credit policy and a great deal of new capital investment resulting in a period of steady growth. Exports rose from 9.5 billion lire in 1922 to 15.6 billion in 1926. During the same period savings stood at a level of 12 per cent of national income, an exceptionally high figure. However, in 1925–6 the measures introduced by the government began to fail and the party's popularity underwent a temporary eclipse. The chief cause was an over-expansion of credit, leading to a serious currency weakness. As yet there had been no real indication of the introduction of a corporative state economy, though at Pesaro on 18 August 1926 Mussolini declared that he would defend the stability of the lira 'to the last drop of blood'.

The continuing fascist concern for the control of labour was also shown in 1926, for on 3 April a law was promulgated making fascist syndics the only representatives of their occupational groups. Strikes and lockouts were expressly prohibited. The only ways of settling labour disputes that were henceforward acceptable were collective bargaining and the decisions of government labour courts. In an attempt to make this decree seem more palatable a vague collection of suggestions, injunctions and aphorisms was devised to provide a gloss; its publication in 1927 under the name of the Charter of Labour was greeted with baffled incomprehension.

Despite these unpromising starts, the period 1926–9 witnessed increasingly effective government intervention. Note circulation, which had reached 21.4 billion lire in 1925, fell to 16.8 billion lire in 1929. Deflationary measures began to take effect. There were reductions in wages, interest rates, taxes and rents. The intention was to make Italian prices fall into line with the rest of the industrial world. In theory a planned economy was gradually introduced, with the avowed intention of making Italy self-sufficient. In practice, at least during this period, the planned economy mainly meant more work for an increasing number of bureaucrats. The personal involvement of Mussolini in economic affairs was high, however, and his enthusiasm was responsible for two important acts. On 29 July 1927 a measure to increase agrarian credits was passed. As well as providing a very much needed stimulus to agricultural production (Mussolini dramatically referred to his campaign as 'the battle for wheat'), the law also established a National Consortium for Agrarian Credit, the first major regulatory body introduced by the fascists. The second important measure was the so-called Mussolini Act of 24 December 1928, which initiated a vast programme of land reclamation. During the next decade actions based upon this measure were highly successful and most of the swampy areas of Italy (amounting to about 7 per cent of cultivable land) were drained. Population resettlement followed and production increased.

The period 1929–34 marked the apogee of governmental intervention. To a very considerable degree fascist policies protected Italy from the worst consequences of the depression. It is true that prices fell and markets dwindled. Industrial production, which stood at 100 in 1928, rose to 109.2 in 1929 but fell to 73 by 1932. Wage reductions were almost inevitable in these circumstances and unemployment rose. In December 1930 Mussolini told the senate that 'fortunately the Italian people were not accustomed to eat much and therefore feel the privation less acutely than others'.[8] None the less Mussolini took a strong interest in economic developments during this period. On 13 November 1931 the *Istituto Mobiliare Italiano* was established in order to provide financial aid to those branches of industry that had suffered most seriously during the depression. The attempts of private industry to find its own solution were taken over by the state under the law of 16 June 1932. Private cartels, known as *consorzi*, had become extremely common since 1929 and were now taken under government control. Indeed, in some cases compulsory membership was introduced in an attempt to regulate certain industries. Some of the leading industrialists, notably members of the Pirelli and Agnelli families, became concerned lest this should prove to be the first step towards nationalization of major industrial companies. These fears were proved groundless in the next few months.

The principal action taken by the fascists was to increase expenditure on public works. In 1928–29 expenditure stood at 1,676 million lire, in 1931–32 this figure had risen to 2,877 million lire. At the same time unemployment insurance was introduced, there were special relief grants, the working week was shortened, and internal migration was controlled. The corporative state had arrived. The concept of the balanced budget, so dear to orthodox economists in the 1930s, was abandoned: the deficit rose from less than half a billion lire in 1930–31 to over three and a half billion lire in 1933–34.

As well as introducing measures, many of which might be only temporary in application, Mussolini set out to create a more permanently fascistized economy. In January 1933 the *Istituto di Recostruzione Industriale* (I.R.I.) was set up. Its function was to provide financial aid to industrial concerns by means of long-term loans, backed by government guaranteed bonds. The problems created by the existence of the *consorzi* were also recognized in the laws of 12 January and 5 May 1933. These were designed to prevent industrial overproduction and to rationalize the process of expansion in a way that would fit in with Mussolini's desire for economic self-sufficiency. It was at this time too that Mussolini's imperial ambitions began to affect the development of the economy. During 1934–5 serious controls on imports were introduced and a system of quotas and licenses created. This and other measures were closely connected with the coming adventure over Abyssinia, but even before involvement in Africa took place there was a serious renewal of working-class unrest. Mussolini sought to meet complaints in characteristic fashion. On 5 February 1934 an act was passed creating councils for the occupational corporations. These councils consisted of an equal number of representatives of workers' and employers' syndics, together with a small number of technical experts and members of the party. It was intended that the councils should act as conciliation boards, but of course their effectiveness was much diminished by appeals for sacrifices in the name of national unity.

The effects of the Abyssinian war were to accelerate both the progress towards the introduction of a corporative system and the drive towards autarky. Sanctions played a significant role in this process after their introduction on 18 November 1935. The system of controls previously introduced by Mussolini acted as a cushion against a sudden change in traditional trading patterns. Additionally, Italy had a large stock of raw materials, upon which the war machine was able to draw. Price controls were introduced and there was rigid protection of Italian gold reserves. Where imports of essential goods were badly affected industries were encouraged to develop substitutes or to revive the production of local resources, previously abandoned as unprofitable. Resistance to sanctions was formidable, not least because many countries ignored the directive of the League, thus not only facilitating Italian resistance but also holding out hope that the policy of sanctions would collapse, as it eventually did. On 23 March 1936 Mussolini, with characteristic bombast, said: 'November 18th is a date which will mark the start of a new phase in Italian history, a phase dominated by the fundamental postulate of seeking to achieve, in the least possible time, the maximum possible degree of economic independence.' The fascists were now totally committed to a policy of economic autarky.

During the brief period of time that elapsed between the end of sanctions and the declaration of war on France the Italian economy failed to make much progress. The goal of autarky was certainly never achieved. In fact, so closely linked was the Italian economy to that of the rest of Western Europe that on 5 October 1936 the lira was devalued, to bring it into line with other currencies. Wage and price inflation existed, as in Germany, and in October 1936 wages were increased by an average of about 9 per cent. Many of the most successful schemes of the past, such as land reclamation, were temporarily abandoned—in fact never to be revived. Rearmament, the readiness of the eight million bayonets, became the immediate goal. Mack Smith accurately summarized the cost of the policies of 1936–40 when he wrote: 'Mussolini confessed to Admiral Maugeri in 1943 that Italy had been much better equipped for war in 1915 than in 1939, so that the seventeen years of fascism had apparently been to no purpose. The regrettable fact was that the long and painful struggle for autarky, far from increasing Italian strength as had been promised, had done the very reverse. Fascism, indeed, was being defeated by its own dogma.'[9]

13 Fascism, Class and Social Change

'The dreadful events in the years that followed were a direct
result of the effect of this period of moral decay on the German
body politic.' Franz von Papen, *Memoirs*, p. 129

In view of the Italian and German experiences, does it make sense to
talk of fascist economic systems? Is it not true that fascist governments responded to situations in ways that were similar to those
adopted by other governments? In order to answer these questions
it does not make much sense to look at the economic systems of other
fascist states, for they almost invariably came into existence in
wartime. The French experience of fascist economics was greatly
influenced by German occupation and, indeed, even though the
Vichy régime was very weak it still prevented the complete application of fascist principles.[1] In other occupied countries it was the
application of German techniques on behalf of German interests
that shaped the economy, not local fascist interests. As Milward has
observed, writing of Norway, 'the relative lack of complexity of the
economy seemed to make it more susceptible of incorporation
within the framework of economic reconstruction which Germany
hoped to erect in Europe than a complex economy, both liberal and
imperialist in nature, such as that of France'.[2] The only useful piece
of information, for the purpose of answering these questions, which
does emerge is that the Germans were committed to a form of
economic self-sufficiency, which was to be attained by conquest and
annexation. The connection between autarky and expansionism,
which was so characteristic of European fascism, exemplified in
Germany's New Order in Europe, could also be found in the
Japanese scheme for East Asia. If it is possible to assume that from
the very start both the German and Japanese governments had the
intention of expanding territorially then certain parts of their economic planning make good ideological sense.

However, to recognize the truth of this fact ought not to lead one
to suppose that there was a great ideological content in fascist

economics, ruthlessly applied at the expense of pragmatism. The fascists, like supporters of democratic governments, balanced ideology against necessity. In many cases, it may be argued, they responded better to   challenges than democratic governments. Knowingly or unknowingly, Hitler and Mussolini applied Keynesian remedies in the 1930s more consistently than Roosevelt. Realities fettered the fascists as much as the democrats or the communists. Absolute control of the economy did not exist in Germany any more than it did in Britain or in the Soviet Union. The fascists had an economic ideology, as did the Marxists, and their leaders tried to apply their rather muddled principles to situations which the ideologists had never envisaged. Inconsistency, then, seems an unimportant charge to level against the fascists—even if the charge were true, does it matter?

The importance of fascist beliefs about the nature of the economy and its relation to the state lies in the effects on society. European societies were very greatly affected by the rise of fascism and the rule of the fascists. Everyone in the state could find some aspect of proposed policy from which he would benefit. Electoral success or elevation to power by some coup followed quickly and naturally from this fact. Unless the fascists were to make all citizens of the state their enemies (by protecting no interests other than their own) or offend some influential groups (by protecting business against the workers or *vice versa*), they needed to find an answer. This they did, albeit by pursuing policies that were apparently self-contradictory. But the fascists rationalized their procedure, first by asserting that perfection could not be immediately achieved (an argument used by most governments to explain reverses of all kinds) and, more importantly, by asserting that all interests, government, party, industrial, agricultural, upper-, middle- and working-class, would benefit from the achievement of self-sufficiency. Autarkic expansionism was the only plausible solution to the problem. If the Germans ruled Eastern Europe and the Italians dominated the Mediterranean then privation and under-privilege would disappear among the Germans and Italians. Although not all fascists recognized the inexorable logic of their attempts to please all sections of the electorate (save for minority groups such as Jews), economic realities forced them to do so. An exaggerated nationalism, characteristic of fascism, pushed the fascists in such a direction from the very start. Experience in power completed the process. The effects on society were, of course, immense. The quest for the economic millennium helped destroy public morality and integrity at almost every level. Often the sacrifices of principle which were made were not recognized until too late: frequently they were never recognized at all. It was, in fact, because fascism was a mass movement, possessing a distinctive economic policy with a mass appeal, that events took the course they did. If fascism had not sought to appeal to any sections of society the pressures on fascist governments would have been much less significant. Probably many of the leaders of the Third Reich failed to perceive the ultimate destiny of their policies. Speer saw the likely outcome and recoiled from the prospect, while Rosenberg, even at his trial, still had blind faith in the rightness of his cause. But these two men, at opposite poles, recognized the consequences of their actions, whereas the performance of those, like Göring and Streicher, who gave in to pressures in the 1930s and similarly surrendered at Nuremberg in 1945, suggests that they always gave way to superior strength and deemed it a virtue. They were the men who helped 'direct' the course of fascism and it is upon them that responsibility must fall most heavily. They were powerful examples of the corruption of fascist society, and it is only by an examination of the personnel of fascism that the face of fascism in practice is fully revealed.

In any examination of the personnel of fascism two questions must be answered: who were the leaders and who supported them? It is much easier to provide an acceptable answer to the first than to the second question. As might be expected the leaders of fascism came from widely different backgrounds. Only two of the major leaders can be described as upper class—Mosley and the Belgian, Degrelle.[3] Many were of middle-class origin. Quisling was an army officer and son of a priest, Clausen a doctor, de Clercq[4] and Déat were both teachers, Mussert[5] was an engineer and van Severen[6] a lawyer. Hitler was the son of a petty official, Mussolini and Doriot were sons of blacksmiths and Darnand[7] was the son of a railway worker. Fascism, like Marxism, thus provided a speedy route to the top for political aspirants outside the traditional ruling classes. This fact itself reveals one of the principal reasons for the impact of fascism—it was a movement which flourished in a period of acute social mobility. The social and economic dislocation created by the war of 1914–18 provided the conditions in which fascism could most obviously flourish. Many people, of diverse social origin, became the prey of fears that had scarcely existed in the years before 1914.

Fascists were particularly successful at convincing people of all classes in many different countries that their dynamism could resolve these fears in a fashion which would protect a wide range of interests.

Despite general agreement about the conditions in which fascism flourished there is little unanimity among historians about the nature of the support given to the fascists. Andreski suggested that 'Indeed, one could even advance the hypothesis that the more devoted a fascist movement was to the defence of the upper classes, the less capable was it of mobilizing mass sentiment for aggressive purposes.'[8] The implications of this comment are clearly that fascism needed a strong populist base and that when its leaders deviated too markedly from a populist policy their position was undermined. Advocates of this theory would probably see Italian fascism as the most obvious paradigm. On the other hand, Solé-Tura has asserted that 'fascism arose as a direct expression of a real state of discontent in one sector of the population (the lower middle classes)'.[9] Acceptance of this argument would imply that fascism could never have any genuine mass support, for its whole success depended upon the appeal of its ideology to a threatened sector of society. These differences of opinion are irreconcilable and it is essential to try to make some judgement between their rival merits.

The balance of evidence would seem to point to the explanation that fascism was a mass movement, not almost exclusively dependent upon one class. It can hardly be doubted that Hitler was genuinely popular in Germany. If his party failed to win outright in any free and competitive election it seems likely nonetheless that at virtually any time between 1936 and 1939 Hitler would have won an overwhelming vote of support from the German people. Until disasters began to occur (after 1936) it seems probable that this would have been true of Mussolini in Italy too. The evidence of such plebiscites as were held in Germany and Italy at the time may be adduced in favour of this assertion, though it must be remembered that considerable elements of compulsion and terror were present. What is more significant is that both Mussolini and Hitler enjoyed some success in coping with the difficult economic problems of the decade and it seems highly unlikely that Italians and Germans would have neglected this fact in giving any verdict on the régimes. After all, conservative and middle-of-the-road politicians in France and England, who enjoyed much less success, encountered little difficulty in securing massive electoral support during the same period.

If a combination of patriotism and moderate prosperity can be held to explain a great deal of the popularity of fascism in the 1930s it can hardly be advanced as an explanation for the support given to fascism in its early, untested, days. During the rise of the fascists to power the significance of class rivalries can hardly be overstated. There are cetain common factors in the Italian and German situations that are worthy of examination. The most important common factor seems to have been a process of economic/political change. In Italy this took the shape of very rapid economic growth, which upset previously stable social patterns. In Germany economic dislocation led to a similar disruption of well-established class relationships. The Italian process of fascist development was quicker and earlier (in part a reflection of the long-standing grievances in Italian society) than that of Germany, so it is to this that attention will first be drawn.

The war of 1914–18 accelerated, as has already been mentioned, the growth of trade unionism and the parties of the Left in Italy. At roughly the same time (1913) there had been a vast expansion in the size of the electorate. In the period after 1918 there were many opportunities for the development of socialist answers to important social, economic and political questions. However, the main obstacle to a real shift in power lay not in the effectiveness of the traditional parties, which had almost disintegrated, or traditionally privileged economic groups, but in the *immobilisme* of the new parties of the Left. As Horowitz has pertinently observed: 'When it appeared that the government forces might not be able to cope with the situation, the Socialist Party sat back, and applauded but offered no leadership or direction, either back to legality or toward insurrection.'[10] Yet if it seemed that the traditional parties and the new parties of the Left were alike unable to cope with working class demands for increased wages and greater political control how was it that revolution was averted? The most probable answer may be seen in the political mobilization of other sections of the electorate. Other sectors of the community believed themselves to be threatened by the advance of labour. Middle-class workers throughout Europe found their social positions threatened on two fronts in the years after 1918. Not only was their standard of living falling (partly because of lack of proper organization) but at the same time their social inferiors were gaining important political and economic concessions which were rapidly closing the gap between the two classes, in terms of both financial standing and prestige. To be a white-collar worker no longer meant automatic social and economic superiority over the blue-collar worker. This was particularly true in Italy and this process generated a further form of socio-political mobilization, that of the threatened classes, which included among them not only the lower middle classes but also skilled and semi-skilled workers. The result of industrialization and political concessions in the shape of a wider franchise was political mobilization on a huge scale, of which fascism sought to take advantage.

It must not be assumed that the interests of these social groups were necessarily in total opposition. Both had important demands to make on the traditional ruling groups in Italy as well as on each other. In that fascists envisaged change as a centre-piece of their philosophy there was some common radical ground between these groups and fascism. The fascists could envisage pleasing both working- and middle-class interests through their programme for the introduction of the expansionist corporate state. The fascist deference to hierarchy proved to be an important asset, for potential recruits could be convinced that they could easily become an important cog in the new hierarchical order. The rise of men such as Hitler, Mussolini and Doriot was visible proof of the correctness of such a belief. In this sense Italian fascism could never be and was not just a defence of the privileges of the wealthy and well-established. The dynamics of the social situation dictated a different course. The suggestion made by Lombardini that 'In its origins fascism was supported mostly by socially frustrated members of the middle class and by landowners who encouraged violence against the peasant movements,'[11] indicates a major failure of understanding about the nature of the political opportunity offered to the fascists. If the fascists had just appealed to these sections of the community their popularity would have been short-lived and their fate virtually indistinguishable from the ineffective parties of the Right in Italy in the early 1920s.

The social significance of fascism was that it sought to create a new hierarchy or élite. The prospect of membership of that élite proved attractive to the politically frustrated of all classes, including the upper class. It was a doctrine particularly suited to a society in which there was a high degree of political mobilization and social mobility. Italy was such a society and, furthermore, had already witnessed a wide acceptance of the desirability of élitist rule in the approbation shown of the doctrines of Pareto. Pareto's hostility to democracy, modernization, liberal humanitarianism and progress had struck a chord in Italian hearts. Fascism, in one respect at least, was the political descendant of Paretoism and was thus enabled to appear as all things to most men. Members of the working class interested in fascism could look at the socialist-oriented programme of 1919 and Mussolini's proposals for much more even social justice. Threatened members of the middle class could welcome the prospect of a revival of status in the new imperial Italy. The upper class recruits could see fascism as a protective barrier against Marxist revolution and as a guarantor of established economic interests. It was possible to hold these contradictory beliefs not only because of the studied ambiguity of many of Mussolini's proposals but also because of greed for status. The fascist movement seemed to offer opportunities for those at the top to secure their places by putting themselves at the head of a new and dynamic élite and for others to improve their status by casting in their lot with a new party un-committed to the defence of the old semi-feudal, non-democratic society which had previously existed in Italy.

If capitalists flourished in Italy (as many, but not all, did) it was for two reasons. In the first place fascism was not anti-capitalist in the sense that fascist economic doctrine allowed a place for enter-prise, as long as it was deemed useful. In addition the fascists wished to move slowly towards a form of state capitalism and this could hardly be achieved by the sudden and violent overthrow of the pattern of private ownership. Indeed, Mussolini saw clearly in 1921–2 that attacking revolutionary elements in Italy would not significantly reduce his prospects of working-class support but would effectively immobilize potential opposition from conservative interests among the industrialists, the church and the army. Events were to prove him right. The conventional Right found itself swept along by fascism, travelling often in directions in which it did not wish to travel. It is interesting that Organski has written: '. . . the evidence seems compelling that the fascists climbed to a position of power because their activities and attitudes pleased all of the existing groupings of élites, with the army and the civil and paramilitary bureaucracies the immediate practical allies in the repression. In other words fascism was a major instrument of the élites seeking to beat down a threat to the existing system.'[12] Much of this is true, but the conclusion is false. It was the Right which surrendered to fascism, not fascism which surrendered to the Right. In the 1930s the King, the army and the church found that little pressure could be brought to bear on Mussolini once he was resolved to move in a particular direction. Opposition, for example, to the Abyssinian war was nugatory. In an earlier period the same thesis holds good. Conservative landed interests initially saw fascism as a protector against land-hungry peasants, but as the fascists became firmly established in power they tended to ignore pressure from these groups because more support could be derived from sections of society with different interests.[13]

Fascism in Italy also leaned heavily upon the notion of a revolutionary approach. The activities of the *gruppi di competenza* naturally focused around the enthusiasm of the young for a new political system, which they believed to be unencumbered and uncompromised by the history of the past. Many middle-class intellectuals were in some way committed to fascism in Italy, although they would have described themselves as radicals—men hostile to the preservation of existing privileges, save one, that of education. The poverty of the intellectual opposition to fascism was further emphasized by the bribes (in the form of status and privilege) handed out to leading writers and teachers in this period. Mussolini spoke repeatedly of the revolution being a perpetual process rather than just an event of 1922. These approaches to politics were designed to appeal to non-conservative forces in society and enjoyed considerable success, at least until the introduction of the racial laws in 1938. At that point the attractiveness of perpetual revolution began to diminish.

Support for fascism came from many different sections of the community. There were thus many different reasons for the support which was forthcoming, but the most important was the belief that fascism could solve Italian problems. The belief was born of, in Villari's words, 'exasperation, the mainspring of the Fascist movement at its outset'.[14] The Italians were 'yearning for peace and order . . . wanted to feel that there was a strong hand at the helm.'[15] The fascists were quick to recognize this feeling. The programme of 1921, devised at the Rome Congress, declared that 'The nation is not merely the sum total of living individuals, nor the instrument of parties for their own ends, but an organism comprising the unlimited series of generations of which individuals are merely transient elements; it is the supreme synthesis of all the material and non-material values of the race.'[16] Mussolini succinctly expressed the attractiveness of his doctrine when he referred to 'everything for the state, nothing against the state, no one outside the state'. All sections of society could draw comfort from the notion that their interests would receive protection in the new state. The hierarchical system advocated by the fascists, having as a result the enlargement of the bureaucracy, still further committed society to value order and obedience.

The fascist state created new opportunities for many people, mainly, admittedly, for the *arrivistes*, but this, of course, could hardly be foreseen in 1922. The fascist appeal was especially attractive to members of the middle class who had, in relation to members of other classes, recently undergone a shattering process of social realignment. There is some truth in Marxist assertions that the fascists derived their main strength from the *spostati*, the displaced persons of society. Those who were suffering from *anomie* were vulnerable to the appeal of fascism, and these were found mainly in the middle class. But recognition of the importance of these factors must not blind one to the fact that new political parties invariably come into existence through dissatisfaction with the existing order of things. After all, the Bolsheviks depended a great deal on disillusioned members of the middle class in Tsarist Russia, so the support of key sections of the middle class for fascism in Italy in the early 1920s should not necessarily be seen as a reliable index of the conservative nature of fascism. Indeed, fascism is inherently revolutionary in the case of Italy. The fact that conservatives misread the fascist emphasis on hierarchy as a welcome reinforcement for defence of the traditional structure of society has deceived far too many observers. The nature of Italian fascism was exemplified in its modernity, its approach to mass politics, the charismatic leader, the disciplined hierarchy and the exaltation of the nation-state. The fascists in reality had little in common with either the aristocracy or the bourgeoisie, those two pillars of traditional conservatism. The major social significance of Italian fascism, and the reason for its mass appeal, which transcended class (deliberately), was that it opened up apparently real prospects of social change.

Many of the factors that influenced the rise of fascism in Italy were also present in the case of Germany, although generally at a later period. But the political history of Germany before 1914 had been radically different from that of Italy and there was already established a large socialist party and a strong trade union movement.

Although apparently ruled by an emperor, Germany was in fact highly democratized in comparison with Italy, ruled by a constitutional monarch. The role of the Left in the rise of fascism was thus rather different, as can be seen from a brief examination of the events of 1914–25.

During the crisis in July and August 1914 the leaders of the Social Democratic Party had fulminated against war, threatening a general strike and to vote against army credits. Yet nationalist feeling ran strong even within this group for, at a private caucus of the parliamentary party, over two-thirds of its members were in favour of war credits; in the debate in the Reichstag the party unanimously associated itself with the war. It was only the pressure of war which seriously upset this unanimity and in 1917 dissident members broke away from the main body. In due course there were further defections from this splinter group which were ultimately to lead to the foundation of the German Communist Party. From 1917 onwards the commitment of the S.P.D. to revolutionary socialism was non-existent and the proclamation of a republic in 1918 was an anti-revolutionary response to a potentially revolutionary situation. On 19 January 1919, the S.P.D., led by Ebert, secured about 38 per cent of the total poll and, in conjunction with two other parties, was able to form an apparently stable government. The new administration was not only anti-Bolshevik but was very willing to work with conservative forces in the armed forces and the police in order to retain control.

Thus far the political history of Germany offered few opportunities for a fascist party. Indeed, attempts by conventional nationalists to secure a government more to their liking were suppressed without much difficulty, as were revolutionary moves from the Left. Although superficially the political structure of the Weimar Republic appeared secure there were in fact very serious defects which, not being remedied, were ultimately to lead to the rise of the fascists who managed to appeal to an ever-rising tide of discontented citizens. It was weak government that allowed threats to security to develop and hence the rise of political mobilization. Governments were weak in Germany because of an unfortunate combination of circumstances. Germany was for most of the 1920s regarded as a pariah in international affairs, and events such as the invasion of the Ruhr hardly corrected the deep national sense of frustration. The strong chauvinism present among most German politicians had in fact been reinforced rather than diminished by the events of 1918. It was much easier to find an explanation in terms of betrayal than defeat. The economic disasters of the 1920s, particularly the inflation of 1923, combined with reparations, also hit Germany harder than other European countries. The forces of democracy in Germany were weakened by unnecessary divisions, by the existence of the Catholic Centre Party (which divided the nation across non-political lines) and by the refusal of the S.P.D. to participate in coalitions at the end of the decade. Furthermore, most of the able politicians were inevitably identified with the revolution of 1918 and the humiliation of Versailles. The cynical attitudes of both the Nationalists and the K.P.D., both growing forces in the 1920s, further limited the small room for manoeuvre possessed by the democratic parties.

However, although all these factors were in the course of time to favour the Nazi Party, fascism was still slow to grow in Germany until the economic catastrophe of 1929. It was repeated disaster rather than the problems of just one era which facilitated the growth of fascism. The process of political mobilization was clearly related to the chaos of the 1920s. As Speer wrote in his autobiography, 'political indifference was characteristic of the youth of the period, tired and disillusioned as they were by a lost war, revolution, and inflation; but it prevented me from forming political standards, from setting up categories on which political judgments could be based'.[17] The experience of Speer reveals only too clearly how Nazism was able to fill the void left by the inability of the conventional democratic parties to cope with the problems of the day.

The process of social disintegration, from which the fascists were able to draw their strength, was much slower in Germany than in Italy. The erosion of middle-class security was also a much more serious phenomenon in Germany, for the simple reason that the middle class was much larger. The alienation of the middle class from politicians and parties of the centre was the result of several developments. There was much less fear of socialism in Germany than in Italy, because of the existence before the war of the S.P.D. On the other hand the phenomenal success of the S.P.D. in the election of 1919, combined with the activities of the Spartacists, led many members of the middle class to believe that their social, political and economic interests were seriously threatened. The progress of the Bolshevik Revolution in Russia hardly allayed these fears. Immediately the politicians of the Right began to take advantage of these basic fears and in the election of November 1922 there was a dramatic revival of the Right from its miserable performance of 10 per cent in 1919. The real failure of the politicians of the centre, throughout the decade, was their inability to prevent large sections of the electorate from deserting the moderate, democratic parties as soon as a crisis arose. The Nationalists, the archetypal German party of the Right, were the principal beneficiaries of these middle-class fears of revolution in the 1920s.

Fear of and dislike for socialism was not the only motivating force for middle-class discontent. Of prime importance was economic distress. The social and political structure of middle-class Germany fell to pieces under the pressure of the inflation of 1923. The inflation led to a sudden redistribution of wealth, favouring on the one hand the owners of the means of production and on the other the wage-earners who, being tightly organized, were able to strike in order to maintain real wages. Those who suffered were investors, savers, salary earners and pensioners. Again, it is worth mentioning the experience of Speer in connection with these events: 'The financial upheaval finally forced my family to sell my deceased grandfather's firm and factory to another company at a fraction of its value in return for "dollar treasury bills".'[18] Naturally the nascent Nazi Party attempted to profit from the resentment caused by these sad events and in the election of May 1924 the proscribed party (banned because of the abortive coup of 1923) participated in the *Völkisch* front, which did extremely well. Divisions over the Dawes Plan, together with the revival of national confidence in the administration of Stresemann and his allies, led to a dramatic reversal of fortune in the election of December 1924. The lesson that should have been drawn from these two contrasting results was plain—that the support of the middle class was vital to the continued existence of democracy in Germany and that economic dislocation would lead to a withdrawal of such support. In a highly developed, industrialized country the staunch support for democracy of the majority of the working class was insufficient if it stood alone. The vote on the enabling legislation in 1933 was to provide a final dramatic proof of this fact.

Middle-class discontent was also fostered by national feeling, born out of surprise at the defeat of 1918. Nationalism was a strong force in Imperial Germany and it probably emerged strengthened by the events of 1918–19. Defeat came hard on the heels of the triumphant treaty of Brest-Litovsk and to many middle-class citizens it appeared as if internal instability (i.e. the deposition of the Hohenzollerns) had caused the defeat. Those who engineered the necessary change in power were also those who signed the ignominious treaty at Versailles and agreed to surrender German territory, economic well-being and honour. It was clear that the 'November criminals' had sacrificed Germany on the altar of S.P.D. power-seeking. The stab in the back legend was only strengthened by the intransigence of the French and the economic problems of Germany in 1923. The bulk of the middle class thus found the Weimar Republic unsatisfactory in many political matters and was, consequently, never ready to defend the system in the way the middle class rallied around the National Government in Britain in the 1930s.

Nazi propaganda was, of course, very well designed to attract members of the middle class. From the start fascism in Germany was violently anti-Marxist. Hitler's party was also intensely nationalistic, hostile alike to Versailles, reparations, the Dawes Plan and Locarno. It ought, therefore, to have easily attained a strong following among the middle class in the 1920s. However, it failed to do so. Retrospectively the reasons seem clear. After the tragic events of 1923 governments recovered their nerve and substantial economic progress was made. Germany's accession to the League of Nations, combined with the delicate and skilful diplomacy of Stresemann restored some self-respect to Germans. Although the K.P.D. grew more powerful, the menace from the Left seemed to diminish and the trade unions played a less important part in middle-class demonology with the gradual return of prosperity. Additionally, Hitler had made himself and his party look ridiculous by their abortive putsch in 1923. Germany had, in no small measure, regained its confidence.

Middle-class discontent throughout most of the 1920s thus focused on politics through one or other of the conventional right-wing nationalist groups. It was the catastrophe of 1929 that changed this pattern and, incidentally, created the opportunities for a strong working-class commitment to National Socialism. Comparisons between the performances of the N.S.D.A.P. in 1928 and 1930 reveal the significance of the economic developments which intervened between the elections of those years. Votes for the party rose from 810,000 to 6,409,000. This faithfully reflected the collapse in the German economy. In the summer of 1928 unemployment had fallen to 650,000, real wages in 1929 were about 10 per cent higher than in 1925, production was well in excess of the golden period just before the war and retail sales marked a steady rise. Upper-, middle- and working-class Germans were hardly likely to support the N.S.D.A.P. in the calm and increasingly prosperous atmosphere of 1928–9.

The depression of 1929 swiftly brought about a renewal of the social mobility that had so terrified the middle class in 1918–23 and, in consequence, a revival of political mobilization. It is at this stage that comparison with the Italian situation falls down badly, for in Germany the fascists began to do well in elections and to lay siege to the seat of power as a political party and not as the political wing of a movement which could only come to power through a coup. It is comparatively easy to identify the supporters of Italian fascism in 1922, but much more difficult to see why the fascists in Germany were so successful in gaining recruits among people of all classes. The sheer pace and scale of the depression was an important factor in causing a panic-stricken rush to the Nazis. Mass unemployment, the destruction of agriculture, the outflow of capital, the end of American co-operation, the reduction of wages and salaries and the fall in exports followed one another in bewildering succession. It was the Nazis who derived the greatest political benefit from the chaos which ensued, through their unique ability to convince large num- bers of the electorate that their party opened up new roads to economic and social change. In that sense, if in no other, the Nazis were lineal descendants of the Italian fascists.

The Nazi appeal to the working-class elements in Germany was in part positive, in part negative. The negative appeal of fascism is easier to explain, principally being derived from the failure of the S.P.D. and K.P.D. to be able to do anything about the rising unemployment figures. In that the S.P.D. had deliberately cut itself off from power and the K.P.D. spent most of its time waging an arid and unprofitable war against its fellow parties of the Left, the boredom of the German electorate with these sterile attitudes may be forgiven. The positive attraction of the Nazis is slightly more mysterious, but may in part be explained by the revolutionary and proletarian nature of the N.S.D.A.P. The revolutionary element of fascism in Germany has been underplayed. It is of interest to read Speer's account of his father's reaction to the Nazi electoral successes of 1930: 'By the time we returned, there had been a Reichstag election on September 14 which remains in my memory only because my father was greatly perturbed about it. The N.S.D.A.P. had won 107 seats and was suddenly the chief topic of political discussion. My father had the darkest forebodings, chiefly in view of the N.S.D.A.P.'s socialist tendencies. He was already disturbed enough by the strength of the Social Democrats and the Communists.'[19] There were those in Germany, therefore, who saw Nazism as a potentially revolutionary force. There was much in the Nazi programme which lent credence to this viewpoint, as has already been mentioned. The fascist appeal to the German working class was based upon the positive proposals of the Strasser wing of the party plus the great heritage of bitterness among the unemployed and those who faced the prospect of unemployment. As Clark wrote: 'The clever linking of revolutionism and nationalism, the appeal to "the plain man who hates politicians", and to the young who were conscious in their minority of intellectual frustration and in their great majority of economic helplessness, the Messianic fervour with which the salvationist mission of the Leader was preached, the cumulative effect of eighteen months' furious propaganda ably conducted with its electoral evidence of steady success—all these worked powerfully on the electorate and flung the older parties back on the defensive.'[20]

Even more significant than their appeals to the ordinary voter was the fact that the Nazis were, in the main, a non-class party. The recruits for the S.A. came from widely different backgrounds. Indeed, the propaganda machine always made great play of the fact that the party was not a class party, but a national institution, unlike the Nationalists or the K.P.D. The Nazis, like the Communists, began to attract the discontented in large numbers. In 1928 the combined vote of these two parties was just over 4 million, in July 1932 it exceeded 19 million. Even allowing for the fact that the Nazis picked up many votes formerly given to middle-class parties, this represented a formidable increase in the number of the discontented. The Nazis also profited among the working class from the fact that, although under Weimar the working class party (the S.P.D.) had been able to win elections, or at least form governments, it had been unable to deliver the social benefits which were, not unreasonably, assumed by working-class voters to be the purpose of voting for a working-class party. The loss of enthusiasm among the leaders of the S.P.D. was a material factor in the growing appeal of the Nazis among their former supporters. The phenomenal success of the Nazis in 'red' Chemnitz in the first presidential election of 1932 shows the working-class appeal of the Nazis was a force to consider. In that astounding election the N.S.D.A.P. secured more votes than the S.P.D., in what had traditionally been an S.P.D. stronghold. Those who refer to the Nazis as a party of the lower middle class would do well to consider this fact.

The Nazis were also extremely proficient at appealing to middle-class fears. The growing economic problems convinced many people that security could only be attained through a process of defensive class conflict. At a time when middle-class standards were thus under attack there also arose a strong feeling that middle-class interests needed stronger protectors than the proven incompetent democratic party system could provide. For most of the people who thought in this way the K.P.D. was impossible, whereas the N.S.D.A.P. seemed a potential protector. The appeal of the Nazis to the middle class has been summarized by Mason, when he wrote: 'The accumulated problems arising out of the unviable structure of German society were even less amenable to solution during the world economic crisis than at any other time. Faced with these problems, the bourgeoisie, the old and the new petty bourgeoisie and the rural population all sought their salvation in an unthinking flight into "pure politics": politics-as-propaganda, national exaltation, the cult of the leader, anti-semitism and anti-communism, a yearning for an idealized pre-industrial community all served as political pseudo-solutions to the structural problems of the social order of Weimar Germany.'[21] The demagogy of Hitler and Goebbels had a profound impact upon these people. As Speer wrote, 'Hitler ... spoke urgently and with hypnotic persuasiveness. The mood he cast was much deeper than the speech itself.'[22] Speer also revealed how it was discipline which was so attractive in times of disorder and the impression of energy at a time when the general feeling was one of hopelessness. Like so many other members of the middle class, for Speer the 'crucial fact appeared to me to be that I personally had to choose between a future Communist Germany or a future National Socialist Germany since the political centre between these antipodes had melted away'.[23] Speer made his choice as early as 1931; in the next eighteen months hundreds of thousands of other middle-class Germans were to travel the same road.

The attractiveness of the Nazis lay in part in their hostility to Marxism. The peril of communism seemed to be unchecked by the normal parties. The Nazi concept of a united and homogeneous nation added an element of idealism to the beliefs of those who would otherwise have seen the struggle in the simple terms of class conflict. Hitler repeatedly asserted the value of such qualities as discipline, hard work, integrity, patriotism and self-reliance. All these had a high appeal to the German middle class and Hitler's judgement was vindicated by the results of 1930. In that election the bourgeois parties' vote fell from a total of 5,547,000 in 1928 to 4,262,000; the decline between 1930 and July 1932 was even more spectacular—to 955,000. Clearly most of these votes were absorbed by the N.S.D.A.P., though some went to the Centre Party and some to the Nationalists. The steadily rising vote for the K.P.D. during the same period convinced many middle-class Germans that their only hope of survival lay in embracing fascism. The appeal of the Centrists had disappeared in the bitterness left by Brüning's harsh measures. Measures introduced by the Chancellor during the years 1930–2 which occasioned particular hostility among his natural supporters included tariff increases, salary cuts, reduction in the employment of officials, increases in both direct and indirect taxation and government by decree rather than with the support of the Reichstag. Hitler's assertion that willpower and determination could overcome economic problems began to seem very much more attractive than the alternative, which was an apparently unending process of tightening belts.

The Nazi promise to supply strong rule also attracted members of the upper classes to the party. As in Italy the chaotic state of democratic politics left many industrialists and other wealthy members of the community anxious about the future of their interests. They believed that there was a power vacuum which, unless a suitable candidate was found, might be filled by the growing K.P.D. The so-called 'non-political' rule of Brüning had been found inadequate by 1932. The result was that 'In the year 1932 all political organizations, with the exception of the Social Democratic Party, were convinced that a completely new system of government was called for, whether a Catholic corporative state, a Bonapartist autocracy (Schleicher), a National Socialist state based on the leadership principle, or a dictatorship of the proletariat.'[24] In these circumstances the attractiveness of a man like Hitler was considerable.

The great mistake made by members of the ruling class was that they imagined Hitler would be easy to control. In part this was pure misjudgement—they forgot the revolutionary slogans and the proletarian background of many members of the party. Fear, greed and complacency operated at different levels within the ruling hierarchy and corrupted political judgement. However, there was some evidence favourable to the belief that Hitler could be controlled. In the first place Hitler had asserted that he would only come to power by constitutional means and, as he depended upon Nationalist support in the Reichstag for any prospect of a majority, this meant readiness to co-operate with others. Those who took this line ought to have recollected Hitler's speech of 18 July 1930, when he declared: 'It is not parliamentary majorities that mould the fate of nations. We know, however, that in this election democracy must be defeated with the weapons of democracy.'[25] Also, the conventional Right should have realized that once enabling legislation had been passed and the K.P.D. expelled from the Reichstag the parties representing their own interests would be as ineffectual as those of the Centre and Left. Just as in the case of Italy the fascist revolution would begin once power had been secured and not before, lest potential supporters be frightened away.

The leaders in German politics and society could also find security against the prospect of a fascist takeover in the setback to Nazi hopes in the election of November 1932. Compared with the election held just over three months previously the N.S.D.A.P. dropped just over two million votes. The prospect of a Hitler enjoying a popular majority receded fast, thus leading the Right to believe that he would be ready to compromise in order to secure power. There was further evidence for this belief not only in Hitler's readiness to come to terms with von Papen but also in the dependence of his party on the subscriptions of the industrialists for financing both propaganda and election campaigns. The heavy expenditure of the Nazis in 1932 had eroded their financial standing and it was believed that this could be used as a lever to control them. The assistance given to the Nazis by Kirdorf, Thyssen and other magnates has already been mentioned; the industrial barons were convinced that Hitler could be controlled by the power of the purse. If such an assumption proved unwarranted there was always the army to be relied upon. Here was the ultimate stronghold of the Right, a bastion which only finally capitulated to Nazism in the aftermath of July 1944. If the generals collaborated with Hitler in the intervening period (1933–44) they did so with their eyes open and unrealistically confident in their ability to direct policy. The Right could not forget that the unpromising situation of 1918 had been redeemed by the entrenched might of the army, that generals had played a vital part in the politics of Weimar and that the army had been instrumental in securing the decree of 14 April 1932, banning the S.A. and S.S. The Right was extremely unwise to abandon its monopoly of legal armed force for, as the decree suggested, 'these organizations form a private army whose very existence constitutes a state within the State, and represent a permanent source of trouble for the civil population. . . . It is exclusively the business of the State to maintain organized forces.'[26] But the army leaders were too confident in their own power and the supposed political abilities of men like von Papen. Furthermore, the nationalist and anti-Marxist drums which Hitler always banged played sweet music to their ears.

Support for Hitler among the upper classes and the conventional Right was thus secured, for the main part, on different terms and later than the support he received from most of the rest of the community. Although the electoral successes of fascism could hardly have been achieved in either 1930 or 1932 without substantial backing from the coffers of the industrialists, the bulk of the ruling class remained aloof from the Nazis until after the events of January 1933. The upper class was fearful of the K.P.D., worried about unemployment and economic decline, pro-nationalist and in favour of preserving its class privileges, but it was only slowly converted to the proposition that these fears could best be allayed and these interests best protected by Hitler. The ruling hierarchy did not throw itself into the arms of the fascists with the abandon born of desperation, which characterized the conversion of most working- and middle-class members of the party. The Right believed it spoke from a position of strength and that it could negotiate with Hitler. The surrender of power to Hitler was, of course, a misjudgement of the man and his movement, but it was a decision deliberately made, based upon what was believed to be a rational calculation of self-interest. The part played by this section of the community was decisive. As Bullock has rightly pointed out: 'Despite the mass support he had won, Hitler came to office in 1933 as the result, not of any irresistible revolutionary or national movement sweeping him into power, nor even of a popular victory at the polls, but as part of a shoddy political deal with the "Old Gang" whom he had been attacking for months past. Hitler did not seize power; he was jobbed into office by a backstairs intrigue.'[27]

The fascist rise to power in Germany was thus, in class terms, both similar to and yet distinctively different from Mussolini's success in Italy. Many fears which influenced the actions of the middle and upper classes in Italy in 1922 also played their part in the Germany of 1929–33. General similarities in the types of situation, the nature of the parties and the forms of leadership must not be allowed, however, to obscure the very real differences in social significance and impact. It is true that the ruling classes in both nations possessed great social power, but the way in which they sought to cope with the challenge to political power was very different. Examples such as this may be found at every level in any comparison between Italy and Germany. Whereas in Italy certain assumptions were made about the nature of society and then acted upon or ignored, as the whim took Mussolini, in Germany the Nazis sought to create a new political consensus. Social disintegration was much more serious in Germany than in Italy, consequently it needed a more radical approach to recreate a viable social system. The fascists everywhere rejected in principle the essence of democracy— the conciliation and integration of widely different social groups within the same community. In practice, however, the use of force, dictatorship and the concept of national unity varied widely. In Italy Mussolini's appraisal of the situation varied from year to year and his actions altered accordingly. In Germany Hitler realized that conventional means could not alone bring about a national recovery. The cartels were too powerful, there were too many people afraid of inflation or deflation, agricultural and industrial interests were in conflict and unemployment was an ever-present spectre. Hitler's success lay not only in defeating the traditional rulers' grip on power and the opposition provided by the S.P.D. and K.P.D. but also in being able to convey a new sense of 'belonging' to many Germans. This was an achievement which Mussolini did not attain.

The importance of the element of propaganda in Hitler's rise to power can hardly be exaggerated. It was direct propaganda, via the speaker's podium, at which the Nazis excelled. Mussolini was a powerful speaker, but he was as nothing compared with Hitler. As Speer recollected: 'Both Goebbels and Hitler had understood how to unleash mass instincts at their meetings, how to play on the passions that underlay the veneer of ordinary respectable life. Practised demagogues, they succeeded in fusing the assembled workers, petits bourgeois, and students into a homogeneous mob whose opinions they could mould as they pleased. . . . But as I see it today, these politicians in particular were in fact moulded by the mob itself, guided by its yearnings and daydreams. Of course Goebbels and Hitler knew how to penetrate through to the instincts of their audiences; but in the deeper sense they derived their whole existence from these audiences. Certainly the masses roared to the beat set by Hitler's and Goebbels's baton; yet they were not the true conductors. The mob determined the theme. To compensate for misery, insecurity, unemployment and hopelessness, this anonymous assemblage wallowed for hours at a time in obsessions, savagery, licence. This was no ardent nationalism. Rather, for a few short hours the personal unhappiness caused by the breakdown of the economy was replaced by a frenzy that demanded victims. And Hitler and Goebbels threw them the victims. By lashing out at their opponents and vilifying the Jews they gave expression and direction to fierce, primal passions.'[28] The voice of Speer is one of personal experience and must not be lightly cast aside. What happened to Speer was repeated among all sections of society. Hitler's vision of a new, socially united Germany, purged of all dissonant elements, was enormously attractive in that it provided simultaneously not only a sense of comradeship and purpose but also targets against which jealousy and resentment could be directed. The greatly increased number of party members and camp followers after 1929 shows how at a time of social and economic pressure and disintegration the N.S.D.A.P. emerged as a new pillar around which each man could build his own reconstructed version of society. The fascist success in Germany therefore in no small measure bore relation to the fact that after the onset of the slump the Nazis became the members of the new 'safe party', the dependable party, the consensus party.

In the period before the Nazi Party was in receipt of large subsidies its style was particularly important. This is not to suggest that its approach to politics was unimportant after 1929, that would be grotesquely inaccurate, but that the life of the party before 1929 was sustained by popular enthusiasm, thus making appeal all-important. From the very first the movement set out to be popular, of wide appeal and universalist (with certain well-defined exceptions, such as the Jews). The element of participation was constantly emphasized. Recruits were urged not just to pay dues to the party but to join one of its organizations. These varied from the politically active S.A. to the relatively non-political N.S.K.K. (the Nazi motorists organization). The S.A. provided a very important stimulus to popular recruitment, not only in the period after 1925, when the party was struggling to establish itself as a serious political contender, but also after the events of 1929. The S.A. appealed to the basic nationalism, the sense of discipline and the military traditions so deeply established among the German people. The S.A. differed greatly from the *squadristi* in Italy or, indeed, the hunger marchers of the revolutionary period in German history. The S.A. was uniformed, organized and disciplined. As the years went by it more frequently became involved in street battles with communists and other groups on the Left, but usually it merely paraded in a menacing fashion and its members acted as stewards at political rallies. Once the party was able to exist in comfortable financial circumstances recruitment by the S.A. increased sharply. In 1923 the S.A. numbered some 15,000 men; by the time of the decree of 1932 this figure had risen to 400,000. At one stroke comradeship and dedication to the party became identified with relief from the problem of unemployment. In this sense the S.A. marked a triumph for the populist wing of the movement, it was the political instrument of Röhm and the Strassers—it in fact represented the revolutionary aspects of the Nazi approach to politics.

Hitler, therefore, needed to control the S.A. very carefully, for it was at one and the same time not only a manifestation of the popular success of fascist propaganda but also a movement which might veer out of control. As long as the right emphasis was kept on discipline and loyalty to the leadership principle the S.A. could be controlled, but once let it loose on the streets and the results could be politically catastrophic. In order to gain power Hitler was prepared both to use and to sacrifice the S.A.; once in power his opinion of the S.A. depended likewise on its utility. The danger of the S.A. was that it united a genuine proletarian (and semi-revolutionary) fervour with the disciplined enthusiasm of the old *Freikorps*. In 1932 Röhm felt the moment had come for his army to invade the streets, to exact full retribution for the foolish provocation of the K.P.D. squads in the late 1920s. It was Hitler's will which triumphed, for, as a politician, he saw that failure to accept the dissolution decree would inevitably lead to a successful coalition of forces against the N.S.D.A.P. He also saw that Röhm and Strasser wished to lead the party in a different direction and in the period between 1925 and 1932 there were constant purges of the disaffected. Matters were only finally resolved in 1934 when Hitler firmly trod on the concept of permanent revolution and purged the S.A. of many leading figures. The S.A. was full of the discontented, those whom the Nazis had attracted into the party at a vitally important period in its growth; it was involved with the very ethos of fascism in Germany and when Hitler turned his back on it he denied the relevance of one of the strongest forces behind his rise to power. As Speer wrote, 'in the Blood Purge of June 30, 1934, the strong left wing of the party, represented chiefly by the S.A., was eliminated. That wing had felt cheated of the fruits of the revolution. And not without reason. For the majority of the members of the S.A., raised in the spirit of revolution before 1933, had taken Hitler's supposedly socialist programme seriously. During my brief period of activity in Wannsee I had been able to observe, on the lowest plane, how the ordinary S.A. man sacrificed himself for the movement, giving up time and personal safety in the expectation that he would some day receive tangible compensation. When nothing came of that, anger and discontent built up.'[29]

Hitler was very conscious of the image of the party, for he, above all others, realized what a rickety coalition of different and conflicting interests it represented. The opportunism Hitler was to display with such cynical abandon in negotiations with foreign powers in the period 1936–41 was applied to domestic politics between 1925 and 1934. In order that he (and Hitler identified the party with himself) should triumph he was ready to knock down those who had helped raise him up. It was a characteristic he was to retain until the very end of his life, as can be seen from his dismissal of Göring in 1945. Goebbels, who himself had a number of fortunate escapes from being purged, as the supreme propagandist was as equally aware of the need to control all the disparate elements that made up the party. Here the leadership principle was a godsend, for the doctrine of infallibility could be used as a cloak to give private assurances to those who would otherwise have been worried by apparently conflicting public pledges. The changing nature of the movement after 1929 reinforced this point of view. Speer observed this fact, remarking that in an editorial in *Angriff* on 2 November 1931 Goebbels 'warned the party against the infiltration of more bourgeois intellectuals who came from the propertied and educated classes and were not as trustworthy as the Old Fighters. In character and principles, he maintained, they stood abysmally far below the good old party comrades, but they were far ahead in intellectual skills: "They are of the opinion that the Movement has been brought to greatness by the talk of mere demagogues and are now prepared to take it over themselves and provide it with leadership and expertise. That's what they think!" '[30] Such was the style of the party—opportunistic under the guise of certain immutable principles all relating to the national welfare. It was a style likely to be immensely successful in opposition, particularly in times of social, political and economic upheaval, as indeed it was. It was much less likely to be successful as a form of government, but once in power Hitler was ready to remove certain old manifestations of his style if they happened to conflict with his will to power. Hitler never forgot the maxim that politics is about power after his humiliating experiences of 1923–4, and his party faithfully reflected its master's image. It was a fundamental reason for its success in acquiring new sources of support in the period immediately preceding the Nazi installation in power.

14 The Incapacity of Political Orthodoxy

'Where has that chap with glasses [Brüning] gone to ?' Hindenburg speaking to his son. Quoted in J. Gunther, *Inside Europe*, p. 43

In addition to the matters that have already been considered it is also essential to try to answer the question: why were the other political parties so enfeebled in their opposition to fascism? The answer in Italy is, for the most part, that the fascist threat was not taken seriously until it was too late. Such an explanation can hardly apply to Germany, where there were politicians not only well aware of the Italian precedent but who had time to reflect on the Nazi potential. After all, the N.S.D.A.P. was a political force for a decade before it secured power. The answer has been partially given in the evidence cited concerning the collapse of Germany in 1918–19, again in 1923 and once more in 1929. Statements concerning the attractiveness of Nazi doctrine and propaganda also give some hints as to the omissions and failures of the movement's rivals for power. However, the social significance of the rise of German fascism was such that it is important to establish clearly some of the points at which other parties missed opportunities to hold back the advance of the Nazis.

Among the most important phenomena was the absence of any unity among the Left. In the 1930s in France the communists, socialists and radicals managed to band together, albeit for only a brief period, in order to vanquish what they believed to be a threat from fascism in France. In Germany no popular front was ever secured. Mutual distrust between the S.P.D. and K.P.D. was deeper than their common fear of the N.S.D.A.P. The directives of Stalin, aimed at the K.P.D., in any event condemned the possibility of co-operation with the 'social fascists'. The K.P.D. forgot that the task of a revolutionary party was to see to the task of promoting a national revolution and became instead the agent of a foreign power. The antics of the leadership of the K.P.D. split the working-class movement and at the same time rendered the task of the S.P.D.

(which was of necessity a major partner in government) virtually impossible. The concept of eliminating all the moderate parties, leaving the K.P.D. face to face with the capitalist enemy (which was later identified as the N.S.D.A.P.), ignored several factors. It ignored the fact that the N.S.D.A.P. might win the struggle, it ignored the fact that in the meantime the K.P.D. was demoralizing its natural potential allies in the coming struggle, and it ignored the fact that the Nazis were themselves revolutionaries. As Clark observed so bitterly: 'In no party in Germany was there more will to sacrifice, more reserves of courage and endurance, and by no party were such will and such reserves more pitiably wasted. . . . As a peril it existed only in the imagination of the bourgeois; the party to which it was most hostile never feared it. . . . Its one positive deed was to stab German democracy in the back and paralyse its resistance to counter-revolution. The monstrous imaginings of National Socialism deceive only those who want to be deceived; Hitler had no better allies, and no one knew that better than Hitler himself.'[1]

In turn, the S.P.D. were bounded in vision by their intellectual revolutionary tradition. Although the party soon became accustomed to working with other parties it did so without enthusiasm and, on a number of occasions, it preferred doctrinal purity to common sense. The inevitable result was inconsistency and, hence, an inability to attract new support. The S.P.D., after the death of Ebert, never accepted either the role of wholehearted co-operation with the other democratic parties or that of outright opposition, which would probably have given the S.P.D. a real chance of picking up many of those discontented voters who put their trust in the K.P.D. or N.S.D.A.P. At a time when the Brüning administration desperately needed positive support, in May 1932, when the fascist danger was fully apparent, the S.P.D. gave it grudging support. The two leading figures in the S.P.D., Breitscheid[2] and Müller[3] opted for the policy of 'the lesser evil'. It was a decision in which responsibility became indistinguishable from cowardice. The S.P.D. wished to break both the fascists and the communists, but it could never decide which enemy was the most immediately dangerous and how it could fight without being ready to spill blood. In the meantime it decided to let Brüning occupy the front line of the battle. In the end the S.P.D. fell into the same trap as the Labour Party in Britain in 1931; it spent all its available energy on trying to protect the class interests of its voters and ignored the political storm that was developing around it. The revolutionary potential of the Nazis, despite all their external paraphernalia (red flags, inflammatory slogans, marches, mass rallies), was assumed not to be a serious threat to the political position of the S.P.D. Yet the S.P.D.'s proportion of votes fell steadily. From the highpoint of 1919, when nearly 38 per cent was secured, the S.P.D. fell to 25.8 per cent in December 1924, to 21.6 per cent in July 1932 and to 20.4 per cent in November 1932. The missing votes went mainly to the revolutionary parties which propounded new, radical solutions to old problems, the K.P.D. or the N.S.D.A.P.

In defence of the S.P.D. it must be said that the members of the party in the Reichstag acquitted themselves with honour in the vote over the enabling legislation. The vote in favour was 441 and against 94. Every S.P.D. man present had voted against the bill—the recognition of danger was too late, but at least the S.P.D. did not let the Weimar Republic pass away without even a gesture being made in its defence. No such honour attached itself to the other democratic parties. The attitude of the Centre Party, led by Kaas,[4] typified the supine behaviour of the democratic parties during the years since the start of the depression. The Centre Party voted for the enabling bill, it voted itself out of existence by so doing. It was a characteristic climax to the shabby policies the party had pursued in its dealings with the Nazis. It fitted in well with the Centrist philosophy of always wishing to be part of the majority, but did not square with the Christian and democratic ideals which it purported to represent. The plain truth of the matter was that Kaas and his followers no longer believed in themselves. So many somersaults had been performed over such a long period of time that one more hardly mattered. The Centre Party, unlike its smaller, non-socialist allies, remained confident in the knowledge that its bloc of votes was virtually unshakable. The party placed its faith in the promises of its enemies, the Nazis and Nationalists, despite the evidence of the election campaign of 1933 (during which Centrist leaders had complained to Hindenburg about Nazi terror) and Hitler's reply to the speech of Wels,[5] the S.P.D. leader, in the debate on the enabling legislation. Stung to fury by Wels' defiance, Hitler had jumped to his feet and declared to the S.P.D.: 'I do not want your votes. Germany will be free, but not through you. Do not mistake us for bourgeois. The star of Germany is in the ascendant, yours is about to disappear, your death knell has sounded.'[6] Even at that moment the Centre Party had the chance to recognize that the death of the S.P.D. would be swiftly followed by its own demise. Its terror and short-sightedness deprived it of the ability to think and to observe. It received, in the course of time, its just reward.

The bourgeois democratic parties placed their faith in illusory promises in 1933. The process by which they arrived in this position was simple. It stemmed in the first place from fear—fear of Bolshevism and the rising K.P.D. vote, fear of the social and economic changes proposed by the S.P.D. and, most importantly, fear of being held responsible for the disasters of 1929–33. The democratic parties saw their own incompetence and were, in a curious way, glad to see the rise of a political movement which had no fears for the future. The smaller democratic parties soon sank beneath the tidal wave of Nazism; their strength had been sapped by repeated failures. The bourgeoisie, that backbone of Imperial Germany, no longer believed in its own parties and politicians. It surrendered to the Nazis because they offered security. The experience of Speer was typical of many members of his class: 'In making this decision to join the accursed party, I had for the first time denied my own past, my upper-middle-class origins, and my previous environment. Far more than I suspected, the "time of decision" was already past for me. I felt, in Martin Buber's phrase, "anchored in responsibility in a party". My inclination to be relieved of having to think, particularly about unpleasant facts, helped to sway the balance. In this I did not differ from millions of others. Such mental slackness above all facilitated, established, and finally assured the success of the National Socialist system.'[7]

The group best placed to halt the fascist rise to power lay on the Right, depending for its strength on the army, the bureaucracy, the police and the courts of justice. Fervently nationalistic and militaristic the Right dominated politics during the Weimar era. Hitler was forced to compromise with the Right—he needed the votes of its parties in the Reichstag, the finance of its wealthy members and the consent of its armed forces to his rule. The Right thus permitted Hitler to rule in a fashion very different from the licence allowed to the democratic governments which preceded the Nazi takeover. Despite all the benefits which the Right enjoyed under Weimar it was never reconciled to the existence of the republic. As Bullock commented: 'Many of them were left in positions of power and influence; their wealth and estates remained untouched by expropriation or nationalization; the Army leaders were allowed to maintain their independent position; the industrialists and business men made big profits out of a weak and complaisant government, while the help given to the Junkers' estates was one of the financial scandals of the century. All this won neither their gratitude nor their loyalty. Whatever may be said of individuals, as a class they remained irreconcilable, contemptuous of and hostile to the régime they continued to exploit. The word "Nationalist", which was the pride of the biggest Party of the Right, became synonymous with disloyalty to the Republic.'[8] The Right struck a sordid bargain with Hitler (for which it also received its just reward in 1944-5) and therefore had no reason to stand in the way of the fascist rise to power.

The nature of fascism in Italy and Germany, some of the reasons for its success and the social composition of its membership ought to have emerged from the discussion of these issues. However, fulfilment of the doctrine, that is to say how closely practice adhered to theory, has only thus far been examined in relation to economic life (admittedly in itself the most important facet). As it would be impossible to examine every aspect of life in detail I shall confine myself to a brief discussion of two further topics, the doctrine of terror and the concept of expansion.

Terror was a fundamental weapon of the totalitarian state. As such it had immense social consequences, it required men to serve the system as well as victims. The heritage of Nazi terror still exists in the form of trials in Germany to this very day. The spectacular trials at Nuremberg did not succeed in relieving the rest of the German people from responsibility for the events of 1933-45. The significance of terror in Nazi Germany was that it was combined with propaganda by Goebbels. Goebbels perceived that if he could conjure up dangers to the newly-found security of most Germans then the régime could act as a national rallying point. It was terror of revenge by the Russians and the Jews, terror of the loss of the status and prosperity won at such great cost in the 1930s which solidified support for the Nazis in wartime. The triumphant success of Goebbels in his speech advocating 'total war' in 1943 illustrates this point; it was made after the defeats at El Alamein and Stalingrad had undermined the confidence of the German people. Terror also existed in a less subtle form—that of the Gestapo and the concentration camp. Yet this form of rule was not much in evidence in

Germany in the 1930s, unless one happened to be a Jew or a communist. The bulk of the German people was left almost untouched by the secret police and security organizations. The reaction of the Austrians to the introduction of persecution of Jews and the Left after the *Anschluss* was, on the whole, to shrug their shoulders and argue that it was what these dissident groups deserved anyway. The system was brutal and could be oppressive, but its philosophy of hate and rage was concentrated upon the abnormal. The average German citizen certainly suffered a serious reduction in personal liberty during the period of Nazi rule but on the whole he was not frightened into submission. The great propaganda success of the Nazis lay in convincing the German people that everything could be explained in terms of a glorious future. A few casualties would be bound to occur, but these would not be among normal members of society. The result was a steady erosion of moral values and the capacity for making moral judgements.

In Italy terror was a much less significant weapon in the armoury of fascism. During their rise to power the fascists had not hesitated to employ the tactics of terror and violence, though the fascist strong-arm squads in Italy were never as powerful as they were to be in Germany. Curiously, in the period immediately preceding the rise to power the Italian fascists were the more violent. The regular forces (the police and the army) viewed the fascists almost benevolently after the events at Bologna in November 1920. Events in the next two years led to a serious growth in beatings, burnings and attacks. In 1921 the number of fascist militants belonging to these squads rose from about 20,000 to nearly 250,000. At the same time hundreds of opponents of fascism were killed or injured. Violence played a key part in creating the atmosphere of terror in which the Right surrendered to Mussolini in October 1922, but thereafter terror was kept firmly under control, particularly after the embarrassment caused by the murder of Matteotti in 1924. Mussolini himself took full responsibility, declaring in January 1925: 'If fascism is an association of delinquents, I am the chief of this association of delinquents.'[9] Of course, Mussolini introduced a secret police organization (the O.V.R.A.) in 1927, but although terror tactics were occasionally used the Italian fascists preferred beatings and castor oil treatment to concentration camps. Additionally, the attention of the O.V.R.A. was, until 1938, largely confined to opponents of the régime rather than to a group identifiable by racial or religious customs. This factor itself made it tread more warily. In Italy, even after German successes, no attempt was made to unite propaganda with popular apprehensions. The Goebbels technique was a notable absentee from the Italian political scene, save for the period of the Abyssinian war when the Duce sought (with some success) to rally the nation behind him. The Italians were never sufficiently interested in Mussolini's imperialist dreams for there to be any real prospect of propaganda successes on the scale of those achieved in Germany.

The programmes of the fascist movements in both Italy and Germany clearly envisaged foreign expansion. During the period 1922–39 Italy occupied Albania and Abyssinia; between 1936–9 Germany occupied the Rhineland, Austria and most of Czechoslovakia, as well as establishing firm control over Danzig and Memelland. Practice, therefore, certainly adhered closely to doctrine in this case, but is it possible to draw any more elaborate conclusion than that the fascist states were expansionist? In fact, the politics of expansion were of vital importance to both the rise of fascism and its retention of popularity. The economic concepts behind the fascist way of thinking have already been mentioned—ultimately it was impossible to satisfy the demands of the different sections of the community unless expansion took place. The social significance of the policy of expansionism went much deeper than this, however.

Germany and Italy either were, or behaved like, defeated countries after 1918. The concepts of imperial expansion and *Lebensraum* thus had primary political significance. Success in attaining these goals would be important not only in that it would apparently herald the dawning of an age of prosperity but also that it would mark a decisive rejection of the past. The psychological need for vindication in fighting in the war of 1914–18 was felt profoundly by many Italians and Germans. The Nazis, in particular, were able to pinpoint this national neurosis and use it as a springboard to power. From the viewpoint of the fascists success in important fields of foreign policy was vital—it would justify their calls for a break with the methods of the past and it would keep alive the prospect of economic autarky, so essential to fulfilment of their promises.

It followed naturally and easily from fascist doctrine about the superiority of the nation that this superiority should receive tangible recognition in the form of expansion. The doctrines of race, economic prosperity and the acquisition of territory were closely allied in the case of Germany. In Italy the connection was less obvious but it was still present. The advantages reaped by the fascists from this extraordinarily belligerent form of nationalism were numerous. In the first place significant resistance from the Right was virtually eliminated—the example of the resistance movement within the German army springs to mind at once. The middle class, fervently nationalistic in both Italy and Germany, was much less likely to resist fascist blandishments. The working class, which included among its ranks many of those who had fought and suffered without reward in the wartime battles, also accepted this appeal. The doctrine placed the blame for misery firmly on the shoulders of others, thus playing on the natural self-exculpatory instincts of all ranks of the population. In the 1933 election campaign Hitler blamed German misfortunes on the makers of the Versailles Treaty, those who had stabbed Germany in the back in 1918 and on the corrupt democratic politicians. At Cologne, on 19 February 1933, Hitler declared: 'I ask of you, German people, that after you have given the others fourteen years you should give us four.'[10] Yet in 1945 Hitler was to declare that the German people had been an unworthy instrument for his genius! The skill of the fascist propagandists lay, in this instance, in finding a cause around which all Germans could rally. Failure in 1918 had been the result of evil work by the identifiable few; success would inevitably attend those who perceived the true destiny of the *Volk*.

The fascist emphasis on militarism and expansionism was thus no accident. It was closely related to history and to the fascist prognosis of the shape of things to come. Fascism played upon basic human emotions of greed, bitterness and disillusionment. Questions of immediate urgency about economic improvement could be deferred by the promise of achievement of a golden land. The fascists played simultaneously upon despair and hope. Fascism preyed upon weaknesses of character and willpower, upon the readiness of the Germans to let the Jews and the Slavs pay for their economic revival, upon the willingness of the Italians to let the inhabitants of a Mediterranean Empire serve their economic needs. When the benefits were so obvious who would ask the awkward questions about the nature of the régimes which the fascists had created?

Totalitarianism was a new phenomenon and the problems of the peoples of Western Europe in the inter-war years were so serious that to a certain extent excuses can be made for those who failed to understand its significance. Those who failed comprised the majority of people in the majority of nations—at least until about 1939. In that sense fascism was a truly international phenomenon. People everywhere failed to understand what kind of a state the totalitarian state would become—this is hardly an excuse but does provide something of an explanation. The reasons for this failure of understanding lie variously in stupidity, obstinacy, fear, greed, wilful blindness, ambition, laziness or just ignorance. As Speer observed: 'Why, for example, was I willing to abide by the almost hypnotic impression Hitler's speech had made upon me? Why did I not undertake a thorough, systematic investigation of, say, the value or worthlessness of the ideologies of all the parties? Why did I not read the various party programmes, or at least Hitler's *Mein Kampf* and Rosenberg's *Myth of the Twentieth Century*? . . . For being in a position to know and nevertheless shunning knowledge creates direct responsibility for the consequences—from the very beginning.'[11] The fascists were dominated by men who, despite poor educational qualifications, understood mass psychology. Hitler and Mussolini knew the fears and aspirations of their people and played upon them, often with apparently uncanny skill. The truth is that fascism in both Italy and Germany responded to deeply-felt emotions running through all sections of society, and the primary reason for its success in attaining power was that its leaders were able to judge and to harness emotions which under democratic governments had merely proved destructive. Inevitably, there were radical changes in the shape of society unforeseen by those who pinned their faith in fascism.

PART III

The Possibility of Fascism in Greece,
Latin America and Africa

15 Greece under Metaxas and the Colonels

'This certainly is what an ancient Greek would put first among his countrymen's discoveries, that they had found the best way to live.' H. D. F. Kitto, *The Greeks*

It is perhaps ironic that the country which gave birth to a particular form of intellectual justification of politics—democracy—and whose language supplied so much of the terminology of political life should be one of the three modern European states (together with Spain and Portugal) most commonly called fascist. The distressing contrast between the romanticized version of life in ancient Greece and the flatulent bombast of the régime of the colonels has been the subject of many a harrowing comparison in recent years. However, it is not the purpose here to compare the golden age of Greece with the present day, but rather to set the politics of modern Greece in its proper historical and contemporary setting. If it is true that the present Greek government is fascist then it is desirable that the reasons for the existence of fascism in a modern European form should be clearly understood.

In common with so many other East European countries, fascism came to Greece in the inter-war years. In Greece it took on an uniquely national form, difficult to compare with the fascism of other European states, although many of the economic and social problems that faced Greece in the 1920s were of the same nature as those of other European nations. The most obvious starting point may be seen in the foundation of the Free Opinion party by General Metaxas[1] in 1920. From the very beginning this party held conventional nationalist and militarist views. Among leading members were many who had shared the pro-German sympathies of the king during the 1914–18 war and who were as equally dissatisfied with the terms of the Versailles settlement and its attendant treaties.

In the event Metaxas' party failed to seize its opportunity, but this may in retrospect be seen as the result of inefficiency rather than the consequence of the institutional strength opposed to it. In fact the political situation of 1918–21 was extremely fluid, owing to the weakness of the monarchy, largely discredited by the exile of King Constantine. Venizelos[2] had led Greece into war against Germany and had expected substantial concessions from the Allies for his assistance. However, despite the reasonably favourable terms of the Treaty of Sèvres, signed in August 1920, Greece found herself at war with Turkey and with no likely source of support from any major power. In October 1920 the new king, Alexander, was bitten by a monkey and died soon after. As Churchill aptly commented: 'It is perhaps no exaggeration to remark that a quarter of a million persons died of this monkey's bite.'[3] In the elections that followed Venizelos' party was routed and King Constantine returned, despite an Allied declaration that if he returned to the throne 'Greece would receive no financial assistance of any kind from the Allies'.[4] Belligerent policies towards Turkey were at once adopted and war was resumed in the summer of 1921. In September of the same year the imperialist ambitions of the Greek monarchists were shattered by their defeat in the battle of the Sakaria River. In August 1922 the Greek Army was put to flight at Afium Karahissar and on 9 September the Turks entered Smyrna. In August 1923 the new balance of power was recognized by the Treaty of Lausanne.

In the midst of this political confusion Metaxas' party missed its opportunity to seize power. Conditions familiar to students of the rise of fascism were in existence in Greece. Conventional politics had failed the country, its king was twice disgraced, its leading politician was in exile, nationalist passions were running high, ex-servicemen were clamouring for rewards which the government could not provide and there was no prospect of Allied intervention to bail out the threatened régime. A model for a Greek coup had already been presented by Mussolini in October 1922, when Italian politics had undergone as tragic and as catastrophic a series of experiences as had those of Greece. Gounaris,[5] the man principally responsible for the return of Constantine, together with a number of other ministers and some generals had been shot in Athens, so violence had been swiftly re-established as part of the Greek political tradition. Metaxas and his followers delayed, however, and the most favourable moment passed. In 1923, it is true, Metaxas made an abortive attempt to seize power, but his putsch was a total failure.

Events in the following decade, however, showed that authoritarianism was still a potent factor in Greek politics. The king,

George II, who had succeeded Constantine in late 1922 was obliged to leave the country by General Plastiras[6] while elections were held. On 25 March 1924 a republic was proclaimed and this remained the official form of government until November 1935. Although nominally a republic the form of government in Greece during these years was on many occasions far from democratic. General Pangalos[7] seized power in June 1925 but was deposed by General Kondylis[8] in August 1926. Later Venizelos, who was rather impatient of opposition, returned as premier (1928–32), but from 1932 until 1935 there was a series of weak ministries, alternating between the Liberals led by Venizelos and the Populists headed by Tsaldaris.[9] After the frustration of an attempted coup by Venizelos in March 1935, conservative forces led by Kondylis managed to procure the return of George II in November of that year. The inability of the democratic parties to come to terms led soon after to the seizure of power by Metaxas on 4 August 1936, when an effective dictatorship was set up.

The purpose of this brief historical review is to set the régime of Metaxas in its proper context. Metaxas was accused of being a fascist both during his lifetime and afterwards and it is essential to see how much, if at all, the practice of his administration was derived from that of these régimes which preceded his coup of 1936. In fact, the brief reign of Pangalos contained many examples of what may be reasonably described as fascist actions. Pangalos was hostile to democracy and his opposition to it in Greece was so much feared that he was exiled to Corfu after 1932. During his period of office he dissolved the national assembly and postponed elections indefinitely. However, it would be wrong to think that he was a fascist, for he had no comprehensive ideas for state action. Indeed, one of the reasons for Kondylis' ability to overthrow his government lay in the aimless and contradictory policies pursued by Pangalos. Pangalos did pursue policies which bore the stamp of totalitarianism—he established press censorship and exiled many of his opponents. Restrictions on freedom of movement were placed on those deemed to be politically suspect and he blatantly rigged elections. On a more trivial note he introduced all kinds of regulations supposed to enhance national dignity, ranging from attempts to control drug trafficking and drunkenness to limitations on styles of dress. Pangalos believed that he had a moral crusade to wage as well as one for total national regeneration.

Pangalos was not a fascist but rather a muddled conservative trying to cope with the problems of a world he did not properly understand. His successors, Kondylis, Venizelos and Tsaldaris were not fascists either. It may be asserted that their devotion to democracy was rather dubious but none of them seriously supported restrictive measures even at the level of those devised by Pangalos. The democrats even managed to survive attempted putsches by republicans in 1933 and Venizelos' more rabid supporters in 1935, although at a price. In the confusion of 1935 Metaxas was brought into office and soon Greek politics began to resemble those of Italy in 1922. Attempted political assassinations went unpunished, the police control led public meetings and all other means of the expression of feeling were checked. Under the influence of Kondylis the Venizelist revolutionaries were sentenced to long terms of imprisonment and the Liberal-dominated Senate was abolished. A manipulated election produced a vote of larger size than the number of electors and, not surprisingly, a verdict of 97 per cent in favour of Kondylis' chosen plan of action—restoration of George II. The king was, of course, dominated by the military men who had placed him on the throne and after the death of Kondylis and the premier in early 1936 Metaxas became premier.

The Metaxas administration lasted from March 1936 to January 1941 and may in some ways be regarded as a primitive fascist régime. Metaxas was not in full control of Greece for the whole of this period, however. From March to April 1936 he was just deputy premier, though as the prime minister was very ill he effectively held power. From April until 4 August 1936 he was premier, but in August he seized full power and with the consent of the king declared himself dictator. The parallel with Mussolini is obvious.

The movement of 4 August was a political response to both short and long-term political problems—an immediate crisis and the rather more complex task of the reconstitution of Greek life according to 'sound principles'. The immediate crisis provides considerable insight into the future development of the Metaxas government. Metaxas was faced with the opposition of both the Liberals and the Populists and responded by banning what he termed seditious political activities, including overriding an adverse note in the assembly. In May 1936 widespread strikes, centring on Salonika, were suppressed with great severity by the police. About thirty strikers were killed and some hundreds injured. In response a general strike was proclaimed for 5 August, and this provided the setting for the coup of 4 August. Metaxas declared martial law and suspended several important constitutional provisions.

Bereft of mass support at this point, Metaxas set about the creation of an authoritarian state, based upon a philosophy which was a mixture of puritanism, nationalism, socialism and totalitarianism. Metaxas attempted, like Hitler and other dictators, to gather the reins of power into his hands and, when convenient, to ignore both the principles and practice of democracy. One of his first moves was to suppress opposing political parties. Metaxas declared that until the task of regenerating Greek national life had been completed political activity would be restricted. The party that came under particular scrutiny was that of the communists, many members of which were arrested. According to some accounts as many as 50,000 communists were arrested, deported or executed during the years 1936–41. It is now generally recognized that this figure was much too high, although it is true that the party's underground organization was left in almost complete ruin as a result of penetration and persecution by the secret police.

Metaxas also set about controlling the press. Newspapers and other forms of communication were censored, there were book burnings just as took place in Nazi Germany. It must be admitted, however, that Metaxist antipathy to authors was not confined to modern radical works but also extended to classical and modern conservative authors. Sophocles' *Antigone* was to be performed only with large extracts (believed to be hostile to authoritarianism) excised, and access to the works of other classical writers was restricted. Where local administrative bodies came into conflict with the régime they were suspended. The Chair of Constitutional Law, being a persistent source of criticism no matter who occupied it, was abolished. The power of the police was increased as were the numbers of the security forces. In 1938 the police force was re-organized upon the model of the totalitarian states. The civil service was filled with Metaxist supporters and an oath of loyalty was extracted from government employees. Serious restrictions upon the freedom of trade unions were also introduced.

It should not be supposed from this brief account that the Metaxist régime was totally negative in its political approach. In fact, Metaxas adopted a strong and energetic domestic policy which gained him a great deal of popularity. Among the most important of his proposals was compulsory arbitration of labour disputes and of disagreements involving collective contracts. Indeed, it was on this issue that the proposed general strike of 5 August was to be called. Metaxas also advocated the introduction of the eight-hour day and the payment of minimum wages. There were to be holidays with pay, Sundays were not to be regarded as work days, health insurance was introduced. There was much in this programme that was attractive to the Greek worker, and although all these proposals were not fully implemented (mainly because of obstruction and delay by reluctant employers) even partial fulfilment guaranteed an increase in the dictator's popularity. If the formal organization of the trade unions fell into the hands of Greek equivalents of Dr Ley the position of the industrial worker was, nonetheless, substantially improved.

There were other surprisingly radical items in the Metaxist programme. The dictator forbade Greek citizens to live off unearned income—the penalty for disobedience was deprivation of civil rights. Wealth had to be used for the good of the community, a sentiment more commonly expected from socialist and populist movements than from one of this type. Metaxas also tackled the thorny problem of agrarian reform, remitting up to one third of agricultural debts, thus enabling peasant proprietorship to become a more common phenomenon. An ambitious housing scheme was partially completed and a ten-year plan for building roads was started. In addition to all these changes another ten year plan of public works (dredging harbours, railway construction, municipal buildings and factory reconstruction) was instituted.

All these schemes cost a great deal of money, but international confidence in Metaxas was high. Substantial improvement loans were secured from American, British and French sources. In addition, in 1937, he secured a loan of 350 million drachmae (at the very reasonable rate of 3 per cent) from the German government. The surprising stability of the régime and its lack of a bellicose foreign policy contributed a great deal towards the successful projection of a favourable international image by Metaxas.

There were also aspects of Metaxist government that seemed to the outside world to have fascist connections. The dictator strengthened his armed forces and his security system. Concentration camps and torture became the destiny of his communist opponents who, on several occasions, made abortive attempts at insurrection or assassination. The principle of leadership, so greatly revered in Italy and Germany, was also introduced into Greece. Youth movements were created in which physical fitness and belief in the ethos of the régime became the two major guiding principles. Paramilitary parades of pro-Metaxist organizations were encouraged and there was much talk (though no prospect of action) of Turkish and Italian oppression of what were regarded as Greek *irredenta*. In a futile attempt to ward off Axis intervention in Greece Metaxas even asserted that since he had come to power Greece had been 'anti-Communist, anti-parliamentary, anti-plutocratic and a totalitarian state. In consequence, the leaders of the Axis powers ought to be regarding the movement of 4 August with sympathy and understanding instead of hostility.'[10] But, at the same time, he made overtures to Britain in an attempt to ensure support in the event of German assistance to the Italians.

How, then, should the régime of Metaxas be evaluated? It is clear that in some respects the Metaxist system should be regarded as fascist, but *in toto* such an impression would be erroneous. It was essentially a Greek version of Franco's Spain. Metaxas used the fascists rather than accepted the validity of their theories. He disregarded opposition and was anti-communist, he was no democrat but it would be untrue to say that he did not attract widespread popular support. If he did much to weaken the standing of the monarchy he also created conservative political forces that were to enable the monarchy to stage a recovery after the defeat of the Axis powers. When Metaxas led Greece into war he led a largely united country and even those who were opposed to his domestic policies were no friends to fascism. Indeed, in 1939 the democratic front, hostile to Metaxas, led by Plastiras from exile in Paris, even withdrew its opposition to his régime because of its conviction that Metaxas was the man most likely to preserve Greek freedom and independence in a threatening international situation. Some high-ranking officials and officers who had supported Metaxas in due course obliged the Germans by collaborating, but these were comparatively few and it is far from clear that any belief in Metaxist doctrines impelled them towards this course of action. The Metaxas period, then, cannot accurately be regarded as fascist. Many of the most notable aspects of fascism were absent and Metaxas may more properly be described as a nationalist and authoritarian leader ready to undertake certain reformist measures than as a fit companion for Hitler, Mussolini and their imitators.

The Metaxas régime is not the only recent system of government found in Greece to be described as fascist. The administration of the colonels has already found a place in anti-fascist writings. The importance of the assertion that the colonels are fascists is clear, if it is true. As in the case of so many other accusations of fascism the charge against the colonels is somewhat discredited by the curt dismissal of all Greek governments since 1944 as fascist by many of those who make the accusation. The fact of the matter is that between 1944 and 1967 Greece was ruled by a series of governments of the Right. The varying degrees of 'Rightness' of these governments were wide; so too were commitments to anti-communist and authoritarian policies. In part these variations reflected the struggles against attempts by E.A.M. (the Communist Party) and E.L.A.S. (its guerilla army) to overthrow the monarchy. The behaviour of governments at elections was very variable too, but a brief examination of governments after 1952 (by which time more or less normal political conditions had been re-established) shows that while they may on occasion have been repressive they were not totalitarian.

On 16 November 1952 the Greek Rally, led by Papagos,[11] won the election securing 239 seats of the 300 at stake. After Papagos' death his successor, Karamanlis, under the banner of the National Radical Union (E.R.E.) won elections in 1956, 1958 and 1961. During the eleven years Papagos and Karamanlis were in power (1952–63) the government pursued strong conservative policies. Agircultural interests received very favourable attention (this in part reflected as well as reinforced the preference of rural areas for a conservative central government). Trade unions were still subject to serious restraint, though it was argued that this was not to be a permanent feature of Greek government. More seriously, these governments were hampered by acute problems of security. When criticizing Karamanlis for acts which superficially seem to indicate a rather tenuous belief in democracy—such as ruling by emergency laws and decrees—it must be remembered that the powerful E.A.M. never formally accepted the role of a constitutional party. In these circumstances it was necessary to maintain large police and security forces as well as such arbitrary devices as exile, confinement to places of residence and detention. The government also turned a blind eye to the formation of paramilitary groups of the Right, such as the Anti-Communist Patriotic Union, the Blue Falange and the Young Aspirants. Political prisoners existed in quite large numbers until the end of 1963, when a political amnesty was declared. Despite all these unpleasing features, the government did permit the communist-penetrated E.D.A. to contest elections.

In the wake of the Lambrakis Affair the Karamanlis government fell and at elections on 3 November 1963 the Centre Union, led by Georgios Papandreou, became the largest party with 140 seats against the E.R.E.'s 128. Four months of political chaos then ensued until the C.U. won 173 seats in the elections of 16 February 1964. Papandreou was perhaps more energetic than politic in his pursuit of the achievement of absolute democracy and social equality in the next year and a half, certainly he was far too careless of the growing power of the E.D.A. and too tolerant of the radical activities of his son, Andreas. On 15 July 1965 King Constantine II (who had succeeded his father Paul I on 6 March 1964) dismissed Georgios Papandreou for permitting Andreas to penetrate the army security service through an officer association known as Aspida. Despite widespread popular resentment a lengthy period of political bargaining led to a substantial number of defections from the C.U. and the formation of a coalition government under Stephanopoulos in September 1965. This administration lasted until the end of 1966, embarking upon the trial of the Aspida leaders and suspending proceedings against some of the minor figures allegedly implicated in the murder of Lambrakis. Stephanopoulos also tried desperately hard to restore external confidence in the capacity of the Greeks to rule themselves democratically, for such confidence had been very badly shaken by the revelations, accusations and counter-accusations of the period between 1963 and 1965.

No settled government had emerged in Greece after the retirement of Stephanopoulos on 21 December 1966, although elections were due to be held in May of the following year. Among military circles were many who feared either a victory of the Left or an E.D.A.-supported coup so on 21 April 1967 a military coup took place, led by Colonel Papadopoulos. The chief prosecutor of the Supreme Court, Constantinos Kallias, was nominated as premier for an *interim* period. The Papandreous were arrested and martial law was imposed. Constantine II, who may have been contemplating the installation of a military dictatorship himself, was caught off balance by the coup, although it was proclaimed in his name. Rather unwisely he eventually agreed to support the coup, probably as a result of pressure from his mother, Queen Frederika, who had always wished to indulge a predilection for firm monarchist rule. This decision was soon seen to be a mistake and in December 1967 Constantine II tried to overthrow the Papadopoulos government. The royal counter-coup was easily defeated by the colonels, who had retained a very high level of support among the armed forces, and the king fled to Rome. Since that time he has eked out an uneasy existence as the pensioner of his royal relatives in the rest of Europe.

What is the nature of the Papadopoulos régime and can it be described as fascist? At first glance it appears to be yet another military dictatorship, bolstered by conservative forces, and looking more towards a paternalistic form of society than to a radical transformation of society and its institutions. However, this impression is, at least in part, faulty. The political appearance of Greece has undergone serious changes during the last five years and the colonels (who have now all resigned their military titles, but not their military power base) seem to have wished to institute such changes from the moment they seized power.

The major innovations since 1967 have been the government control of all trade unions, syndics, corporations and cartels. In fact, the industrial life of Greece, making allowance for differences of scale, bears a marked resemblance to that of Nazi Germany. It is true that representatives of the workers and management serve on governing councils which supervise industries, but these representatives are almost invariably appointed by the government. Additionally, the government has appointed special commissars to investigate the operation of industry at all levels. These commissars are empowered to take many important decisions and their recommendations are rarely ignored by the governing councils they advise. Industrial development has, rather surprisingly, been largely taken out of the hands of private enterprise. In that conservative interests in business and industry generally welcomed the 1967 coup this seems a poor reward for either support or tolerance for the existence of the régime. The fact of the matter is that business interests in Greece have proved no more able to control the colonels than business interests were able to control Hitler in Germany after 1933. The success of the colonels' economic policies has come as a surprise to many observers. In 1969 the G.N.P. rose by over 8 per cent in real terms and similar figures were achieved in 1970 and 1971. The great industrial and shipping barons, Niarchos and Onassis, have been obliged to protect their interests by co-operating with government consortia on terms that have not been as favourable to the magnates as was the case in the past.

If the government of the colonels has taken a rather unconventional line in economic policy it has compensated for this radicalism by a steady display of conservatism elsewhere. The régime has sought to place some political power in the hands of the peasants, at the expense of the urban population. In order to secure the loyalty of the peasants attempts have been made to better their living standards. Since 1967 an elaborate programme of public works has been undertaken. Most notable among the schemes have been housing projects, health schemes, sanitation, road building, irrigation and the provision of expert advice in order to improve the yield from the land. The implementation of these measures has significantly strengthened the power base of the colonels. On the other hand, restrictions on public meetings and festivals (save those of the most obviously non-political kind) have not been popular. The abolition of free school meals and the postponement of the extension of school-leaving age have had more impact upon the urban than the rural population but these measures have hardly added to the régime's popularity.

There are features of the present government that are familiar to all students of totalitarianism. The most obvious feature is censorship of news and comment. Several prominent Greeks have fled the country because of their inability to comment upon the régime in security: several of these have been deprived of their citizenship. A heavy hand has fallen not only upon editors of newspapers but also upon authors and playwrights, both of the present and the past. In conjunction with censorship the government has also introduced a whole range of measures which add up to a significant restriction upon personal liberty. Newspapers were compelled to publish articles and editorials supplied by the government agencies and any attempt to refuse was severely dealt with. There was also heavy restriction upon political activities. Many communists were arrested and, additionally, many who were merely suspected of harbouring sympathy for communism. Politicians of all beliefs were denounced as corrupt and inefficient (both accusations were frequently made by fascist régimes in the 1930s in order to discredit respectable opponents) and many were taken into custody. Military courts were appointed to examine the charges brought against the detainees and few were released from prison or house arrest.

The colonels were not so stupid as to ignore totally the task of maintaining the appearance of democratic government. Even after the flight of Constantine II they asserted merely that the king had chosen voluntarily to abstain from his duties. Indeed, the government appeared quite willing to allow the king to return as long as he abstained from political activity independent of the tasks they wished to assign to him. However, the government also set up a constitutional commission to inquire into the operation of the law and the constitution. They also had the task of devising a new constitution more to the liking of the colonels. When finally drafted the major innovations were seen to be the suspension of parliamentary democracy, the separation of the legislative and executive branches of government and the strengthening of the power of the executive. The new constitution was ratified by a plebiscite in September 1968. Great pressure was put on voters to comply with the wishes of the régime and there was a strong undercurrent of violence throughout the period leading up to and during voting.

The colonels have also been increasingly successful in their attempts to present a favourable image to the outside world. The growing economic strength of Greece has had some effect, but so too has the increasing confidence of the colonels. Pattakos, one of the leaders of the coup, has openly admitted that concern about the Greek image abroad is no longer one of the problems of the régime. The Greek government has been sensitive to any symptoms of hostility from the U.S.A. but, in practice, American assistance has usually been forthcoming. In 1972 a new aid programme was confirmed. In these circumstances the strictures of the American ambassador or the Council of Europe count for very little. Recently some damage has occurred to the image owing to the colonels' support for the attempted political comeback of Grivas in Cyprus, but the hostility aroused in Britain and Turkey by this mistaken attitude is unlikely to be of long duration once it is seen that President Makarios can look after his own interests.

The colonels have even felt so confident of their position that they have divested themselves of military rank and have undertaken sweeping measures involving an army purge. Many senior officers were prematurely retired, thus strengthening the control of the revolutionary junta. At the very top the puppet president was recently dismissed, apparently without affecting the stability of the régime. Benefits have been showered on the rest of the officer class, which has profited from its unwavering loyalty. The appeal for an army coup to oust the junta, made by Karamanlis, fell on deaf ears. The colonels have been very careful to promote only those who are fully committed to the new régime. Thus the government has been able to emerge gradually from the shadow of external disapproval. It has become clear that the colonels have every intention of being more than a caretaker administration. Civil servants, in consequence, have been obliged to take an oath of loyalty to the government; failure to comply has led to dismissal.

Further examples of confidence have been seen in the shape of relaxation of the regulations regarding political prisoners. In December 1970 it was announced that political prisoners would be released during the first few months of the following year; in due course this promise was kept. However, some prisoners were kept in jail or under house arrest on the grounds that they were dangerous enemies of the state. Many of these either were or were accused of being communists. A number of them had been arrested in a security drive in November 1970. Certainly, there are some prisoners (perhaps about one hundred) held in custody without having been charged. But the signs are that the government is confident enough to take the risk that some released prisoners will resume clandestine political activity.

Do all these characteristics add up to fascist practice? On the whole the verdict must be against the proposition that the colonels are fascists. They fit more easily into the political tradition of the *pronunciamento*, well-established as a characteristic of political life in Spain, Greece and some banana republics. The life-style and intellectual approach of the colonels may be more accurately seen as characteristic of conservative reaction rather than radical dynamism. The colonels dislike social change rather than welcome it as a political force from which they can benefit. Their model is Franco rather than Hitler. They have the same views about the position of the middle class, agrarian interests, the church and education as the *Caudillo*. Like Franco they are obliged to lean heavily on the support of the army and the security forces.

If the colonels are conservatives (of a very rightist hue) rather than fascists, there are good social reasons for this approach. Although Greece is undergoing a process of industrialization the agrarian sector is still very powerful. Much of the industrialization programme, in any event, has been developed under the colonels. The social and political mobilization which is so commonly found in societies where fascist governments have existed is thus not much advanced. Constant concessions to agrarian interests have helped to slow down the drift to the towns, thus impeding the growth of a large and underprivileged urban proletariat. The colonels have a truly conservative fear of urbanization but have adopted a solution to their problems that is hardly characteristic of the Right. They have been prepared to use current economic developments in order to consolidate their position within the state in the hope that changes will come about only at an acceptable rate. In this sense the régime marks a surprisingly radical break with the recent political past of Greece. It would be wrong, however, to regard this radicalism as a Greek version of fascism, not only because the social and economic conditions conducive to the rise of fascism are absent in Greece, but also because this radicalism is based upon a desire to smother rather than to take advantage of mass political mobilization and participation.

16 Vargas, Perón and Some Signposts for the Future

> 'Dictatorships of the past needed assistants of high quality in the lower ranks of the leadership also—men who could think and act independently. The authoritarian system in the age of technology can do without such men. The means of communication alone enable it to mechanize the work of the lower leadership. Thus the type of uncritical receiver of orders is created.' Albert Speer, Final statement at Nuremberg, September 1946

Latin America, apart from Greece, is the only area of the world in which fascism is popularly supposed to have existed in both the period before and after the Second World War. Is this popular belief well-founded? It is certainly true that the conclusion of the war of 1939–45 did not lead to a sudden decrease in the number of dictatorships in Latin America. Nor has there been a very remarkable decline in the intervention of the army, or one of the other armed forces, in internal politics during the years since 1945. Men such as Batista,[1] Perón[2] and Duvalier[3] have been as prominent in post-war politics as Vargas[4] and Trujillo[5] were in pre-war politics; some of their careers even spanned the war and lasted well into the post-war period. Argentina and Brazil, in particular, have been the scenes of numerous armed interventions in political life. More recently an upsurge in guerilla movements, both urban and rural, has reflected growing dissatisfaction with the apparent norms of political conduct. The Latin American experience of the last half-century is thus of great significance, for although the area's cultural patterns ensure that its political development is unique, nonetheless the impact of modernization on a traditional way of life may give important pointers to the future development of politics in Africa and other unindustrialized parts of the world.

As in the case of Europe it would clearly be impossible to follow the development of all the régimes described as fascist. An attempt has been made, therefore, to pick out several of the most relevant examples—the most important of which is that of Vargas' rule in

Brazil. Vargas' dictatorship has to a very serious extent been mis-represented, both insofar as its nature and its intentions have been concerned. In 1930 a presidential election was due in Brazil amid an atmosphere of economic panic. Interest and service charges on foreign loans had risen to the incredible sum of $200 million (which was about five times as large as the favourable balance of trade) and coffee prices had almost completely collapsed—even in 1938 coffee was selling at only a third of the price it had fetched before the slump. In São Paolo alone in 1930 there were sufficient supplies of coffee stockpiled to last the world demand for more than a year. At this highly unfavourable moment a major internal political dispute arose, the result of which was a coup placing Vargas in power in October 1930.

From the very start Vargas sought to create a national party of reform, albeit through an authoritarian system. Vargas wished to free Brazil from dependence on foreign capital and to industrialize the economy. The measures he took fitted in well with the concept of economic autarky, they aimed at the creation of a national economic state. The first priority was to try to restore economic stability. This Vargas achieved (in part by accident)—he ordered the coffee supplies to be stockpiled, which at least halted the catastrophic decline in price. It had an important side-effect too in that investors were encouraged to put their money into industry rather than coffee plantations—it was obvious to them that the market for coffee would be highly unprofitable for some time to come. This in turn produced a sharp rise in production of other goods, particularly textiles and minerals. Cotton products rose from 3.4 per cent of exports in the 1920s to 14.3 per cent in the following decade; there were similar expansions in rubber, chemicals, cement, steel, iron ore, tobacco and manganese. The diversification of the economy and the increase in prosperity which followed proved an important popular ingredient in Vargas' rule.

The keynote of Vargas' rule was direction. What happened in Brazil in the period 1930–45 was not accidental but part of a de-liberate scheme. Government intervention in economic and political life became increasingly frequent. The first moves were made against foreign dependence; soon after coming to power Vargas introduced controls on foreign exchange, import quotas and tariffs. He followed this up by limiting foreign investment within some industries and in others a degree of expropriation took place. Public investment and government-dominated corporations were introduced in order to encourage new industries. In the new constitution of 1937 it was resolved to create a corporative organization of the national economy—an echo of policies being pursued by Mussolini at this time. A vast programme of public works was begun. Swamps in the state of Rio de Janeiro were drained and turned over to agriculture. Roads and railways were built. In 1938 the National Petroleum Council was founded, with the hope of making Brazil independent of foreign supplies. This was followed in 1939 by the creation of the National Council of Hydraulic and Electrical Energy and two years later by the National Steel Company.

The economic system of control was paralleled by political control. Vargas called his government a 'disciplined democracy', but there is more evidence of discipline than democracy. All appointments were made by Vargas and he ruled by decree. There was a continuing demand for constitutional rule throughout the 1930s, exemplified by uprisings in July 1932, November 1935 and May 1938. All these revolts were put down without undue difficulty. The dictator treated his political opponents well, for he preferred to exile or imprison them for short periods of time rather than execute them. Vargas did make some concession to the demand for democracy by convening a constituent assembly in 1933. The result of the meetings of this body was the constitution of 1934, which named Vargas as president for a four-year term. In 1937 a complete seizure of power took place when Vargas dissolved congress and proclaimed himself president for another four years. Another constitution was drawn up (with the aid of his Minister of Justice) entitled *Estado Novo* in which a state of emergency was declared, which could only be ended by a plebiscite. Article 180 of the constitution effectively transferred all power to the president, declaring that until elections took place 'the president of the Republic shall be empowered to issue decrees on all matters of legislation'.[6]

Like other dictators Vargas was obliged to use various forms of political control. Censorship was an important weapon in his armoury. From the very first a rigid censorship over the press was introduced. The press, radio and all forms of education were placed under the control of the D.I.P., which assigned a censor to each newspaper. Preference was given to sympathetic foreign correspondents and others were encouraged to leave Brazil. One of the country's leading newspapers, the *O Estado de São Paolo*, an organ of liberal democracy, having run foul of the dictator in the period after 1937, was confiscated in 1940 and publication was only resumed under the direction of a Vargas nominee as editor. During wartime this practice was intensified, the D.I.P. censored news favourable to the Allies in the early part of the war, only reversing its tactics when Brazil entered the war on the Allied side in the summer of 1942.

Vargas also sought to control labour. As in Italy and Germany this was a vital area of concern, both economically and politically. In the constitution of 1934 provisions for the control of labour were formally introduced. At the same time social legislation for both agricultural and industrial workers was implemented and votes were given to women. Wages, however, were kept low without the aid of any statutory instrument. The combination of a developing industrial economy and a declining subsistence economy regulated wage levels without need of resort to strict government control. After Vargas' coup of 1937 a new social programme was introduced. It included medical assistance for all workers and for pregnant mothers, insurance, restrictions on night work and child labour and the promise of an eight-hour day. Henceforward trade unions were to be controlled by the state, through a labour front, but collective bargaining was recognized as an inalienable right. All resources were deemed to be national, including labour and investment, and the ultimate goal was declared to be the corporative state. Labour unions in reality lost the little power they had previously enjoyed. Towards the end of Vargas' dictatorship inflationary pressures undermined his popularity still further, thus necessitating still stricter control.

How much of a fascist was Vargas ? In appearance it would seem that to call him fascist is well justified. The essential elements of control—lack of elections, censorship, lack of bargaining power by the unions, repression of political parties and emphasis on the national interest, both economic and political, are all present. Furthermore, such expressions of ideology as Vargas ever made are certainly open to interpretation as fascist. In 1940, for example, he asserted that 'Virile peoples must follow their aspirations . . . we are advancing towards a future different from established economic, social and political organizations . . . we believe that old systems and methods are on the wane.'[7] This was a clear indication of sympathy for fascism and was widely interpreted as such by shocked members of the State Department. Yet Vargas was a man of inconsistency. He used the war as a lever to improve Brazil's position. During the years before 1939 he had built up trade with Germany; in 1942 Brazil entered the war on the Allied side in return for some heavy loans. Ideological sympathy did not lead him to make a cardinal misjudgement in foreign policy.

There is other evidence to support the view that Vargas was not a real fascist. If, outwardly, he followed economic and social policies similar to those of Hitler and Mussolini his internal practice was very different. Police activity was minimal, political opponents were rendered harmless rather than eliminated. Other Brazilians were entrusted with real power, notably the commander of the army and the Minister for War. Still more important is the way Vargas dealt with the *Integralista* movement, which had some real claim to be fascist. Headed by a fanatic, Salgado,[8] this group came to prominence in the mid-1930s. Its programme was a compound of religious mysticism, anti-Semitism, devotion to the principle of leadership and advocacy of the corporative state. Salgado's followers, known as legionaries, wore green shirts, had their own salute and were always in the forefront of political unrest. The movement began to penetrate conservative circles, probably as a result of the money (some supplied by the German embassy) it was able to spend. When Vargas declared a state of emergency in 1937 Salgado offered the services of a hundred thousand legionaries to protect the republican régime. Vargas' coup completely undermined the *Integralista* movement and henceforth the Germans invested their money in and pinned their hopes on Vargas. Vargas continued his authoritarian and anti-Marxist policies, thus simultaneously pleasing the Germans and not offending the Americans.

It is hard, therefore, to label Vargas as a fascist. By the standards of Hitler and Mussolini he was not a fascist. His régime fitted in well with Latin American political traditions and with the needs of the time. The industrial development that took place during the fifteen years of his rule produced many benefits for Brazil. Vargas was a nationalist, he was enthusiastic about promoting Brazilian interest, he had some conception of the national interest. He was a political juggler rather than a savage tyrant. He remained at the top of the greasy pole for so long because he was so adroit and not because he crushed all opposition. He did not enrich himself at the public expense nor did he tolerate maladministration by his appointees. If he sought to create a fascistic economic system, which he did, he failed. He never succeeded in conquering labour problems as Hitler did. Unlike most of the fascist leaders he always encouraged ability among his subordinates. He did not attempt to secure his own power by creating rival organizations, each seeking a favourable decision from him, as did Hitler. If Vargas is to be regarded as a fascist, then he must be seen as a fascist with a human face.

Another favourite target for the description 'fascist' is the régime of Perón, which lasted from 1943–55. Perón's movement has continued to be of political importance in Argentina to the present day, so it is too early to speak of its demise. Far more than the system of Vargas does it warrant the description of fascist. Perón's movement was based upon mass support, upon proposed radical policies and resulted from a combination of political confusion and high political mobility derived from the events in economic and political life since 1929. Perón was also a demagogue and an organizer, a nationalist and a socialist. He also created the archetypal image of the anti-imperialist, hating and fearing the power of other countries, whether political or economic.

Perón held power through his control of a mass movement. In 1943 a coup brought a junta of pro-Axis generals to power. Within a few months they had allowed German activity to reach unprecedented heights. The Jewish press was banned, as were organizations working for Allied victory. Repression was the chief characteristic of the régime. Only in early 1944 was there a reversal of this policy. During the intervening months Perón had been consolidating his power. He was leader of the trade union movement through his post as head of the Ministry of Labour. In February 1946 he was elected president, despite an unsuccessful attempt to strip him of power in October 1945.

Perón's control of the proletariat was in part secured through the activities of his wife, Eva.[9] The secret of their success lay in action to protect working-class interests, and they retained great loyalty from the working class until the very end of the régime. The C.G.T. (General Federation of Labour) was impotent in the face of the largesse showered upon its members. The poor peasants and the underprivileged industrial workers were awarded high wages and given favourable social legislation. Perón's wife organized a charitable foundation, named after herself, which did a great deal of good work as well as providing a lucrative source of private revenue for the dictator. The poor, the sick and the old all benefited from the foundation's operations. It became, in fact, a kind of national social insurance, to which unions, employers and foreign corporations contributed. The threat of a general strike was enough to topple Perón's opponents in 1945 and secure for him a decade of almost unrestricted power.

The *peronista* economic policy was based on fascist principles. Belief in government control of all aspects of economic life dominated Perón's actions. In 1946 he simultaneously published plans for a five-year period and set up a National Economic Council to supervise its working. The plan was exceptionally ambitious, based as it was on the thesis that industrialization alone could cure Argentina's problems. It was Perón's view that Argentina should become the Germany of Latin America. Consequently about half of the projected expenditure was allotted to the construction of power plants, mainly hydroelectric. Argentina did not have large resources of coal or oil so these schemes depended entirely on completion of the hydroelectric plants. Similarly, government control was extended into other important economic areas. Before coming to power, in 1944, Perón had been the brains behind the creation of the Industrial Credit Bank. The overall result of the reforms of 1944–6 was an enormous increase in industrial production, so that prospects for large-scale industrial expansion looked rosy.

However, closer inspection reveals some of the weaknesses of Perón's economic policy. In general he neglected agriculture which, as only 28 per cent of the population was employed in industry and another 39 per cent in commerce, transport and government, meant that a vitally important sector was being ignored. In 1946 he created the A.I.P.E. (the Argentine Institute for the Promotion of Exchange), the function of which was to handle grain exports and secure for the country the most favourable terms. In the post-war world this organization enjoyed immense success for a few years, so much so that trading in meat and other supplies was handed over to its control. Perón's dealings with Britain were particularly successful and resulted in a number of important concessions. But successive British governments became less and less willing to submit to blackmail and by the end of Perón's rule British beef imports had fallen to a third of their 1943 level. The consequences of the neglect of agriculture were very serious. Argentina's shaky industrial prosperity was based upon the balance of payments surplus achieved by agricultural production. Indeed, as Bryan had observed in slightly different circumstances: 'Burn down your cities and leave our farms, and your cities will spring up again as if by magic; but destroy our farms and the grass will grow in the streets of every city in the country.'[10] Perón was foolish enough to allow agriculture to decline, partly because of his wish to placate the industrial worker, partly because he failed to see that the food-importing nations would not always be prepared to pay any extortionate price he chose to demand. The production of wheat fell to less than a third of the 1940 figure by the end of the 1940s. Belatedly, in 1952, Perón tried to introduce subsidies for grain and cattle farming, but the damage had already been done. The new prosperity of Argentina had been built on sand.

Peronista economic policy involved, naturally enough, control of foreign economic interests. It had proved easy enough to obtain concessions from Britain, in particular the ending of British control of the railways, but in other cases *peronista* policy was less fortunate. Attempts to deal hardly with the U.S.A. met with scant success after the end of the war. In 1946 Perón seized the Central Bank and transferred to it control of the numerous foreign banks established in Argentina. The telephone and telegraph companies, owned by Americans, were also acquired in the same year, although compensation had to be paid. But economic nationalism did not really pay and in 1950 the U.S.A. bailed out Argentina to the tune of $125 million. Only through this loan was Perón's policy able to be pursued until 1955. It is ironic to record that, if anything, the humiliation of having to accept the loan encouraged the dictator in his paranoid outbursts against the U.S.A. If in economic terms it was a losing policy, in political terms it drew support from the anti-Yankee feelings of the bulk of the population.

The principal problem with which Perón had to grapple was inflation. It was a battle he could not win, for his power rested upon the support of labour and constant wage increases merely accelerated the inflationary spiral. The amount of currency in circulation increased rapidly and the rate of capital investment fell dramatically. Total production even began to decline and reserves dipped sharply. Outwardly it seemed as if *peronista* policy had brought prosperity and economic diversity. In fact, industrial development was largely fictitious. Argentina did produce some steel, machinery and other industrial products, both in light and heavy industry, but at astronomic cost. It proved impossible to create an autarkic system without a very large industrial complex, which Argentina did not have, and without a high degree of internal demand, which was also absent. The domestic market could not sustain industrialization, as Perón had believed. Perón tried to implement fascist economic policies, as they were pursued in Nazi Germany, but local conditions were totally unfavourable.

In the end Perón's position depended on mass support. The death of his wife in 1952 and his increasing inability to handle the economy undermined his support even among the unions. Perón, however, although he leaned heavily on the support of the poor working class did use other forces to sustain him in power. There were many fascist characteristics of his domestic policy in the non-economic field. Like Vargas he came to rely increasingly on censorship. The Buenos Aires mob was turned on those who disagreed with him, as can be seen from the riots inspired in 1953. As early as 1951 *La Prensa*, the famous oracle of democracy, had been expropriated and turned over to direction by a government board. Other newspapers, less bold, became increasingly reluctant to utter any criticism at all.

Control of business and industrial interests also appealed to Perón. Until the pressure of events forced a change in 1952, he repressed the political power of the landowners. Confiscation of assets followed immediately upon any unwise political initiative. Similarly, Perón controlled the political parties. He did not ban other parties but the full range of government propaganda was deployed against them. Dissident politicians were accused of neglecting the national interest and of being in the pay of the U.S.A. or some other foreign (and even Latin American) power. When pressure became too great mobs were incited to burn the buildings and murder the leaders of the hostile parties. Controlled violence, as in Italy and Germany, became a standard technique of power. As in Germany and Italy the dictator attempted to come to terms with the Catholic hierarchy. In his early years this was very successful, for the hierarchy of the church endorsed Perón's candidature in 1946, despite protests from many in the lower ranks of the priesthood. Later the bishops were to learn that their goodwill too could be ignored. After the death of Eva, the dictator legalized divorce, advocated the taxation of church property, the separation of church and state and indicated that he intended to end the connection between the church and education. These proposals created great unrest amoung former supporters and Perón exiled two of the more recalcitrant bishops in the summer of 1955. However, the enmity of the church certainly facilitated the fall of Perón in September 1955.

It should not be forgotten that Perón also had strong support within in the armed forces. His route to power had been found through his participation in the insurrection of 1943. The army soon became suspicious of his intentions and attempted to remove him in 1945. Although the army was defeated, Perón knew that unless he was able to conciliate this immensely powerful pressure group he could not hope to hold power for long. The officers who had plotted against him were removed and steady promotion was given to those who showed their loyalty conspicuously. Non-military, high-ranking posts were found for supporters and pay was increased at frequent intervals. The budgets for the armed forces were very generous, amounting to about 20–25 per cent of the national budget throughout the period. Obsolete equipment was replaced and rearmament proceeded apace. During the years 1950–5 Argentina's officers were in real terms the most highly paid in the Western world. The programme of industrialization with its strong nationalistic overtones also had considerable appeal among the military. As in the case of Germany the army sold its loyalty to the dictator.

On the face of it, then, Perón's Argentina would seem to merit the term 'fascist'. Close inspection of the social pressures reinforces this belief. The coalition that Perón created bore some resemblance to that devised by Hitler, although the different nature of the states makes a complete comparison impossible. In Argentina there was a high degree of political mobilization in this period. Economic growth had been rapid in the period after the war of 1914–18 and had been followed by migration from rural to urban areas. This process had been intensified by heavy immigration from Spain, Italy and Portugal. Social mobility bred political mobilization, which did not immediately secure action from the conservative groups which dominated politics in the inter-war period. The limited voting system that had existed before 1914 was expanded but still did not include either those of foreign birth or the urban proletariat. There thus existed a section of the population concentrated in the urban centres which was both economically and politically disaffected. It was to this mass that Perón successfully directed his appeal.

The *peronista* movement was in essence a populist coalition, drawing together support from certain sections of the army, the urban proletariat, the landless peasant, some members of the clergy and a considerable number of industrialists and entrepreneurs. In class structure, then, the movement was heavily tilted towards the underprivileged members of society. Even the support for the movement among the upper classes tended to be drawn from those who were socially not completely accepted, the *arrivistes*. The process of social change wrought by Perón's rule was surprisingly profound. The old élite trade unions, for example, were coerced into becoming large, mass bodies and were given a larger role in political affairs. The organizations of the mass of the urban working class were rewarded for their steady support with social benefits. Labour came to play a critical part in politics and membership rose to about four million by the time of Eva Perón's death.

The success of Perón in retaining loyalty among the urban workers was not ephemeral. It has been estimated that even in the 1970s the *peronista* vote in Argentina is as large as 30–35 per cent of the votes cast. Clearly, this form of fascism, if that is what it is, is different from the European model. Because it is the view of many writers on fascism that the movement represents a final stand by the élites to protect their position, the interpretation of the *peronista* movement creates certain problems. Organski rejected the charge that Perón was a fascist on these grounds, remarking that 'political mobilization in the peronist system led to social and economic gains. Nothing could be more alien to fascist experience. Perón did the one fundamental thing that all fascist systems (whatever their other characteristics) are designed to prevent. He permitted the integration of economic systems and enabled the newcomers to use their newly found power to meet some of their social and economic demands.'[11] This definition is simple but seems to me to fail to understand that fascism can be popular and can lead to social benefits for the underprivileged. It is surely wrong to write off the mass support which Hitler and Mussolini received as the result of delusion on a vast scale. Is it correct to assume that fascists everywhere not only were incapable of fulfilling their supporters' hopes but never had any intention of so doing? The *peronista* movement produced a form of fascism which was distinctively Latin American, suitable for the conditions that existed in developing countries soon after the war of 1939–45. In this movement labour played a much larger part than in Italy or Germany, and this was true from start to finish. The unique nature of the régime may also be discerned in the fact that the middle class and intellectual support for the system also vanished much more quickly. Few industrialists, merchants, clergymen, soldiers or bankers supported Perón by 1955. Even fewer support his movement now. Perón's fascist form commanded support from the bulk of the urban proletariat and a minority from the upper and middle classes; the European fascist model was based on massive middle- and upper-class support together with a sizeable minority from the working class. These differences are extremely important, but similarities between the ideological basis, the *modus operandi*, the social and economic conditions preceding the seizure of power, and the social effects make a comparison between the European and Latin American forms valid. It is not seriously misleading, therefore, to see *peronismo* as a form of fascism.

Since so many of the new nations are undergoing processes of modernization and industrialization it is a matter of importance to try to determine how relevant the Argentinian experience is to present-day Latin America. Conditions favourable to the development of fascism (in a modern form) are widely prevalent in Latin America. Among those worth mentioning are the privileged position of élites, low educational standards, potential social and political mobilization, xenophobia and belief in economic autarky. It is not necessary that these conditions should lead to the imposition of a fascist solution, but Latin American attempts to deal with their problems in other ways have been pretty unsuccessful. Unless the institutional and social structure common to most Latin American countries undergoes fundamental changes within the comparatively near future then a whole range of new problems will be created which may only be solved through the adoption of a fascistic solution. There are already signs of such development.

One of the most important characteristics of Latin American countries is the strength of feeling against what is described as economic imperialism. The relationship between the U.S.A. and its Latin neighbours has been increasingly bedevilled by this problem. It is, of course, hardly new. Perón constantly posed as the friend of other Latin American countries and as the enemy of the greedy, capitalist U.S.A. Obviously the relationship between the U.S.A. and Latin American states varies from country to country, but the general pattern is clear. The financial relationship basically signifies liability to non-residents. Liability may be owed to banks, corporations, governments, international bodies and to individuals. Usually the liability has been built up over a long period of time. Necessarily these liabilities carry with them certain political consequences and may in some instances seriously affect the options open to a country. In a period when great emphasis is laid on national independence it is natural that Latin American attitudes should have come to be characterized by xenophobia, mainly directed at the U.S.A., and by popular demands for economic autarky.

The simplest answer to the problem, and that advocated by Marxist politicians, is confiscation of foreign assets, nationalization of industries and of banks. Such a policy has been followed in Cuba during the last decade and, to a limited extent, in Chile since the presidential victory of the Marxist coalition in 1970. Unfortunately for the advocates of this solution, it is hardly a success. Latin America is an area which needs capital and international agencies are as dependent on the wealthy nations for the supply of capital as any other body. Confiscation of American assets is hardly likely, therefore, to be followed by massive indirect American subsidies sent through some United Nations agency. The more perceptive régimes in Latin America have realized that their countries need investment in roads, power stations, dams, harbours, railways, refineries, smelting works and all the other trappings of a process of industrialization. Leaders of these governments have, in fact, adopted a solution which bears some resemblance to fascist practice in Europe in the inter-war years. Foreign involvement in economic affairs has been consistently denounced, and in some cases involving private assets action has been taken, but in general little action has been taken. The most notable examples of this attitude may be seen in Peru, Bolivia and Brazil. The commitment of these countries to the goal of economic autarky is apparently wholehearted; opportunities are frequently taken to embarrass the U.S.A., as in the case of Peru's ridiculous claim to a 200-mile territorial waters limit. In reality, however, bilateral aid agreements with the U.S.A. and some European countries are still sought. At the same time private foreign investment (that is to say the type that is most readily recognized by the native inhabitants of the country) has been subjected to a rigorous process of control. Several governments seem to have realized, as in the case of Nazi Germany, that appearances count for a great deal. What Peru has done has not in practice been very different from Chile, but the impression left on the observer is very different. The government in Peru, for example, is not fascist but it is of interest that in its conduct of complex politico-economic issues it has operated along lines which, both ideologically and in practice, existed in inter-war fascism.

Another factor favouring the development of fascism is the domination of Latin American society by élites, particularly when this is coupled with very low average educational attainments. In most Latin American countries can be found an aristocracy, accepted as socially superior for a long period of time. The same families have virtually monopolized political power, have been very wealthy and have been socially prestigious. They have dominated the army, the legal profession, political life and the diplomatic service. Although in many cases much direct political influence has been lost—and not least through the rise to power of men like Vargas and Perón—social mobility into this class is still low. The middle class has only been able to break into the upper echelons of society by a process of association, through education and through a willingness to accept aristocratic values. Clearly this state of affairs is highly dangerous, for it opens the way for the rise of unscrupulous demagogues, who are able to convince the bulk of the population that nothing can be lost by destroying the traditional fabric of society.

The effect of demagogy can be felt in two principal ways, by the adoption of a communist solution or by the adoption of a fascist solution. Until the fall of Batista the communist solution was ruled out in Latin America, and, after the dangerous episode of the Cuban crisis, it is at least doubtful whether most Latin American countries would wish to adopt Marxist ideas, for these seem to involve dependence on another foreign power even more alien than the U.S.A. The possibility of a fascist solution can hardly be ruled out. Fascism takes an anti-communist form, so in its initial stages is hardly likely to encounter hostility from the U.S.A. Nor, for that matter, would a fascist state, for the same reason, appear so dreadful to the privileged élites. The sympathy shown by the hierarchy of the Catholic Church to Perón shows also how another important potential source of opposition could be immobilized. Fascist doctrine also embraces a number of propositions dear to élites. Fascism is essentially nationalistic and militaristic. It accepts the concept of hierarchy and leadership. It thus simultaneously leads existing élites to believe that their power will be left intact (at the price of admitting a few into the ruling circles) and the underprivileged to believe that they can rise through the movement to dominate political life. Élites that are under challenge are especially vulnerable to the rise of fascist movements, for they are resisted less strongly than revolutionary movements of the Left and their appeal is nicely gauged in terms of the existing political mobilization to be attractive to the multitude. In Latin America there can be little doubt that the political conditions exist which could favour the growth of fascism. Industrialization, the decay of the political domination of the conventional Right and increasing awareness of the benefits of education have combined to produce in Latin America populations which are only too ready to follow the lead of a demagogue.

Inadvertently some encouragement has been given to this process by the involvement of the army in politics. As in the case of Nazi Germany a dangerous state of affairs can arise from military misjudgement. For many years it was only the army which provided a safe route for social mobility, and new political aspirations tended to be expressed in terms of military interventions in politics. The intensely militaristic and nationalistic characteristics of fascism have a considerable appeal to the privileged armed forces, so their resistance to any mass fascist movement would in all probability be feeble. Once again the example of Perón is worth bearing in mind.

Traditional political groupings have been slow in the past to see the dangers that have threatened them. This short-sightedness seems unlikely to disappear. Despite the weakening of the grip of the landowners on government, in no Latin American country has it proved possible to implement a full scheme of land reform. Unless there is a sudden change in the tempo of political development it is possible that the drift from the land will be intensified. Latin America is unlike other underdeveloped areas in that its countries already have large urban populations. Add to these disaffected peasants and the parallel with the situation in the Weimar Republic of 1929–33 becomes obvious. Neither a fascist nor a communist solution can easily be ruled out of the reckoning. The traditional parties have also weakened the framework of government. While in power they have been obliged to bow to realities and the old adherence to liberal democratic doctrines has been loosened. Government intervention in all spheres of life is now accepted as commonplace. This in turn advances the possibility of the totalitarian state, particularly as means of communication favour ready obedience to orders from a central authority. Scope for individual judgement, the backbone of liberal democracy of the classical kind, has been steadily eroded.

Although low educational standards make the notion of mass participation in political life unreal in most Latin American countries, there have been some concessions to this ideal. Most Latin American régimes have in common a degree of authoritarianism. The activities of ordinary political parties are in some way curtailed and the power of the executive (the makers of decisions) is, on the whole, on the increase. It is interesting to note that with the collapse of the Marxist coalition in Chile its leaders, who formerly advocated collaboration with the Christian Democrats, now complain bitterly about the obstructions put in the way of executive power by the party system. A few changes in the names of the parties and the personnel and the words would not have seemed inappropriate in the mouth of Hitler. Mass participation is encouraged through acceptance of a charismatic leader, a man of the people for the people. However, the facade of parliamentary democracy can easily conceal an authoritarian régime, whether the country be situated in Europe or Latin America. Mexico has had the good fortune to be ruled for the last half-century by men who have, on the whole, been able administrators, but the government has still been authoritarian. This has not precluded the existence of widespread public support for the system. Governments in Latin America are constantly seeking new ways of keeping in contact with popular feeling. Plebiscites, referenda, direct reform outside the constitutional process have all been tried. This system is far removed from the Westminster model, though it does have some affinity with the Gaullist approach to politics. It is a version of 'neo-populism' and as such is particularly vulnerable to a fascist challenge.

The position of the Latin American countries in relation to a revival of fascism is, therefore, of great interest. Systems that could reasonably be regarded as fascist have existed in the sub-continent in the past. Economic, social and political conditions favour the simultaneous development of industrialization, a decline in the importance of the primary sector, and political mobilization. It is very far from clear that fascism will be revived in a unique Latin American form but it would also be wrong to dismiss the possibility. It would be wrong to label any of the existing régimes in Latin America as fascist, but several contain within their political systems features which could easily be made to serve the interests of a fascist demagogue. The political fears of the conventional Right, the ambitions of the underprivileged, acute national feeling and devotion to the concept of economic autarky could combine in a new system. In view of the European experience would it be wrong to regard such a system as fascist ?

17   Africa: Some Contemporary Political Trends

'Ex Africa semper aliquid novi.' Proverbial, from Pliny, *Historia Naturalis*

At first sight it would seem absolutely extraordinary even to consider the possibility of the existence of fascism in Africa (South Africa excepted) because so many of the régimes in that continent which have attained independence in the last decade or so describe themselves as anti-imperialist. It is also extremely common for them to be described as socialist, multi-racial, progressive and nationalist. The validity of many of these claims is, on closer inspection, somewhat dubious. Many of the characteristics of European fascism may be found in certain of the African countries, though it is rare for any number to be found at the same time in one country.

In order to facilitate analysis Africa has been divided into two major areas—those still ruled by whites and those that are ruled by native Africans. The northern areas of Africa, dominated by Arab traditions, have been left out of this survey. Some of the European characteristics of fascism are, of course, totally absent from the African scene, so attention will be devoted very largely to the nationalist, socialist, militarist and racial aspects of current African politics in relation to fascism and, in addition, to the concept of leadership as presently understood in Africa.

The concept of nationalism is naturally very strong in an area where memories of colonial domination are still vivid. Most African states only became independent in the 1960s, and the continued existence of Portuguese involvement in Angola, Mozambique, Guinea and the Cape Verde islands, as well as the rather more securely based régime in South Africa, serves as a permanent reminder of the imperial past. Nationalism in Africa is thoroughly muddled up with internationalism and pan-Africanism, which are two very un-fascist movements. A major contributory factor to this state of affairs was the approximately simultaneous departure of colonial administrations throughout Africa, which thus helped create the impression that all the African nations had common interests and common goals. Busia, in his fascinating *Africa in Search of Democracy*, recognized the problem as pan-African when he wrote: 'It is right that Africa should seek her own institutions, and not pattern her institutions on those of Britain or France or American or Russia or any other country.'[1] It is significant that he writes of Africa in general terms rather than making reference to one particular state.

However, the passage of time has made it clear that there is not only a form of African internationalism which is manifest in terms of united action at the United Nations over certain issues (an ever-declining number), but also more normal forms of nationalism. Indeed, according to Rotberg, contemporary nationalism 'connotes the consciousness of belonging to a particular nation, with pride in its cultural heritage (rather than in that of any particular ethnic group), together with an articulate demand for the self-government of that nation in place of alien control.'[2] Nationalism has led inevitably to the development of international disputes. Various attempts at federation have collapsed, including, most recently, all effective association in East Africa. It would indeed be a matter for surprise if the chauvinism of the colonial period had disappeared as suddenly as the European administration.

An examination of attempted unions between African states shows how strong nationalism is. On 23 November 1958 the Ghana-Guinea union was formed, to be joined by Mali (itself the remains of a failure to unite with Senegal) on 24 December 1960. The association was, in the words of its own articles, 'to promote a common economic and monetary policy'. Ghana, under the leadership of Nkrumah, was clearly the dominant partner and it was not long before there were discontented rumblings in the other states about attempted exploitation by the dominant partner. The fall of Nkrumah in February 1966 put an end to the experiment, but not before Senghor, the leader of Senegal, had scathingly criticized his narrow nationalism: '. . . the actual deeds of independent African governments contradict their pan-African declarations. As soon as independence is acquired, most African States, still afflicted by European viruses, begin to secrete a conquering imperialism. They argue over their present borders, claim portions of neighbouring territories, maintain in their countries, at considerable expense, emigrants and shadow governments or, in other countries, subsidize fifth columns in their service. I do not see how one can possibly create the United States of Africa if one starts by disuniting the States of the Continent, if one does not begin by respecting their integrity and their frontiers.'[3]

National integrity has also proved to be fragile under pressure. In Nigeria the racial antagonism, religious disunity and economic differences between Hausa, Ibo and Yoruba have contributed not only to the Biafran War but also to several changes of government during a mere decade of independence. The earlier experience in the Congo was still more terrible and it seems likely that national integrity will be challenged again in the future by tribalism, which is, after all, merely a miniscule form of nationalism. The experience of Malawi, where Banda was attacked by other African leaders for the slow advance of his government towards the achievement of goals they deemed desirable, has shown how quickly nationalism can turn into authoritarianism of the fascist mould. When confronted with opposition, Banda sacked his enemies, declaring: 'What are the four cornerstones on which our Party, our Government, our State, was built ? . . . they are unity, loyalty, discipline and obedience . . . once these four cornerstones are broken away . . . there is no Malawi government in this country, and there is no State . . . what do we get ? Another Congo ? Is that what anyone in this country wants ?'[4] Repression and rebellion swiftly followed, although Banda's policy proved successful in the end. A not insignificant factor in his success was the folly of his opponents in launching a military attack on his régime based upon external support from Zambia and Tanzania. Banda's appeals to crude, but strong, sentiments of nationalism in Malawi were well received during the crisis.

Nationalism has found its most obviously totalitarian and fascist outlets in the formation of one-party states and domination by leaders who either possess or seek charismatic qualities. The one-party state is frequently seen as absolutely essential on national grounds. Sir Abubakar Tafawa Balewa based the case for a one-party system on his political experience in Nigeria: 'I have told people all along that we are not ripe for a system of government in which there is a full-fledged opposition. In Nigeria, no party can agree to be in opposition for long. A political opposition in the Western accepted sense is a luxury that we cannot afford.'[5] President Nyerere of Tanzania went even further, suggesting that 'The politics of a country governed by a two-party system are not, and cannot be, national politics; they are the politics of groups whose differences, more often than not, are of small concern to the majority of people.'[6] Justification for Nyerere's point of view is found in the peculiar traditions of African society, the belief that opposition can best be expressed within the party grouping, the need to pull together in order to achieve social progress. The fact that they lead to the installation of tyrannical régimes such as those of Nkrumah and Karume is almost everywhere ignored by African apologists.

It is sad, too, to record that many Europeans (most of whom were presumably bitterly hostile to fascist régimes in Europe) have surrendered their critical faculties in their inability to see fascist tendencies in newly emerged states. It is true that African states on the whole lack the social attitudes and social groups which, in the West, have been the backbone of democracy, but this provides an explanation of the phenomenon rather than a justification. Calvo-coressi has suggested that one-party states are not undemocratic: 'In the West opposition was almost automatically regarded as loyal opposition; in new states it was equally automatically branded as disloyal to the concept and very existence of the state, besides sabotaging the essential tasks of peaceful economic development. It is not to be disputed that this view of opposition led in places to unjust and excessive repression, but it was wrong to generalize from these examples that the basic political philosophy was either intrinsically vicious or inappropriate to Africa.'[7]

The more perceptive Africans have themselves seen where sympathetic consideration of this viewpoint has led. Dr Azikiwe condemned the one-party system which had led to the murder of Dr Danquah in Ghana, pointing out that 'I am sorry that Dr Danquah died in a detention camp. I am of the considered opinion that if independence means the substitution of indigenous tyranny for alien rule, then those who struggled for the independence of former colonial territories have not only desecrated the cause of human freedom but have betrayed their people.'[8] Similarly, at the 1961 Lagos conference of African lawyers, organized by the International Commission of Jurists, it was agreed that 'Governments should adhere to the system of democratic representation in their legislatures'. Furthermore, as Professor Lewis has pointed out, no party in West Africa ever fought a successful election on the platform of wishing to create a single-party system. This lack of success, he suggested, stemmed from the simple fact that a one-party system 'fails in all its claims. It cannot represent all the people; or maintain free discussion; or give stable government; or, above all, reconcile the differences between various regional groups. . . . It is partly the product of the hysteria of the moment of independence, when some men found it possible to seize the State and suppress their opponents. It is a disease from which West Africa deserves to recover.'[9] The point is that adoption of such a system is likely in most cases to lead to a political society that is intrinsically vicious and is inappropriately viewed as democratic whether it is in Africa or Europe. No doubt Nyerere and Banda have the purest and most unselfish motivation in their suppression of opposition, but Mussolini and Hitler viewed themselves and their actions in the same way. Those Africans who genuinely believe in democracy, like the late Dr Danquah, can be forgiven for not wishing to run the risk that one-party states turn out badly. They rightly believe that Africa should in this matter be ready to learn from the European experience.

Where one-party rule leads is to the organic state. Sékou Touré, the President of Guinea, once observed: 'There are two ways of governing a country. In the first way, the State may substitute itself for all initiative, all men, all consciences. At that moment it deprives the people of their liberty of initiative, places them under conditions, and in consequence passes itself as omniscient by trying to solve general problems and problems of detail simultaneously. Such a State can only be anti-democratic and oppressive. We have adopted the second way and chosen to be a democratic state.'[10] Yet it was Touré who introduced a one-party state, allegedly based upon Marxist theories, in which the party itself became a substitute for the state and for all personal initiative. The judiciary was not allowed any independence from party control, indeed Touré himself asserted that 'The party is interested in every facet of political life without exception . . . if the attitude of an attorney creates a political problem, then it is the duty of the local administrator and party officials to intervene.'[11] Once the party became the sole judge of the public good, the sole arbiter of the justice or injustice of legal proceedings and the sole legal medium for the expression of public feeling, as it did in Guinea, then democracy was dead.

The party, of course, needs, in these circumstances, to behave very much as fascist parties behaved in Europe in the inter-war years. It is essential for there to be an endless flow of propaganda, not only in the form that the party must sponsor every public activity but also that it must control the press and the other media of communication. Under Nkrumah in Ghana exactly this process was followed. Censorship was introduced and even higher education was made to depend upon political reliability. The party also finds itself compelled to organize groups within the state, so that zeal and energy may be put at the disposal of the party. In Mali in 1961 all existing youth organizations were forcibly amalgamated into a party-controlled body. All those over 18 were obliged to join and to participate in compulsory labour schemes and para-military training. In Nkrumah's Ghana the trade unions became a party organization, thus losing their bargaining power, or, at least forcing those who wished to exercise it to seem factional and rebellious. The fascist tactics of Goebbels and Ley have found many parallels in the one-party states of Africa.

It would not be totally unreasonable for much of the history of the twentieth century to be seen in terms of the history of heroic leaders. The fascist myth encourages such a belief and Africa, as much as Europe, has seen the rapid rise and fall of charismatic folk-heroes. Belief in the leadership is, of course, an almost essential prerequisite for the maintenance of a one-party state. As Harris has observed: 'The single party, it is claimed, has many virtues in a modern African context particularly when headed by a charismatic figure-head. A single leader is seen as capable of making a quick decision on a matter of complexity, and he can change his alliance, alter his goals, direct his organization and mobilize his party-state.'[12] The leader, in many cases, symbolizes the power, unity and independence of the state; in addition he is usually not only the founder of his party but leader in the successful struggle for independence. Consequently the cult of the leader has often acquired almost religious qualities. Nkrumah was, for example, often described as the 'Redeemer' by the sycophantic clique that surrounded him. It was also used, at first enthusiastically, later ironically, by the mass of the Ghanaian people.

Inadvertently some encouragement to this process was given by the colonial powers, particularly by Britain. Wishing to see a solid government established at the time of their departure, British administrations frequently allowed the domination of the political scene by one party and one leader. Although this presumably made for easier negotiation and a smoother transfer of power it had serious political implications for the future of democracy in those states. The party that won the elections was given much help and advice, it had prestige and patronage from holding office, its leader was seen by the public to be associating on apparently equal terms with the colonial administration. When the leader found himself in difficulties the civil servants usually rushed to protect him from the consequences of his own or his party's incompetence or error. By contrast the opposition was habitually ignored, despite the apparent British desire to install parliamentary government on the Westminster model. The opposition received no help and was constantly exposed to the damaging charge of the ruling party that the main function of the opposition was to impede the peaceful achievement of independence. As Busia rightly commented: 'Neither at the centre nor at the local level can it be said that strong foundations for democratic rule were laid. The shoot was very tender, easy to smother under the authoritarian framework that is bequeathed at independence.'[13]

The consequence of this state of affairs was that leaders who were in control of their parties began to emerge as formidable figures. While this personalized leadership continues it is hardly surprising that peoples used to rule by direction rather than by participation accept the prime importance of the leader even against the party. The success of Banda in stifling rebellious elements within his own party is a vivid example of this tendency. In practice the domination of states by personalities has, almost everywhere, seriously damaged the already weak democratic structure. The domination of Touré, Nkrumah, Kaunda, Banda, Olympio and Mobutu, to mention but a few of those who have enjoyed, or still enjoy, virtually unchallenged power has shown a depressing toleration for authoritarianism and an amazing inability of educated Africans to resist surrender to the all-embracing personality cult. The triumph of the concept of direction has fitted in well with the African tradition. As has been pertinently observed: 'An African ruler is not to his people merely a person who can enforce his will on them. He is the axis of their political relations, the symbol of their unity and exclusiveness, and the embodiment of their essential values. He is more than a secular ruler; in that capacity the European government can to a great extent replace him. His credentials are mystical and are derived from antiquity.'[14] The skill of contemporary African politicians has been to absorb this tribalist tradition into a modern system. The abiding influences of tribalism and paternalism have thus been seized upon by leaders and turned to their own advantage. The consolidation of power has often been achieved by the promotion of relations of the leader or the very evident preference for men from the same tribe. In the long run this process has tended to bring about bureaucratization of the leadership and the formation of separatist groups demanding tribal autonomy and even independence, as in the case of Biafra and Chad. Once the gloss has worn off, the structural weaknesses of systems based upon the leadership principle have been ruthlessly exposed. Obote and Nkrumah survived to become petty pensioners of sympathetic imitators. Others, like Lumumba and Olympio, were fortunate enough to be killed before their personalities had been thoroughly exposed to the glare of critical publicity; as a consequence their reputations have largely remained intact and new men still follow their example.

In view of the dominance of the party and the leader in most African states it seems misleading to suggest, as does Wallerstein, that 'single party systems in the African context are often a significant step towards the liberal state, not a first step away from it'.[15] It is perfectly true that African political practice ought to be regarded with some tolerance, as many of the problems that confront these emergent nations have hardly been of their own making, but this form of reasoning seems likely in the long run to do a disservice to the cause of democracy in Africa by implicitly encouraging a type of régime to emerge which would be deemed intolerable in Europe or the rest of the Western world.

If national socialism is seen as a fundamental characteristic of fascism then there is an abundance of evidence to suggest that most African countries are in that sense fascist. Virtually all of them claim to be socialist for the purpose of promoting national well-being. In reality there is very little that is internationalist about their philosophy. The very wide variations of policy among governments purporting to be socialist is in itself a piece of evidence to support the contention that socialism is national rather than international, or Marxist, or revolutionary, or part of any other more general category. A few examples from African political practice serve to demonstrate the extent to which socialism is national socialism. While a number of former French territories sought a wide cultural and economic association based on their common ties with France, Guinea refused to co-operate. The Yaoundé powers were able to create a restricted form of economic union in 1961, calling their pilot scheme, with some justice, socialist and internationalist. Guinea in the meantime adopted a very different attitude, withdrawing from the franc zone, a move justified by Touré in terms which were both socialist and nationalist: 'We could never subject our political revolution to such conditions. No more could we align ourselves with the African territories of the Community financially or economically. To continue the *status quo* would have led inevitably to reintegration with the French Community by the back door and the renunciation of our political, social, and economic revolution.'[16] Touré also accepted the need for a planned economy in order to achieve social evolution in Guinea. Once more, he saw this in terms which may be described as nationalistic, socialist and autarkic: '. . . in the economic field we are in a state of national mobilization. Ours is a non-developed rather than an under-developed land. It is essential to remember this difference in order to understand the objectives of national economic mobilization.'[17]

If it was the avowed aim of the Ghana-Guinea-Mali federation to bring about Marxist socialist states, contrary views were held among many other African states, also claiming to be socialist. There were, for example, very marked disagreements about the desirability and extent of nationalization. In those states aiming at a Marxist society nationalization was extensive and disastrous. Ghana and Guinea were obliged to abandon these policies, while in Mali Keita was forced to admit that 'it would be a poorly advised policy to break down the traditional pattern of collective life in village communities'.[18] In other words, Mali was to revert to a well-tried national form of economic socialism rather than continuing to adhere to Marxist dogma. The experience of Kenya was expressed at a conference advocating nationalization only when 'national security is threatened, high social benefits can be obtained, or productive resources are seriously and clearly being misused, where other means of control are ineffective, and financial resources permit, or where a service is vital to the Government as part of its responsibility to the nation'.[19]

National socialism is a completely explicable phenomenon in Africa. Although it is closely associated with economic autarky, as it was in fascist European countries, it is not in reality a form of fascism. It is a response to recent colonial occupation and to the African desire to avoid foreign involvement in internal affairs. Socialism provides a dogma which Africans believe to be acceptable to both East and West (each of which blocs puts their own inaccurate glosses on the meaning of African socialism) and it is inevitably associated with national progress and well-being in the African mind. African governments, however, have been slow to recognize fascist trends within the doctrines they practise and with the best of intentions have often made important mistakes. It is clear that the Kenyan government had no intention of introducing a fascist state when it observed that 'if discipline is rejected, so is planning, and with it, African socialism'.[20] But this is a dangerous path on which to start one's way, as many African governments have already found. As Busia commented: 'Socialism is beneficial when it is democratic; but it can exist without democracy, and then it can be very despotic. . . . Some African countries, such as Ghana, are already on the road where the wrecks of freedom and justice are warning signposts. Socialism in essence is a moral doctrine which rests on human dignity and social justice. Its perversion becomes frightening oppression and tyranny.'[21] Busia and other politicians have, therefore, been well aware that nationalism and socialism form a dangerous heady brew, as likely to prove damaging to democracy in Africa as in inter-war Europe.

Having looked briefly at some of the nationalist, socialist, authoritarian and allied aspects of African political life, it is worth examining the phenomena of racialism and militarism. Within the European political framework it has already been shown that these were constituent parts of fascist operational doctrine. In Africa each of these phenomena have rather different places within the political system. Militarism exists as a result of two divergent political trends—the opposition of African nations to South Africa and the colonial territories of Portugal and, secondly, the involvement of armies in internal politics. The tremendous hostility that the racial policies of South Africa have created has led to demands for military intervention. African leaders have spoken of their nations being embattled citadels and have strongly supported guerilla movements in South African and Portuguese territories, with a total lack of success in the former and only limited success in the latter. In 1964 FRELIMO began its operations to liberate Mozambique and the following year an organization to co-ordinate African action against the Portuguese territories was set up. But all the African committees on these and allied matters suffered from the disadvantage of being extremely aggressive on paper and poor in achievement. Nyerere expressed

African frustration when he remarked that the African Liberation Committee 'was supposed to be, at its origin, an instrument of liberation and not a political committee having the power to pass resolutions'.[22] Support for military activities has been largely in the form of words rather than weapons. The African states discuss the problem of white-ruled areas in militant and militaristic terms but hardly act upon their own recommendations. Indeed, in the 1970s Banda and some other African leaders have even attempted to open some form of dialogue with South Africa, thus exposing themselves to hostility from their African brethren.

The other major form of militarism may be discerned in the form of military intervention within African states. In some states the military have played an extremely significant part in politics. In Dahomey General Soglo overthrew three governments between 1963 and 1965: in other countries intervention has been less frequent and possibly more effective. African armies play an important part in the cultural as well as the political life of their countries. They are seen as guarantors of national security and well-being. There seems comparatively little evidence of hostility towards them in the conceptual sense; few Africans seem to hold the common European view that all military expenditure is a waste. This form of militarism, however, is more closely related to an immature nationalism than to genuinely fascist militarism. In fact most army coups have been undertaken in some trepidation. General Ankrah's action in Ghana was justified by Afrifa in the following terms: 'A *coup d'état* is the last resort in the range of means whereby an unpopular government may be overthrown. But in our case where there was no constitutional means of offering a political opposition to one-party government the Armed Forces were automatically made to become the official opposition of the government.'[23] Military intervention has not been primarily the result of soldiers' desires to embark upon militarist policies but rather to restore decency and honesty to public life. Of course, there have been notable exceptions from this pattern (Mobutu in Zaire, Amin in Uganda), but the example of Gowon is more typical. As Busia wrote, 'Even the best examples of one-party régimes smother some essential democratic rights, and the freedom of associations like trade unions . . . others are flagrant dictatorships which afford no democratic avenues for change, and, as the records abundantly testify, offer only the alternative of military coups.'[24] In view of these comments and the bulk of the evidence provided during the years since 1957 it would be wrong to see African militarism as fascist in either intention or practice.

Racialism within African states certainly exists. In Uganda and other areas of East Africa there has been considerable discontent over the position of Asian immigrants, many of whom had acquired large commercial interests. In Zanzibar Karume resolved that only pure or half-caste Africans could share in the privilege of ruling the country. In Uganda Amin has gone even farther. Throughout Africa there is widespread resentment against whites. Policies of Africanization have been followed by almost all governments and some, like Zambia and Uganda, have been quick to criticize others that have been less enthusiastic about ejecting administrators merely because they happened to be white. The Zambian government was also ready to annul legal decisions given by its own courts on the grounds that important law officers were white. These are serious reflections upon the honesty and integrity of those governments that are so ready to abhor the policies of South Africa.

Racialism in Africa is, in fact, of two distinct kinds—one aggressive and proto-fascist and the other a relatively innocent form of defence mechanism. The aggressive racialism, examples of which have been given above, stems principally from two causes. Firstly, it is widely believed that the colonial nations exploited African natural resources and that, in a neo-colonialist era, all non-African nations wish to continue this process. Secondly, the continuance of racialist policies in South Africa (in conjunction with South Africa's evident economic prosperity) has stoked the fires of hatred and caused reprisals to be taken against white office-holders in other countries. The more innocent form of racialism is the belief in negritude. This was in its original form a revolt against the widely spread belief that negroes were inferior. At first it was a gospel of hate. As Senghor admitted: 'The negro students of whom I was one in the years 1930–4 were negativists, I confess we were rascists. We were delirious in our negritude. No dialogue was then possible with Europe.'[25] The passage of time, however, brought Senghor round to a different view. In a famous speech at Oxford in October 1961 he declared: 'Our revised negritude is humanistic. I repeat, it welcomes the complementary values of Europe . . . but it welcomes them in order to fertilize and reinvigorate its own values, which it then offers for the construction of a civilization which shall embrace all mankind. Let us stop denouncing colonialism . . . examined in historical perspective colonialization will appear at first glance as a general fact of history. Races, peoples, nations, and civilizations have always been in conflict. To be sure, conquerors sow ruin in their wake, but they also sow ideas and techniques that germinate and blossom into new harvests.'[26]

It is quite clear that Senghor's concept of negritude, whatever its origins, is not racialist but internationalist. It is the type of philosophy that deserves, though it rarely receives, more attention than the narrow racism of Karume and his countless imitators. Africans have as much right as others to be proud of their heritage and their future. Negritude is in this sense a public expression of what is normally regarded in the European world as noble patriotism or cultural pride. As Dadie of the Ivory Coast observed at the Abidjan Conference of April 1961 : 'Negritude is nothing but our humble and tenacious ambition to rehabilitate the victims and to demonstrate to the world what has been specifically denied up to this time: the dignity of the black race.'[27] To view this aspect of race as fascist would be totally inaccurate and betoken a failure to understand the important contribution made by Senghor, Dadie, Busia and others to Afro-European reconciliation.

As we have seen, there are aspects of modern African politics which may be described as proto-fascist; there are others which, if unchecked, might lead to a repetition of the European experience of the inter-war years. However, the presence of the South African political system in close proximity to a number of African states perhaps makes such a development seem less likely. In South Africa has arisen a form of political life which is in many aspects fascist, including institutions, policies, philosophy and personnel. Such is the detestation of black Africa for South Africa that it seems improbable that there is likely to be toleration for any period of time of any system that is directly comparable.

Superficially the institutions of South Africa are democratic. In practice there is some falling away from that ideal state. There is a multi-party system, but since 1949 only one group has held power—the Nationalist Party. In order to hold onto power this party has been compelled not only to place formidable restrictions on the operations of their principal rival, the United Party (which is at best a feeble thing), but, more importantly, has virtually strangled significant activity by the Progressives, the group most favourable to liberalism. Political activity by the non-white sections of the population (which amounts to about 80 per cent of the total population) is so insignifi-cant that it might be more accurately described as non-existent.

How closely, then, does the South African system approximate to fascism ? A brief examination of the roles of nationalism, economic autarky, racialism, militarism and authoritarianism shows conclu-sively that South Africa has many of the trappings of a fascist state. In addition to the formal political and institutional evidence it is also worth bearing in mind two other characteristics that are so remi-niscent of European fascism in its heyday. The first, and most obvious, is the almost hysterical reactions of South African poli-ticians to criticism, be it well or ill-founded, constructive or destruc-tive. The belief that the internal affairs of a country can be totally separated from all aspects of external relations is a characteristic of totalitarians of all kinds. It is also an argument accepted by those who can either only see totalitarianism selectively (that is to say, those who could see that Hitler's Germany was totalitarian but not Stalin's Russia, or *vice versa*) or are unable to see totalitarianism at all. The second important general factor to bear in mind is the very close identification of many of the leading Nationalist Party poli-ticians during the Second World War and the years immediately preceding that war with fascist and proto-fascist movements. It should not perhaps altogether have occasioned surprise when these men put into practice those beliefs that they held so strongly only a few years before.

It is, of course, the South African policy of *apartheid* that provides the most obvious parallel with fascist practice. The very real restrictions on individual liberty that have followed adoption of this policy have, in turn, led to further attacks on human dignity. It is true that the South African government claims that its policies are not racialist but based upon an attempt to afford recognition, albeit a different recognition, to the political aspirations of black Africans, but in practice this means white supremacy. As van den Berghe observed: 'The ideology of Afrikaner nationalism is a complex blend of provincialism, isolationism, xenophobia, pastoralism, egali-tarianism within the *Herrenvolk*, and a deeply ingrained colour prejudice with a touch of condescending benevolence so long as the master-servant relationship is unthreatened.'[28] The policy of *apart-heid* is based upon a siege-mentality and the enforcement of laws which not only create further racial inequalities (over and above the economic inequality that already exists) but also involve the exercise of almost unlimited power by the government. Since 1948 a stream of punitive and restrictive legislation has poured forth. The most notable laws are the Group Areas Act (1950), the Suppression of Communism Act (1950), the Mixed Marriages Act (1949), the Separate Amenities Act (1953), the Native Laws Amendment Bill (1957), the Public Safety Act (1950), the Improper Interference Act (1968), a number of other measures relating to alleged communist activities, and detention without trial.

The result of these acts has, of course, been an almost unbelievable restriction of individual rights. The apparently major difference of emphasis between *verligte* and *verkrampte* groups with the Nationalist Party pales into insignificance by their agreed acceptance of these restrictions. As the Johannesburg *Star* pertinently commented: 'The majority of Afrikaners support the Nationalist Party for two main reasons: to promote their Afrikaner identity and to protect their position of advantage as whites in South Africa.'[29] The central and dominant characteristic of South African politics is, thus, race. The major secondary characteristic is state control of individual rights. In both cases the similarity between South African practice and fascist practice is plain.

In South Africa, too, the fascist characteristics of militarism, nationalism and economic autarky also fit together in a coherent fashion. Economic prosperity has been based upon use of immense mineral resources and a large and politically powerless labour force. Part of this prosperity has been used to develop highly skilled and efficient armed forces. The tremendous superiority of the South African forces in terms of technology, discipline and logistics in relation to any other African power has not only promoted belligerence among South Africans but caused fear among the black African states. In South Africa militarism and nationalism, as well as being linked to racialism, are also linked to the concept of economic autarky. South Africa would dearly love to be totally self-sufficient. In those circumstances no attention at all would have to be paid to the many voices of its divided enemies.

The South African government has attempted to combine its economic and racial policies in the development of native states. Although these states have nominal political autonomy or even independence, the harsh realities of the power politics of the area and their own economic position in relation to South Africa force them into subservience. They have, in fact, all undergone the same political process as Banda in Malawi. This process has been aptly dubbed 'domestic colonialism';[30] and in Transkei the political impotence of the non-white 'rulers' has been plain for all to see. The true worth of these apparently liberal gestures by the South African government can only be seen in the context of a wish for continued economic exploitation of the situation. As in the case of Lesotho, the South African government can clearly make or unmake the administrations of these separate areas.

Africa is, therefore, an area in which fascist tendencies may be found amongst both black and white régimes. Nationalism is a vigorous force, though at times it has been obliged to make concessions to internationalism, especially among some of the more enlightened and genuinely progressive states. Racialism and economic nationalism are also primary characteristics of the Continent, though again these are rejected by some leaders. Fulsome adulation of petty dictators and one-party domination may also be widely found. Militarism and socialism have in Africa a meaning of their own, so it is not really possible to make valid comparisons with the European past. Yet the wholesale application of fascist ideas has taken place in one country—South Africa. Other countries, black African countries, have from time to time sunk under dictatorships into a period of proto-fascism, but these have either been or are likely to be transitory phenomena. When we speak of fascism in a modern African context we should not think of the regrettable neglect of or indifference to democracy which may frequently be discerned among the nations of black Africa, but that systematic and ruthless application of racialist and totalitarian doctrines in South Africa.

18   Conclusion

The comments on fascism made in the preceding pages are not intended to be definitive. Indeed, they could not be definitive, for many works have already been written on fascism and there exist major areas of disagreement among those interested in the topic. Some indication of the range of views held by historians and sociologists about the political experiences of Italy and Germany has already been given. There is still plenty of scope for fresh interpretations. The important facts about fascism are hardly contested, it is interpretation which is the major cause of disagreement. Anyone interested in fascism must bear this in mind.

Why, then, bother to write about fascism? I have strong reasons for believing that it is worthwhile expressing a personal view of the development and significance of fascism. In the first place it seems to me that fascism is not a dead ideology, it still has political potential, particularly in non-European areas of the world. It is thus relevant to current political developments to examine the fascist experience of the past. Secondly, it is very easy to confuse régimes that are ultra-conservative or reactionary with fascist systems and this is a confusion which some attempt ought to be made to dispel. Finally, all Europeans should be aware of the influence of European ideas in the rise of fascism—they should not be content to dismiss fascism as an unfortunate product of a few misguided or diseased minds. This is an aspect of fascism that has been too much neglected in the past.

There is one further justification for writing a general study of this kind. During nearly a decade of teaching I have heard any number of complaints from students that historians will not write general works, that they prefer to play safe by producing highly specialized articles the contents of which are difficult to follow and still more difficult to criticize. This is an over-simplification of a current trend but contains a serious element of truth. The educative process is above all concerned with the task of making people think. That is why I have thought it worthwhile writing this kind of book. I am under no illusion as to some of its defects. There will be many historians, sociologists and economists who will disagree with many of the things I have said or implied. I make no claim to a monopoly of virtue or to correctness of interpretation. It is easier to tear a general work to pieces than one of a specialized nature, but in so doing part of the educative process is accomplished. It is right that one's ideas should be exposed to the biting critical gaze of fellow academics, for we are ready enough to dissect the notions of our students. To be unwilling to expose general ideas about a controversial subject to criticism is to suffer a failure of nerve. As much is learned from reading criticisms of general works as from reading the works themselves. If some discussion of the nature and relevance of fascism is stimulated by this book then it seems to me that this is justification enough for having written it.

Notes to Part I

I

1. *The Journal of Contemporary History*, Vol. 1, No. 1, p. 14.
2. *Three Faces of Fascism* by E. Nolte, p. 6.
3. *The Theory and Practice of Communism* by R. N. Carew Hunt, p. 21.
4. Alfred Rosenberg (1893–1946) was born in Estonia, thus being a Russian citizen, but later came to live in Germany, joining the Nazi Party in 1919. He was the author of a number of turgid books on race theory, including *Blut und Ehre* and *Der Mythus des 20 Jahrhunderts*. Throughout his political career he was a negligible force, protected from the ambitions of others by Hitler.
5. Jacques Doriot (1898–1945) was originally a leading French Communist but moved into the fascist camp in the 1930s. He became a prominent collaborator under the Vichy régime and was killed early in 1945 when his car was strafed by an aeroplane.
6. Roberto Farinacci (1892–1945), Italian politician. At first a Socialist he joined Mussolini's group soon after its foundation. He was General Secretary of the Fascist Party, 1925–6, and a member of the Fascist Grand Council, 1935–43. He was executed by partisans in 1945.
7. Count Arthur Gobineau (1816–82), French author, widely believed to be the creator of racial theory and hence very popular in Germany. His most famous work was *Essai sur l'inégalité des races humaines*.
8. Georges Sorel (1847–1922), French author of *Réflexions sur la violence*. He was a prominent syndicalist and anti-racialist writer. He had a philosophy that was much influenced by Marx and Bergson.
9. Johann Herder (1744–1803), German author of *Ideen zur Philosophie der Geschichte der Menschheit*. One of the most influential of German thinkers and an opponent of Kant and his school.
10. Charles Darwin (1809–82), English naturalist, author of the *Origin of Species*. His theories on natural selection were later to be misused by those who believed in racial superiority.
11. Friedrich Nietzsche (1844–1900), German author of *Also sprach Zarathustra*. A philosopher of violence and the will to power. He died before completing his definitive work, *Wille zur Macht*.
12. Filippo Marinetti (1876–1944), Italian writer and founder of the literary Futurist movement. The author of *Futurismo e Fascismo*, he was protected by the Mussolini government.
13. Oswald Spengler (1880–1936), German author of the inter-war years; chiefly famous as a leading anti-democratic theorist and author of *The Decline of the West* and *The Hour of Decision*.
14. Houston Stewart Chamberlain (1855–1927), an English political philosopher who later took German nationality. His most important work was *Die Grundlagen des neunzehnten Jahrhunderts*. He was both anti-Semitic and an enthusiast for Aryan culture.

2

1. Gabriele D'Annunzio (1863–1938), Italian poet and novelist. He was a colourful nationalist who played a large part in causing Italy's entry into the war in 1915. In 1919 he was responsible for the seizure of Fiume, his 'lyric republic'.

2. D'Annunzio to Hérelle (his French translator), 1895. Quoted in *The Poet as Superman* by Anthony Rhodes, p. 50.

3. Johann Fichte (1762–1814), a German philosopher, frequently accused of atheism. Influential as Rector of Berlin University, 1810–12. In 1813 his lectures on the concept of a true and just war brought him a great deal of attention. They were published as *Über den Begriff eines wahrheften Kriegs*.

4. *Reden an die deutsche Nation*. Part IV.

5. Friedrich Jahn (1778–1852), the German 'founder of gymnastics'. He believed that German morals during the Napoleonic Wars could be restored by development of moral and physical powers through gymnastics.

6. Ernst Arndt (1769–1860), German poet and patriot. A prominent liberal who was instrumental in causing the liberation of the serfs in Swedish Pomerania and Rügen in 1806. Despite a chequered academic career he became Professor of History at Bonn in 1818 and Rector in 1841.

7. Friedrich von der Marwitz (1777–1837), Prussian general. Conservative politician and author; highly respected among the Junkers.

8. Joseph von Görres (1776–1848), German Catholic writer. Founder of the *Rheinischer Merkur*, 1814. In 1927 he became Professor of History at Munich.

9. *Das Wachstum der Historie*.

10. For further discussion of this and related points see *Father of Racist Ideology: the social and political thought of Count Gobineau* by M. D. Biddiss.

11. Richard Wagner (1813–83), German composer whose music reflected his political views. Prominent believer in racial myths.

12. Eugen Dühring (1833–1921), German political economist and philosopher. He was a follower of List (q.v.) in economics; his most famous work was *Cursus der National- und Sozialökonomie*.

13. Paul Lagarde (1827–91), German biblical and oriental scholar who was a professor at Göttingen. He was anti-Semitic and chiefly famous for *Deutsche Schriften*.

14. Karl Pearson (1857–1936), English mathematician and statistician. In 1911 he became Professor of Eugenics at University College London. He was founder and editor of *Biometrika* and author of many books.

15. Benjamin Kidd (1858–1916), English sociologist who was originally a minor civil servant. Chiefly famous for *Social Evolution*.

16. *Grundzüge des neunzehnten Jahrhunderts*. Quoted in *The Roots of National Socialism, 1783–1933* by R. D'O. Butler, p. 168.

17. *National Life from the Standpoint of Science* by K. Pearson, p. 46.

18. Ernst Haeckel (1834–1919), German biologist who had his own ideas about evolution. Professor of Zoology at Jena from 1865. In *Die Welträtsel* he tried to apply these ideas to philosophy, politics and religion.

19. *Social Revolution* by B. Kidd. Quoted in *Imperialism and Social Reform* by B. Semmel, p. 33.

20. In November 1900. *National Life from the Standpoint of Science*, pp. 26–7.

21. Fifth Earl of Rosebery (1847–1929), British Prime Minister 1894–5. A Whiggish member of the Liberal Party and a staunch imperialist.

22. 14 February 1902, at Liverpool. *Miscellanies: literary and historical*, Vol. II, by Lord Rosebery, pp. 250–51.

23. Sir Halford Mackinder (1861–1947), English geographer and formulator of geo-political theories. Academic at Oxford and L.S.E. An M.P. 1910–22. Author of *Democratic Ideals and Reality*.

24. Joseph Chamberlain (1836–1914), English politician. One of the most able men in late nineteenth-century politics. He left the Liberal Party over Home Rule

and was later associated with the Conservative Party through his Unionist Party. In the government of 1895–1900 he was a very successful Colonial Secretary.

25. Cecil Rhodes (1853–1902), English empire-builder. Prime Minister of the Cape, his political standing was largely destroyed by the fiasco of the Jameson Raid.

26. Rudyard Kipling (1865–1936), English author who won the Nobel Prize for Literature in 1907. He believed that all non-British were 'lesser breeds'.

27. *Recessional* by R. Kipling.

28. Rudolf Virchow (1821–1902), German pathologist. He was a professor at Berlin from 1856 and a staunch opponent of Haeckel's theories. He was a Liberal Progressive member of the Reichstag and an enemy of Bismarck.

29. Alfred von Tirpitz (1849–1930), German admiral, responsible for the Navy Laws of 1898 and 1900. Advocate of U-Boat warfare and leader of a nationalist party.

30. Heinrich Class (1868–1953), German propagandist, editor of *Odin*. In favour of expansionist policies for Germany.

31. Friedrich von Bernhardi (1849–1930), German general. Author of numerous books on expansionist policies, particularly *Deutschland und der nächste Krieg*.

32. *Germany and the Next War* by F. von Bernhardi (translated A. H. Powles), p. 18.

33. Friedrich Ratzel (1844–1904), German, Professor of Geography at Leipzig from 1886. Author of numerous works on geo-politics.

34. Karl Haushofer (1869–1946), German general and author. He later became hostile to the Nazis after he saw their misapplication of his ideas.

35. Friedrich Naumann (1860–1919), German author, famous for *Mitteleuropa*.

36. *Mitteleuropa*.

37. Houston Chamberlain to the Kaiser, November 1901. *International Affairs*, Vol. XVII, pp. 667–8.

38. The Kaiser to Houston Chamberlain, *International Affairs*, Vol. XVII, pp. 667–8.

39. *Die Sklaverei, ihre biologische Begrundung und sittliche Rechtsfertigung* by Franz Haiser.

40. *The Hour of Decision* by O. Spengler, p. 202 (translated by C. F. Atkinson).

41. Adolf Stöcker (1835–1909), German priest and political agitator. Founder of the Christian-social movement, powerful in the 1880s.

42. *Die Judenfrage als Racen-, Sitten-, und Kulturfrage* by E. Dühring.

43. Ibid.

44. Georg von Schoenerer (1842–1921), Austrian politician and writer. Basically a conventional right-wing figure with some anti-Semitic views.

45. Karl Lueger (1844–1910), controversial Austrian politician of uncertain affiliation. At one time Mayor of Vienna. Also an anti-Semite, though possibly through necessity rather than belief.

46. Édouard Drumont (1844–1917), French writer and deputy. Founded *La Libre Parole*. A firm anti-Dreyfusard on anti-Semitic grounds.

47. Hilaire Belloc (1870–1953), British writer, poet and historian. Liberal M.P. 1906–10. Author of a number of political tracts as well as numerous books.

48. *Annual Register*, 1910, p. 25.

49. Anton Drexler (1884–1942), German locksmith, founder of what was to become the Nazi Party. In 1921 he was replaced by the more dynamic Adolf Hitler.

50. Erich Ludendorff (1865–1937), German general, famous for his victories in the First World War. He also participated in the abortive Munich coup of 1923.

51. *The World in the Making* by H. Keyserling. Hermann Keyserling (1880–1946)

was of aristocratic origin and had been greatly influenced by Houston Chamberlain.

52. Julius Streicher (1885–1946), German propagandist and pornographer. The founder and editor of *Der Stürmer* in 1923. Hitler derived much inspiration from his frenzied outpourings.

53. Artur Moeller van den Bruck (1876–1925), German writer and thinker, chiefly remembered for *Das Dritte Reich*. A prophet of gloom and pessimism.

54. First Viscount Milner (1854–1925), English politician. He did important work in South Africa after the Boer War and as a member of the cabinet during the First World War.

55. Sir Oswald Mosley (1896–), English politician of changeable political views. Having resigned from the Labour government of 1929–31 he founded his own Fascist movement, which he has continued to support to the present day.

56. *Fascism: 100 Questions, No. 93*, by Sir O. Mosley. His views on birth control are given in the answer to Question 76.

3

1. *Ideen zur Philosophie der Geschichte der Menschheit.*
2. Immanuel Kant (1724–1804), German philosopher of immense influence. His *Critique of Pure Reason* was perhaps his best known work.
3. Johann Schiller (1759–1805), German poet and dramatist. A romantic whose political ideas sometimes conflicted with his basically liberal views.
4. Johann Hölderlin (1770–1843), German poet and romantic, close friend and contemporary of Hegel.
5. Georg Hegel (1770–1831), German philosopher and political scientist. The founder of many modern approaches to the study of political problems. As a teacher he was widely influential in his own lifetime after an initially cool reception.
6. Quoted in Butler. op. cit. pp. 161–2.
7. *Mein Kampf* by A. Hitler, p. 374. (Translated by J. Murphy.)
8. Thomas Carlyle (1795–1881), Scottish writer and historian, his most controversial work was probably *Heroes, Hero-Worship and the Heroic in History*.
9. The case of E. J. Eyre, Governor of Jamaica, who suppressed a negro rising in that country in 1865. The political and legal repercussions were a regular topic of debate for some years afterwards.
10. Charles Dickens (1812–70), English novelist, a great optimist by temperament and a radical who had no real concept of radicalism.
11. John Ruskin (1819–1900), English writer and artist. He was fond of social experiments upon which he dissipated his father's fortune.
12. Charles Kingsley (1819–75), English clergyman and historian. A radical who contributed to *Politics for the People* in his youth, but who in middle age became much more conservative.
13. Ferdinand Lassalle (1825–64), German Jewish writer, a theoretical socialist of strong nationalist convictions. He later completely broke away from socialism.
14. See Wagner's essays *Modern* and *Heldentum und Christentum*.
15. *Also sprach Zarathustra* by F. Nietzsche, R. Pascal (ed.), p. 115.
16. Ibid., p. 4.
17. *Ecce Homo* by F. Nietzsche. Quoted in introduction by Pascal to *Also sprach Zarathustra*, p. xiii.
18. *Also sprach Zarathustra*, R. Pascal (ed.), p. 79.

19. *Ecce Homo*. Quoted in introduction by R. Pascal to *Also sprach Zarathustra*, p. xiv.
20. Alfred Espinas (1844–1922), French philosopher and academic. In later life he became interested in psychology and sociology. The author of *Les Sociétés animales*.
21. Gustave Le Bon (1841–1931), French doctor and sociologist. A man of eccentric, but sometimes perceptive, views.
22. Maurice Barrès (1862–1923), French writer and deputy. An influential figure at the close of the nineteenth century, particularly through his works *L'Ennemi des lois* and *Du sang, de la volupté et de la mort*.
23. Paul Déroulède (1846–1914), French writer and politician. He was a regular supporter of unconstitutional action, as in the case of the projected coups of Generals Boulanger and Roget.
24. *Georges Sorel, Prophet Without Honour* by R. Humphrey, p. 29.
25. Sigmund Freud (1856–1939), Austrian founder of modern psychology. Refugee from Nazism in 1938. His approach to problems of the human mind, though not his verdict, was influenced by the writings of Sorel and Nietzsche.
26. Chiefly remembered for *Our Country: its possible future and the present crisis* (1885).
27. William Sumner (1840–1910), American social scientist, Professor of Political Science at Yale, 1872–1909. A Social-Darwinist who viewed poverty, for example, as a natural result of inherent inferiorities.
28. *The Challenge of Facts and other Essays* by W. Sumner, p. 90.
29. Enrico Corradini (1865–1931), Italian journalist and writer. Author of *Giulio Cesare*, a work exalting the heroic leader. Founder of *Il Regno*, an important journal, 1904.
30. Scipio Sighele (1868–1913), Italian sociologist. Author of *Morale privata e morale politica* and a number of nationalistic works.
31. Rocco de Zerbi (1843–1893), Italian journalist, politician and man of letters. A corrupt and unstable advocate of imperialism, purification of the race and élitism.
32. Pasquale Turiello (1863–1902), Italian journalist and political theorist. He was much embittered by the failure of a united Italy to revive Italian greatness.
33. Karl Lamprecht (1856–1915), German political thinker and polemicist. This extract is taken from his principal work, *Zur jüngsten deutschen Vergangenheit*.
34. Quoted in *Benito Mussolini* by C. Hibbert, p. 76.
35. Ibid., p. 74.
36. Engelbert Dollfuss (1892–1934), Austrian politician. Leader of Christian Socialist Party. Chancellor 1932–4. Murdered by Nazi enemies.
37. Quoted in *Hitler Speaks* by H. Rauschning, p. 49.
38. Vidkun Quisling (1887–1945), Norwegian politician and traitor. He became world famous for his treachery in 1940, but had earlier, in the 1930s, been apparently a strong nationalist. See *Quisling: the career and political ideas of Vidkun Quisling, 1887–1945* by P. M. Hayes.

4

1. *Behemoth: The structure and practice of National Socialism, 1933–1944* by F. Neumann. Quotations are, respectively, from pp. 467, 464, 462 and 463.
2. Heraclitus (*c.* 540 – *c.* 480 B.C.), Ephesian philosopher. Subject to much misinterpretation by later writers, mainly owing to the fragmentary remains of his writings.
3. *The Open Society and Its Enemies* by K. Popper, Vol. II, p. 30.

4. *Heraclitus: the cosmic fragments*, G. S. Kirk (ed.). See fragments 1, 2, 32, 41, 50, 78, 108 and 114.
5. Ibid., Fragment 80, p. 238.
6. *Gesammtwerke* by F. Lassalle.
7. *The Republic of Plato*, F. M. Cornford (ed.), p. 112.
8. Ibid., p. 119.
9. Ibid., pp. 159–60.
10. *The Politics of Aristotle*, E. Barker (ed.), p. 331.
11. *The Political Thought of Plato and Aristotle* by E. Barker, p. 291
12. Wilhelm Stapel (1882–1954), German theologian and political thinker. A generally conservative figure. Author of *Der christliche Staatsmann: eine Theologie des Nationalismus.*
13. *The Politics of Aristotle*, E. Barker (ed.), p. 17.
14. Niccolo Machiavelli (1469–1527), Italian diplomat and political thinker, born in Florence. His two main works *Il principe* and *Discorsi* relied heavily on his personal observation of diplomacy and statecraft.
15. *Discorsi* by N. Machiavelli. Book III, Ch. 41.
16. Jean Bodin (1529–96), French political philosopher, much influenced by the political disorders caused by the French Wars of Religion.
17. *Les Six Livres de la république* by J. Bodin. Preface.
18. Thomas Hobbes (1588–1679), English philosopher. Extremely influential and particularly remarkable for his philosophical definitions. Author of *Leviathan* and *Behemoth* inter alia.
19. *Leviathan* by T. Hobbes, p. 92.
20. Popper, op. cit., Vol. II, p. 32.
21. Arthur Schopenhauer (1788–1860), German philosopher, famous for his search for truth. A strong influence on Nietzsche. Author of *Die Welt als Wille und Vorstellung.*
22. Albert Schwegler (1819–57), German philosopher; professor at Tübingen. Author of *Geschichte der Philosophie im Umriss.*
23. *The Lost Leader* by R. Browning.
24. *My Life with George* by I. A. R. Wylie.
25. Quoted in Popper, op. cit., Vol. II, p. 63.
26. Ibid., p. 31.
27. *Ordenstaat* by A. Rosenberg.
28. *Der christliche Staatsmann: eine Theologie des Nationalismus* by W. Stapel.
29. Quoted in Popper, op.cit., Vol. II, p. 73.
30. *Das Schwarze Korps*, Editorial 1938 (Journal of the S.S.)
31. Karl Jaspers (1883–1969), German psychologist and philosopher. Author and professor of great influence.
32. Martin Heidegger (1889–   ), German professor of philosophy.
33. Edmund Husserl (1859–1938), German philosopher of great influence.
34. Friedrich Gogarten (1887–1967), German theologian and philosopher. Author of numerous works, including a book on Fichte.
35. Max Scheler (1874–1928), German philosopher and sociologist.
36. Adam Müller (1779–1829), German romantic and conservative. He served Austria and was ennobled by Metternich. Author of *Die Elemente der Staatskunst.*
37. Hermann Harris Aall (1871–1952). Scandinavian political theorist and philosopher. Go-between in the negotiations between Quisling and the Nazis. Author of *Social Individualism.*
38. Quoted in Butler, op. cit., p. 69.
39. *Hitler Speaks* by H. Rauschning, p. 128.
40. *The Moral Basis of Socialism* by K. Pearson, pp. 307–8.

41. Ibid., p. 307.
42. *National Life* by K. Pearson, pp. 50–1.
43. *Darwinism, Medical Progress and Eugenics* by K. Pearson, p. 29.
44. *Leviathan* by T. Hobbes, p. 109.
45. Bernhardi, op. cit., p. 20.
46. Ibid., p. 25.
47. Heinrich Treitschke (1834–96), German historian and political writer. Nationalist and pro-Prussian. Author of *Deutsche Geschichte im neunzehnten Jahrhundert.*
48. Friedrich Schleiermacher (1768–1834), German theologian and evangelist. Author of *Dialektik* and numerous religious works.
49. *Die Politik* by H. Treitschke.
50. *Dialektik* by F. Schleiermacher.
51. Rudolf Kjellén (1864–1922), Swedish biologist and political thinker. Pro-German. Author of *Staten som livsform* and *Die Grossmächte der Gegenwart.*
52. *Staten som livsform* by R. Kjellén, p. 35ff.

5

1. Friedrich von Hardenberg (1772–1801), German philosopher and writer. Poet and historian. A member of the Romantic School.
2. *The Nation and the Empire*, speeches by A. Milner. 'The Imperialist Creed', 14 December 1906, p. 139.
3. Ibid., p. xxxv.
4. *War Memoirs* by D. Lloyd George, pp. 64–5.
5. *L'Opera di Nitti* by V. Nitti. Quoted in Rhodes, op. cit., p. 175.
6. *Rivelazioni* by F. Nitti. Quoted in Rhodes, op. cit., p. 175. Francesco Nitti (1868–1963), Italian politician and premier. A man of liberal and democratic views forced to operate in a hostile political environment.
7. Quoted in *Italy* by D. Mack Smith, p. 448.
8. The name was selected in response to the signature of the Versailles Treaty on 28 June 1919.
9. Paul Ernst (1866–1933), German author with strong nationalist influences visible in all his written works. Essayist and novelist.
10. Hans Grimm (1875–1959), German writer. Author of *Volk ohne Raum*. One of the major literary figures supporting nationalism in Germany.
11. *The Hour of Decision* by O. Spengler, p. 56.
12. *Hitler's Secret Book*, p. 88.
13. Alfred Hugenberg (1865–1951), German politician and businessman. Leader of the right-wing faction of the D.N.V.P. Lost all influence under Hitler.
14. Fritz Thyssen (1873–1951), German industrialist, owner of major steelworks and other concerns. Persuaded into financing Hitler's 1929 campaign.
15. *I Paid Hitler* by F. Thyssen, p. 118.
16. A pan-German study group of which Dollfuss was a zealous member.
17. Nikolaus Horthy (1868–1957), Hungarian admiral and head of state. Conservative by temperament, he had great difficulty in controlling fascist movements.
18. Corneliu Codreanu (1899–1938), Romanian politician, leader of the Legion of the Archangel Michael. Later leader of the Iron Guard.
19. *The Foreign Policy of Poland, 1919–1939* by R. Debicki, p. 17. Ignacy Paderewski (1860–1941), Polish composer and statesman. Influential in persuading Woodrow Wilson to set up an independent Poland.

20. Frits Clausen (1893–1947), Danish fascist politician. A collaborator during the German occupation of Denmark.
21. *Quisling: the career and political ideas of Vidkun Quisling, 1887–1945* by P. M. Hayes, p. 126.
22. Giovanni Giolitti (1842–1928), Italian politician and premier. One of the foremost practitioners of transformism as a solution to political problems.
23. Ivanoe Bonomi (1873–1951), Italian politician and premier. A reformist socialist, the rejection of whose administration precipitated the crisis of 1922.
24. Luigi Facta (1861–1934), Italian politician and premier. A follower of Giolitti, a lawyer by training. Totally unsuited to hold high political office.
25. Luigi Albertini (1871–1941), Italian senator, journalist and writer. Editor of *Corriere della Sera*, 1900–25.
26. Notably the conservative *Giornale d'Italia* and the liberal or radical *Corriere della Sera*, *La Stampa*, *Il Messagero* and *Secolo*.
27. Walther Funk (1890–1960), German national socialist politician; particularly important for his advice on economics and propaganda.
28. Hjalmar Schacht (1877–1971), German economist, director of banking enterprises. He played a key role in fascist economic successes in the 1930s.
29. Albert Vögler (1877–1945), German industrialist and nationalist. Important as a leading figure among steel magnates.
30. Gustav Krupp (1870–1950), German industrialist and entrepreneur. One of a large business circle who took advantage of Hitler's rise to power.
31. Emil Kirdorf (1847–1938), German industrialist and coal magnate. He played a critical part in financing Hitler's campaign of 1929.
32. Quoted in *Der Führer* by K. Heiden, p. 271.
33. Aristide Briand (1862–1932), French socialist. Chiefly remembered for his profound influence on church and foreign affairs. Largely responsible for Locarno, 1925.
34. Camille Chautemps (1885–   ), French radical-socialist politician and premier. He withdrew from politics in 1940, being disillusioned with Pétain.
35. Joseph Paul-Boncour (1873–1972), French politician. Syndicalist and socialist. An opponent of Vichy. Signatory of the U.N. Charter.
36. Edouard Daladier (1884–   ), French radical-socialist politician and premier. He with Chamberlain bore much responsibility for the appeasement of Hitler.
37. Léon Blum (1872–1950), French politician and premier. Writer and polemicist. One of the most influential politicians of the 1930s.
38. Marcel Déat (1894–1955), French politician. Philosophy professor, later minister. Founder of the R.N.P. in 1940. A Vichy collaborator.
39. Adrien Marquet (1884–1955), French politician. Accused of being a fascist. He played a key role in the events of 1940 as a capitulationist ally of Laval.
40. Pierre Renaudel (1871–1935), French politician. One-time editor of *L'Humanité*. Excluded from the S.F.I.O. after 1933.
41. Socialist Party Manifesto, 1936.
42. *Le Parti Unique* by M. Déat.
43. Pierre Drieu la Rochelle (1893–1945), French writer and politician. His major work was *Socialisme fasciste*, published in 1934.
44. Charles Maurras (1868–1952), French writer. After 1908 he was director of the policy of *L'action française*. A defender of Vichy and a collaborator.
45. Robert Brasillach (1909–45), French writer and collaborator. Editor of *Je suis partout*. Literary critic and poet.
46. Maurice Bardèche (1909–   ), French man of letters. Author of *Qu'est-ce que le fascisme*.
47. Quoted in *1918–1936: vom Selbstschutz zur Frontmiliz* by H. Arthofer, p. 39.

Ignaz Seipel (1876–1932), Austrian politician and academic. Leader of Christian Socialist Party, 1921–9. Chancellor on several occasions.
48. Othmar Spann (1878–1950), Austrian, Professor at Vienna. The philosopher of Universalism. Author of *Vom wahren Staat*, a semi-fascist tract.
49. Richard Steidle (1881–1938), Austrian lawyer, based on Innsbruck. A leader of the Heimwehr and a thorn in Dollfuss' side.
50. Thorvald Aadahl (1882–1962), Norwegian journalist and politician. Prominent in Agrarian Party politics he later lent his support to *Nasjonal Samling*.
51. Gil Robles Quiñones (1898–   ), Spanish politician, lawyer and journalist. The leader of C.E.D.A. An opponent of Franco until 1950. Exiled in Lisbon for some years. See his speech of 19 May 1936, in the Cortes.
52. Indalecio Prieto (1883–1962), Spanish socialist politician. Editor of *El Liberal*. Republican minister. See *El Socialista*, 2 May 1936.
53. Hermann Göring (1893–1946), German Nazi politician; in charge of the Luftwaffe. At first a close confidant of Hitler, but lost his confidence late in the war.
54. Ernst Röhm (1887–1934), German Nazi politician; an early member of the party and leader of the S.A. Shot, on Hitler's orders, in the purge of 1934.
55. Franz von Epp (1868–1947), German soldier; violent nationalist and organizer of a Free Corps in Bavaria in 1919. Minister of Colonies, 1941–45.
56. *Hitler: a study in tyranny* by A. L. C. Bullock, pp. 68–9.
57. *Hitler's Secret Book*, p. 84.
58. Pietro Badoglio (1871–1956), Italian soldier; conqueror of Abyssinia in 1936. Made head of Italian government after the removal of Mussolini in 1943.
59. Quoted in Rhodes, op. cit., p. 168.
60. Open letter (Aveux de l'Ingrat) from D'Annunzio to the French nation.
61. Rhodes, op. cit., p. 168.
62. *The Decline of French Patriotism 1870–1940* by H. Tint, p.192.
63. François de la Rocque (1886–1946), French soldier and politician; President of the *Croix de Feu*. Served the Vichy regime, but was later exiled for supporting the Resistance.
64. *France in Ferment* by A. Werth, p. 282.
65. Walter Pfrimer (1881–1940), Austrian politician and Heimwehr leader; the leader of an attempted putsch in 1931.
66. *Der Panther*, 24 May 1930.

6

1. Quoted in *Freedom in Science and Teaching* by E. Haeckel, pp. 89–90.
2. See *Versuche einer neuen Theorie des Geldes* by A. Müller.
3. Karl Rodbertus (1805–75), German political thinker. His concept of State Socialism was to be immensely influential in Imperial Germany.
4. Butler, op. cit., p. 129.
5. Quoted in *Bismarck* by A. J. P. Taylor, p. 60.
6. Quoted in Butler, op.cit., p. 134.
7. Quoted in Butler, op. cit., p. 207.
8. Friedrich Ebert (1871–1925), German Social Democrat politician. One of the founder figures of the Weimar Republic and later elected President.
9. Gustav Noske (1868–1946), German Social Democrat politician. Responsible for crushing the attempted left-wing revolution in Berlin in 1919, as Minister of the Army.

10. Karl Liebknecht (1871–1919), German revolutionary, hostile to the war of 1914–18. Leader of the Spartacist rising, murdered by a Free Corps battalion.
11. Rosa Luxembourg (1871–1919), German revolutionary. Joint leader of the Spartacist revolt, also murdered. Founder of the German Communist Party.
12. Eduard Bernstein (1850–1932), German Social Democrat politician. Always on the left of the party he later became a stern critic of rightist deviation.
13. Gottfried Feder (1883–1941), German Nazi politician. An engineer by trade, he played an important part as a party theoretician before 1933.
14. Gregor (1892–1934) and Otto (1897–   ) Strasser, German Nazi politicians. At first followers, later enemies, of Hitler. Both believers in the socialist part of national socialism. Gregor was murdered in the putsch of 1934.
15. Walther Rathenau (1867–1922), German industrial entrepreneur and politician. Foreign Minister in 1922, he was assassinated by an extremist.
16. Thomas Mann (1875–1955), German writer, editor and satirist. Although of ostensibly radical views he held some strong nationalist beliefs.
17. Quoted in Butler, op. cit., p. 242.
18. *The Decline of the West* by O. Spengler (translated by C. F. Atkinson), Part I, p. 138.
19. Ibid., Part I, pp. 361–62.
20. Quoted in Butler, op. cit., p. 264.
21. Quoted in Bullock, op. cit., p. 157.
22. Pierre Joseph Proudhon (1809–65), French socialist writer, author of the famous phrase 'Property is theft'. Author of many works on economics and socialism.
23. Pierre Laval (1883–1945), French politician. Originally a socialist, he gradually moved to the right, ending as effective head of the Vichy régime.
24. Quoted in *The European Right* by E. Weber, p. 112.
25. *Socialisme Fasciste* by P. Drieu La Rochelle.
26. Maurice Thorez (1900–64), French Communist politician, a faithful follower of the Moscow line, participating in governments between 1944 and 1947.
27. *Refaire la France* by J. Doriot.
28. *Le Parti unique* by M. Déat.
29. Enrico Malatesta (1853–1932), Italian anarchist, friend and follower of Bakunin. Founder in 1913 of the newspaper *Volonta*.
30. Interview of Suckert with *La Stampa*, 23 December 1924.
31. Achille Starace (1889–1945), Italian fascist politician, a deputy from 1924, he was extremely influential within the party in the 1930s. Killed in 1945.
32. Giacomo Matteotti (1885–1924), Italian socialist of considerable wealth. Prominent opponent of Mussolini, he was murdered by fascists in 1924.
33. Vilfredo Pareto (1848–1923), Italian philosopher. He was also a sociologist of international reputation, concentrating his studies on the concept of the élite.
34. Gaetano Mosca (1858–1941), Italian politician and political philosopher, interested in sociology. A prolific writer, influential during his own lifetime.
35. Sidney Webb (1859–1947), English politician. Prominent member of the Labour Party. Created Baron Passfield in 1929. His wife insisted on being known as Beatrice Webb.
36. George Bernard Shaw (1856–1950), English author and playwright. One of the most prolific and influential writers of this period. A prominent member of the Fabians.
37. *The Decline of the West* by O. Spengler, Part I, pp. 370–1.
38. Fabian News, IX, No. 10, December 1899, pp. 37–38.
39. Samuel Hobson (1864–1940), British Guild Socialist. Author, inter alia, of *National Guilds*.

40. *Pilgrim to the Left: Memoirs of a Modern Revolutionist* by S. G. Hobson, pp. 63–5.
41. *Fabianism and the Empire*, G. B. Shaw (ed.), p. 6.
42. Herbert George Wells (1866–1946), English writer. Author of many books, fiction, science and history. Chiefly remembered for his scientific predictions.
43. Leopold Amery (1873–1955), English politician. He held a number of high offices, particularly in ministries connected with the colonies. *The Times* correspondent in the Boer War.
44. Leopold Maxse (1864–1932), English journalist and Germanophobe. Immensely influential in his campaigns for expansion of the Navy in the period leading up to 1914.
45. Robert Blatchford (1851–1943), English socialist patriot. Author of *Merrie England* and a number of tracts. One of the leading advocates of social-imperialism.
46. John Strachey (1901–63), English politician and prominent member of the Labour party. Author of a number of important books on politics.
47. Arthur Cook (1883–1931), English socialist and trade unionist. Diehard leader of the miners. Prominent in the General Strike of 1926.
48. *Revolution by Reason* by O. Mosley and J. Strachey.
49. William Morris (1877–1963), English industrialist and philanthropist. Founder of many institutions for the benefit of others.
50. Aneurin Bevan (1897–1960), English socialist politician. Husband of Jennie Lee. The holder of many important ministerial posts. Deputy leader of the party at his death.
51. William Brown (1894–1960), English politician. At first a Labour M.P.; later he sat as an independent. General Secretary of the Civil Service Clerical Association.
52. Oliver Baldwin (1899–1958), English politician. Son of Stanley Baldwin and much disliked by the Conservatives for his apparent disloyalty to his father.
53. Mosley Manifesto, December 1930.
54. *Fortnightly Review*, May 1931. Article by C. F. Melville.
55. Diary of Beatrice Webb, 24 February 1931.
56. Quoted in *Tomorrow is a New Day* by Jennie Lee.
57. Rotha Linton-Orman (1895–), English founder of fascism. Granddaughter of a Field-Marshal. An eccentric spinster of great determination.
58. Arnold Leese (1877–), English fascist, extremely sympathetic to Nazism. A former veterinary surgeon who turned into a fascist and anti-Semite.
59. Quoted in *The Menace of Fascism* by J. Strachey.
60. Tidens Tegn, 24 May 1930.
61. Tidens Tegn, 4 June 1930.
62. Jose Antonio Primo de Rivera (1903–36), Spanish political leader, shot at Alicante by order of the Republican government. Leader of the Falange 1933–6.

7

1. Frederick Roberts (1832–1914), English soldier, created Earl Roberts in 1901. After a very distinguished military career he devoted his life to promoting military readiness.
2. Hippolyte Taine (1828–1893), French historian, philosopher and critic. Founder of several important reviews. An acute observer of both French and British society.
3. *Les Origines de la France contemporaine* by H. Taine.

4. *Briefwechsel, Denkschriften und Aufzeichnungen* by Freiherr vom Stein.
5. Karl vom Stein (1757–1831), German statesman. Important for the political reforms he introduced as a result of Prussian reverses in the Napoleonic wars.
6. Carl von Clausewitz (1780–1831), German soldier and military theoretician who served in the Napoleonic wars. Extremely influential on later military thinking.
7. *Vom Kriege* by C. Clausewitz. Vol.I, p.25.
8. *What is Wrong with Germany?* by W. H. Dawson.
9. Leopold Ranke (1795–1886), German historian. Professor at Berlin from 1834–71. One of the most influential historians of the century; founder of a school of thought.
10. Ewald Banse (1883–1953), German geographer, notable for his influence on military thinking, a geo-politician.
11. *Politisches Gespräch* by L. Ranke.
12. Quoted in Butler, op. cit., pp. 148–9.
13. *Ecce Homo* by F. Nietzsche.
14. *Also sprach Zarathustra*, R. Pascal (ed.), p. 39.
15. Bernhardi, op. cit., p. 41.
16. Ibid., p. 116.
17. Ibid., p. 225.
18. *Raum und Volk in Weltkriege* by E. Banse.
19. *Wehrwissenschaft* by E. Banse.
20. Erich Kaufmann (1880–   ), German expert on law, who later emigrated to Holland. His views later in life were very different from those before 1914.
21. *Das Wesen des Völkerrechts* by E. Kaufmann.
22. Fritz Lenz (1887–1946), German expert on eugenics and genetics. A prolific writer on race and other subjects of great interest to the Nazis in the 1930s.
23. *Die Rasse als Wertprinzip* by F. Lenz.
24. *Deutsche Wehr*, 1932.
25. *Failure of a Mission* by N. Henderson, p. 14. Nevile Henderson (1882–1942), English diplomat. Ambassador in Berlin 1937–9. Unfortunately a disastrous choice.
26. *Proceedings of the International Military Tribunal*, Vol. III, 4 January 1946.
27. Léon Gambetta (1838–82), French politician. Organizer of national resistance in 1870.
28. *Discours et plaidoyers politiques de Gambetta*, Part 7, p. 82.
29. Quoted in *The Decline of French Patriotism, 1870–1940* by H. Tint, p. 41.
30. Georges Boulanger (1837–91), French general and politician. A clever but hesitant man who failed to grasp the political opportunity of 1887.
31. Théophile Delcassé (1852–1923), French politician and maker of the Entente Cordiale. Foreign Minister 1898–1905 and 1914–15, retiring then from politics.
32. Barrère to Delcassé, 18 November 1904.
33. Bernhardi, op. cit., pp. 146–7.
34. In a speech at Issoudun, at which he was unveiling a war memorial.
35. Maurice Paléologue (1859–1944), French diplomat and ambassador to Russia from 1914–17. Friend of Delcassé and a violent Germanophobe.
36. Charles Péguy (1873–1914), French man of letters. Originally a socialist, but in later years rather nationalistic. He was a friend of both Sorel and Bergson.
37. *Péguy* by R. Rolland, p.114.
38. *Echo de Paris*, 1914. Paul Bourget (1852–1935), French writer and journalist; in later life he wrote many articles of a sociological and psychological nature.
39. Delcassé to his wife, 5 August 1914.

40. *The World of Yesterday* by S. Zweig.
41. Quoted in *The Decline of French Patriotism, 1870–1940* by H. Tint, p. 111.
42. Marcel Bucard (1895–1946), French fascist politician, editor of *Le Nouveau Siècle*. A collaborator under the Vichy régime, he was shot in 1946.
43. Eugene Deloncle (1890–1942), French fascist. Leader of the *Cagoule*. Killed by the Gestapo while resisting arrest.
44. Quoted in Weber, op. cit., p. 106.
45. *Lord Roberts Message to the Nation* by Earl Roberts, p. 40ff.
46. *The Clarion*, 1 November 1912.
47. *The Clarion*, 11 November 1899.
48. *Germany and England* by R. Blatchford, p. 45ff.
49. Ibid., p. 90ff.
50. *Democratic Ideals and Reality: a study in the politics of reconstruction* by H. J. Mackinder.
51. Bernhardi, op. cit., p. 99.
52. Ibid., pp. 155–6.
53. Quoted in *The Price of Glory* by A. Horne, p. 79.

8

1. François Quesnay (1694–1774), French thinker and writer. The leading 'physiocrat'. He was extremely hostile to commercial restrictions.
2. Adam Smith (1723–90). Scottish philosopher and economist. Author of *An Inquiry into the Nature and Causes of the Wealth of Nations* (1776). From 1752 he was Professor of Moral Philosophy at Glasgow, retiring in 1763.
3. Richard Cobden (1804–65), English merchant and economist. In partnership with Bright a great influence on mid-Victorian thinking. He played a major part in repeal of the Corn Laws.
4. John Bright (1811–89), English economist. At first a lieutenant of Cobden he later became even more influential than his mentor. A strong supporter of liberal and radical causes and a man of honour and honesty.
5. David Ricardo (1772–1823), English financier and economist. A partisan of Free Trade, he was a prolific and influential writer.
6. James Mill (1773–1836), English historian, economist and philosopher. A disciple of Bentham and a firm adherent of Free Trade.
7. Thomas Malthus (1766–1834), English economist and expert on population studies. Extremely influential though by no means universally popular.
8. Quoted in Butler, op. cit., p. 26.
9. *Der geschlossene Handelsstaat* by J. Fichte.
10. Henry Clay (1777–1852), American politician, leader of the Whigs. Unsuccessful candidate for the Presidency on several occasions.
11. Hezekiah Niles (1777–1839), American journalist, founder and editor of *Niles' Register* (1811–49). A town in Ohio has been named after him.
12. Henry Carey (1793–1879), American economist. At first a Free Trader, later he went over to protectionism. Extremely influential in the U.S.A.
13. David Syme (1827–1908), Australian journalist of Scottish birth. Editor of the *Age*. Author of *Outlines of an industrial science* (1876).
14. Quoted in *Political Economy in Australia* by J. A. La Nauze, p. 123.
15. Cobden to Bright, 18 October 1846.
16. Jean de Sismondi (1773–1842), Swiss economist. Widely regarded as a founding figure in the field of socialist economics. *Nouveaux principes d'économie politique* (1819).

17. Claude Saint-Simon (1760–1825), French philosopher and economist. A member of a distinguished intellectual circle, including Thierry, Comte and Halévy.
18. *Lettres à un Américain, Oeuvres* by C. Saint-Simon, Vol. II, p. 189.
19. Jérôme Blanqui (1798–1854), French economist, successor to J. B. Say's chair. Author of numerous works, most notably *Les Classes ouvrières en France* (1848).
20. Théodore Fix (1800–46), Swiss economist. Founder in 1833 of the *Revue mensuelle d'économie politique*. Hostile to trade unions.
21. François Droz (1773–1850), French historian and economist. One of the first writers on economics to think in 'historical' terms.
22. Quoted in Butler, op. cit., p. 101.
23. *Das nationale System der politischen Ökonomie* by F. List, p. 143. Friedrich List (1789–1846), German economist. Professor at Tübingen 1817–19, lived in the U.S.A. 1825–32.
24. Quoted in Butler, op. cit., p. 102.
25. *A History of Economic Doctrines* by C. Gide and C. Rist, p. 298.
26. Wilhelm Roscher (1817–94), German economist, professor at Leipzig from 1848. Author of *Grundriss zu Vorlesungen über die Staatswirtschaft nach geschichtlicher Methode* (1843) and *Das System der Volkwirtschaft* (1854).
27. Karl Knies (1821–98), German economist, professor at Heidelberg. Author of *Die politische Ökonomie vom Standpunkte der geschichtlichen Methode* (1853).
28. Bruno Hildebrand (1812–78), German economist and academic. Author of *Die Nationalökonomie der Gegenwart und Zukunft* (1848).
29. Gustav von Schmoller (1838–1917), German economist, professor at Berlin from 1882. Immensely influential, particularly through *Grundriss der Volkswirtschaftslehre* (1904).
30. *Die Nationalökonomie der Gegenwart und Zukunft* by B. Hildebrand, p. 73.
31. Cliffe Leslie (1825–82), Irish-born economist, professor at Belfast. The leading English exponent of the school of Historical Economists.
32. Frédéric Bastiat (1801–50), French economist. A notable optimist in contrast to the pessimism of the Manchester School.
33. *Harmonies* by Bastiat, pp. 552–3.
34. Charles Dupont-White (1807–78), French economist. Advocate of state intervention.
35. Rodbertus to R. Meyer, 17 October 1872.
36. *Physiokratie und Anthropokratie* in *Briefe und Sozialpolitische Aufsätze* by K. Rodbertus, p. 519.
37. *Jahrbücher für Nationalökonomie und Statistik*. Vol. VIII, pp. 446–7, note. Article by K. Rodbertus.
38. *Schriften* by F. Lassalle, Vol. II, p. 99.
39. Quoted in Butler, op. cit., p. 177.
40. Ibid., p. 179.
41. William Cunningham (1849–1919), English cleric and economist. Ardent nationalist. His principal works divide clearly into pro- and anti-Free Trade periods.
42. William Ashley (1860–1927), English historian and economist. A disciple of Toynbee. Professor at Toronto, Harvard and Birmingham.
43. *Alien Immigrants to England* by W. Cunningham, p. 266.
44. *Case against Free Trade* by W. Cunningham, pp. 136–7.
45. *Politics and Economics* by W. Cunningham, p. 275.
46. Ibid., p. 159.
47. *History of Economic Analysis* by J. A. Schumpeter, p. 822 note.
48. *Surveys Historic and Economic* by W. J. Ashley, p. 385.
49. *Political Economy and the Tariff Problem* by W. J. Ashley, p. 266.

50. Frédéric Le Play (1806–82), French economist and engineer. A strong believer in religious and family values.
51. Léon Bourgeois (1851–1925), French politician. Interested in economics he was the leading figure in the solidarist movement.
52. *Zur jüngsten deutschen Vergangenheit* by K. Lamprecht. Quoted in Butler, op. cit., p. 195.
53. *Die Agrarkrisis und die Mittel zu ihrer Abhilfe* by W. Skarzynski, p. 12.
54. *Raum and Volk im Weltkriege* by E. Banse.
55. Bernhardi, op. cit., pp. 82–4.
56. Ibid., p. 263.
57. Quoted in Butler, op. cit., p. 206.
58. Ibid., pp. 207–8.
59. *Mitteleuropa* by F. Naumann.
60. *Weltpolitik, Imperialismus und Kolonialpolitik* by E. Hasse.
61. *The Decline of the West*, op. cit., Vol. II, pp. 470–1.
62. Karl Menger (1840–1921), Austrian historian and economist. From 1879 professor at Vienna. Author of *Untersuchungen über die Methode der Sozialwissenschaften* (1883).
63. Enrico Barone (1859–1924), Italian historian, economist and journalist. Editor of *La Preparazione*. Author of *Principi di economia politica* (1908).
64. Richard Schüller (1860–1918), Austrian official and economist. Protectionist and author of *Schutzzoll und Freihandel* (1906).
65. *Economic History Review*, 1953, p. 6.
66. *The Times*, 18 August 1927.

9

1. *Il Principe*, op. cit., pp. 97–100.
2. Hugo van Groot (1583–1645), Dutch lawyer. Hostile to the House of Orange, he had a chequered political career. Author of *De Jure Belli ac Pacis* (1625), also his *De Jure Praedae*, unpublished in his lifetime, though written in 1604.
3. *De Jure Belli ac Pacis* Prolegomena 22 by H. van Groot.
4. *Leviathan*, op. cit., p. 64.
5. *The Mornings of the King of Prussia, Frederick II, called the Great* by Colonel S. H. S. Inglefield.
6. Quoted in *Cobden and Bright* by D. Read, p. 112.
7. Karl von Haller (1768–1854), Swiss political writer, extremely prominent figure in the Romantic period. A diplomat by profession.
8. Quoted in Butler, op. cit., p. 33.
9. *Handbuch der allgemeinen Staatenkunde* by K. Haller.
10. Quoted in Butler, op. cit., p. 120.
11. *Briefe*, Vol. I, No. 146.
12. Quoted in Butler, op. cit., pp. 147–8.
13. *Mein Kampf*, op. cit., pp. 377, 740.
14. Ibid., p. 91.
15. Quoted in Butler, op. cit., p. 151.
16. A. L. von Rochau (1810–73), German political theorist. His *Grundzüge der Realpolitik* (1853) put forward the concept of 'Der Staat ist Macht'.
17. *Grundzüge der Realpolitik* by A. von Rochau.
18. *Politik* by H. Treitschke, pp. 552–3.
19. Rauschning, op. cit., p. 149.
20. *Also sprach Zarathustra*, op. cit., p. 254.

21. Quoted in Butler, op. cit., p. 159.
22. *Also sprach Zarathustra*, op. cit., pp. 41–3.
23. See footnote 17 to section 3.
24. *Ecce Homo*. Quoted in introduction by Pascal to *Also sprach Zarathustra*, p. xiii.
25. *Der Mythus des 20 Jahrhunderts* by A. Rosenberg, p. 424.
26. *The Moral Basis of Socialism*, p. 308.
27. *National Life*, p. 27.
28. Ibid., p. 56.
29. *Germany and England* by J. A. Cramb, p. 53. Cramb gave a series of lectures in reply to Bernhardi's work.
30. Bernhardi, op. cit., p. 23.
31. Ibid., p. 32.
32. Ibid., p. 34.
33. Ibid., pp. 111–12.
34. *Kriegsaufsätze* by H. S. Chamberlain.
35. Quoted in Rhodes, op. cit., p. 237. D'Annunzio to Mussolini, 13 December 1937.
36. Quoted in Butler, op. cit., p. 249.
37. *The Hour of Decision* by O. Spengler, p. 22.
38. Ibid., pp. 92–3.
39. *The Decline of the West*, op. cit., Vol. II, p. 364.
40. From a speech by Goebbels at Weimar, 30 October 1938.
41. *The Disinherited Mind* by E. Heller, p. 172.
42. Hans Frank (1900–46), German Nazi politician. Minister of Justice in the Third Reich. Hanged at Nuremberg.
43. Speech by Frank, October 1935.
44. *Der Mythus des 20 Jahrhunderts* by A. Rosenberg, p. 21.
45. Inglefield, op. cit.
46. *Mein Kampf*, op. cit., p. 151.
47. *Geschichte auf rassischer Grundlage* by Johann von Leers (1936).
48. *The Decline of the West*, op. cit., Vol II, p. 368.

<h3 style="text-align:center">*10*</h3>

1. Butler, op. cit., p. 299.

Notes to Part II

<h3 style="text-align:center">*11*</h3>

1. A. F. K. Organski in *The Nature of Fascism*, S. J. Woolf (ed.), p. 20.
2. S. J. Woolf in *The Nature of Fascism*, p. 119.
3. Ibid., p. 119.
4. Bernhardi, op. cit., p. 260.
5. *The Spark* (1963).
6. *The Early Goebbels Diaries*, H. Heiber (ed.). Entry for 23 October 1925. Paul Joseph Goebbels (1897–1945), German Nazi politician and brilliant propagandist. His work in Berlin prior to 1933 was vital to Hitler's success.
7. Domsarkiv. Quisling file. Undated note.
8. Proceedings against Charles Maurras, 1945.
9. Reich Defence Committee. 15 December 1938. Bundesarchiv, Koblenz.
10. Quoted in *Inside the Third Reich* by A. Speer, p. 211. Albert Speer (1905–), German Nazi politician. In 1942 he took over the direction of war industry.

11. *Account Settled* by H. Schacht, p. 55.
12. *Germany's Economic Preparation for War* by B. H. Klein, p. 17.
13. *Die Auflösung der Weimar Republik* by K. D. Bracher, p. 645ff.
14. Walther Darré (1895–1953), German Nazi politician. Minister of Agriculture under Hitler. Removed from office in 1942.
15. *The Speeches of Adolf Hitler, 1922–39*, N. H. Baynes (ed.), Vol. I, p. 867. 13 July 1933.
16. Ibid., p. 865. 6 July 1933.
17. Kurt Schmitt (1886–1950), German captain of industry. Reich economic minister, 1933–5.
18. Rudolf Hess (1894–   ). German Nazi politician. One of the earliest members and Hitler's deputy. He flew to Scotland in 1941 and has been imprisoned in Spandau since 1946.
19. S. J. Woolf in *The Nature of Fascism*, p. 135.
20. T. W. Mason in *The Nature of Fascism*, p. 167.
21. Speer, op. cit., p. 213.
22. Robert Ley (1890–1945), German Nazi politician. Leader of the Labour Front in Germany from 1933.

12

1. S. Lombardini in *The Nature of Fascism*, p. 153.
2. *Politicians and the Slump* by R. J. A. Skidelsky, p. 433.
3. *Fascist Economic Policy* by W. G. Welk, p. 160 (footnote).
4. Ibid., p. 35.
5. Ibid., p. 34.
6. A. F. K. Organski in *The Nature of Fascism*, p. 41.
7. Alberto de Stefani (1879–   ), Italian economist and politician. He shaped the early development of fascist economics in Italy.
8. Quoted in D. Mack Smith, op. cit., p. 403.
9. D. Mack Smith, op. cit., p. 467.

13

1. For further details see *The New Order and the French Economy* by A. S. Milward.
2. *The Fascist Economy in Norway* by A. S. Milward, p. 3.
3. Léon Degrelle (1906–   ), Belgian politician. Founder of the Rexist movement in 1935, which enjoyed considerable success in the period before 1940.
4. Gustave de Clercq (1902–1942), Belgian politician. Flemish nationalist and founder of the V.N.V. Always pro-German, he was a fairly successful leader in the period up to 1940.
5. Anton Mussert (1894–1946), Dutch politician. Founded the N.S.B. in 1931. This party reached its peak in 1935–7, but thereafter declined in influence.
6. Joris van Severen (1894–1940), Belgian politician. Leader of the V.D.N.S., founded in 1931. Modelled on the Nazis, his party enjoyed limited success, despite competition from the V.N.V.
7. Aimé-Joseph Darnand (1897–1945), French politician of the Right. Always a man of action, he was leader of the notorious *Milice Française* and one of the most active collaborators after 1940.
8. S. L. Andreski in *The Nature of Fascism*, p. 100.
9. J. Solé-Tura in *The Nature of Fascism*, p. 43.

10. *The Italian Labour Movement* by D. L. Horowitz, p. 139.
11. S. Lombardini in *The Nature of Fascism*, p. 155.
12. A. F. K. Organski in *The Nature of Fascism*, p. 37.
13. For a full discussion of this topic see M. Rossi-Doria in *Il Fascismo*, C. Casucci (ed.).
14. *The Fascist Experiment* by L. Villari, p. 35.
15. Ibid., p. 41.
16. Ibid., p. 43.
17. Speer, op. cit., p. 8.
18. Ibid., p. 10.
19. Ibid., p. 14.
20. *The Fall of the German Republic* by R. T. Clark, p. 310.
21. T. W. Mason in *The Nature of Fascism*, pp. 169–70.
22. Speer, op. cit., p. 16.
23. Ibid., p. 19.
24. T. W. Mason in *The Nature of Fascism*, pp. 170–1.
25. *Hitler's Words*, G. W. Prange (ed.), p. 42.
26. Quoted in Bullock, op.cit., p. 204.
27. Bullock, op. cit., p. 253.
28. Speer, op. cit., p. 17.
29. Ibid., p. 53.
30. Ibid., p. 20.

14

1. Clark, op. cit., pp. 202–4.
2. Rudolf Breitscheid (1874–1944), German politician. Prominent leader of the S.P.D. After 1933 he lived in exile in Paris until 1940.
3. Hermann Müller (1876–1931), German politician. Chancellor, 1928–30. One of the most influential of Weimar politicians and professor. Leader of the Centre Party, 1928–33. After 1933 he retreated to safety in Rome.
4. Ludwig Kaas (1881–1952), German theologian and politician. Professor at Trier, 1918. Member of Reichstag, 1920–33, as Centre Party representative. Member of Brünings administration.
5. Otto Wels (1873–1939), German politician. Leader of the S.P.D. who defied Hitler. In exile in Prague until 1938, thereafter in Paris.
6. Quoted in Bullock, op. cit., p. 270.
7. Speer, op. cit., p. 20.
8. Bullock, pp. 254–5.
9. *Mussolini's Enemies* by C. F. Delzell, p. 16.
10. Baynes, op. cit., Vol. I, p. 250. 19 February 1933.
11. Speer, op. cit., pp. 18–19.

Notes to Part III

15

1. Ionnis Metaxas (1871–1941), Greek general and statesman. Dictator from 1936–41. Founder of the Free Opinion Party and holder of authoritarian views.
2. Eleutherios Venizelos (1864–1936), Greek pro-Allied Powers statesman. Premier on several occasions and leader of the Liberal Party.

3. *The World Crisis: the aftermath* by W. S. Churchill, p. 386.
4. Joint Allied Note, 4 December 1920.
5. Demetrios Gounaris (1867–1922), Greek politician, monarchist and pro-German. Finance Minister, 1908. Later premier, executed in 1922.
6. Nikolaos Plastiras (1883–1953), Greek general of important political standing. He rejected German overtures in 1941. A leader against E.L.A.S. in 1944–5.
7. Theodoros Pangalos (1878–1952), Greek general and dictator. Exiled in Corfu from 1932. Wrongly accused of collaborating with Axis forces during 1940–5.
8. Georgios Kondylis (1879–1936), Greek general and politician. In 1923 a republican, but by 1935 a committed monarchist. Responsible for the restoration of George II.
9. Konstantinos Tsaldaris (1884–   ), Greek politician. Leader of resistance against the Germans 1941–4. Prominent in post-war politics.
10. Speech of 6 December 1940, and in many others between 28 October 1940 and 29 January 1941.
11. Alexander Papagos (1883–1955), Greek politician and soldier. Victor of the Grammos-Vitsi campaign against the Communists.

16

1. Fulgencio Batista (1901–   ), Dictator of Cuba 1934–59. At first he brought relief to a maladministered country but later merely became a tyrant.
2. Juan Perón (1895–   ), Argentinian dictator with a strong popular following. The real ruler of Argentina from 1943–55, he based his power on the labour unions. In 1973 he made a political comeback.
3. Francois Duvalier (1907–1971), Dictator of Haiti 1957–71. A man who based his rule on voodoo and black magic. Popularly supposed to be omniscient and immortal.
4. Getulio Vargas (1883–1954), Brazilian dictator 1930–45. A man of immense ability who helped modernize Brazil. His period as a constitutional president (1950–4) was not a success.
5. Rafael Trujillo (1891–   ), Dictator of the Dominican Republic 1930–   . The most able and ruthless of the dictators of small states, he amassed a huge fortune at the expense of his unfortunate country.
6. Brazilian Constitution, 1937.
7. Speech, June 1940.
8. Plinio Salgado (1901–   ), Brazilian fascist leader who came to prominence in 1934. He was outmanoeuvred by Vargas and retired into obscurity.
9. Eva Perón (1919–52), Argentinian leader of labour. Immensely influential and popular among the urban workers in Buenos Aires. Wife of the dictator.
10. Speech, 9 July 1896.
11. A. F. K. Organski in *The Nature of Fascism*, p. 41.

17

1. *Africa in Search of Democracy* by K. A. Busia, p. 143.
2. R. I. Rotberg in *World Politics*, Vol. XV, 1962.
3. *African Socialism* by L. Senghor, p. 91.
4. Parliament of Malawi, *Official Report of the Proceedings*, 8 September 1964.
5. *West Africa*, 29 January 1966, p. 114.

6. *Democracy and the Party System* by J. Nyerere, p. 7.
7. *World Politics Since 1945* by P. Calvocoressi, p. 313.
8. Quoted in Busia, op. cit., p. 128.
9. *Politics in West Africa* by W. A. Lewis, pp. 34–5.
10. See article by A. Cesaire in *Présence Africaine*, No. 29, 1960.
11. *L'Action politique du P.D.G. pour l'Emancipation Africaine*, p. 422.
12. *Studies in African Politics* by P. B. Harris, pp. 47–8.
13. Busia, op. cit., p. 51.
14. *Values in African Tribal Life* by E. Evans-Pritchard and M. Fortes, p. 55.
15. *Africa: the politics of independence* by I. Wallerstein, p. 163.
16. *La Planification économique*. Quoted in *African One-Party States*, G. Carter (ed.), p. 220.
17. *La Planification économique*, p. 316.
18. *International Affairs*, Vol. xxxviii, 1961, p. 436.
19. *Republic of Kenya: sessional paper*, para. 142, 1963/5.
20. Ibid.
21. Busia, op. cit., pp. 89–90.
22. *Africa: the politics of unity* by I. Wallerstein, p. 171.
23. *The Ghana Coup* by Colonel A. A. Afrifa, p. 31.
24. Busia, op. cit., p. 143.
25. Speech of 2 October 1959, in France.
26. Quoted in Busia, op. cit., pp. 46–7.
27. Quoted in Busia, op. cit., p. 45.
28. *Apartheid, Fascism and the Golden Age.* (Paper) by P. L. van den Berghe.
29. *Star*, 29 April 1967.
30. By G. Carter, T. Karis and N. Stultz in their *South Africa's Transkei: the politics of domestic colonialism*.

Bibliography

The bibliography has been divided into two sections—original works and those of a secondary nature. In the first section will be found memoirs, monographs and basic texts by important authors. In the second section can be found critical works, biographies and more general books, including a number touching on fascism in a wide range of European countries which have not always received detailed attention in the text. Interested readers should thus be able to follow up points relating to fascism in, for example, Spain or Scandinavia. There is also a small sub-section of articles. Not all the books used by me have been mentioned in this biography, for many have had only peripheral relevance.

On a technical note, those names prefixed with von, le or some similar modification have been listed under the first letter of the major name, e.g. Le Bon appears under 'B'. This classification is not perfect, but is simple and easy to follow. Finally, all reference to very obvious sources, e.g. *The Times* has been omitted from the bibliography. A long list of the major newspapers in a dozen different countries would tell the reader nothing.

Primary Sources

H. H. Aall, *Social Individualism* (Oslo, 1942).

W. J. Ashley, *Surveys Historic and Economic* (London, 1900).

W. J. Ashley, *The Tariff Problem* (London, 1920).

E. Banse, *Raum und Volk im Weltkriege* (London, 1934).

M. Bardèche, *Qu'est-ce que le fascisme?* (Paris, 1961).

M. Barrès, *Du sang, de la volupté et de la mort* (Paris, 1894).

M. Barrès, *L'Ennemi des lois* (Paris, 1893).

F. Bastiat, *Les Harmonies économiques* (Paris, 1848).

N. H. Baynes (ed.), *The Speeches of Adolf Hitler* (Oxford, 1942).

F. von Bernhardi, *Deutschland und der nächste Krieg* (London, 1914).

J. Blanqui, *Les Classes ouvrières en France* (Paris, 1848).

R. Blatchford, *Germany and England* (New York, 1914).

R. Blatchford, *Merrie England* (London, 1895).

R. Blatchford, *My Eighty Years* (London, 1931).

G. Le Bon, *Le Déséquilibre du monde* (Paris, 1923).

I. Bonomi, *From Socialism to Fascism* (London, 1924).

H. S. Chamberlain, *Die Grundzüge des neunzehnten Jahrhunderts* (London, 1911).

H. S. Chamberlain, *Kriegsaufsätze* (Munich, 1915).

C. Clausewitz, *Vom Krieg* (Berlin, 1867).

E. Corradini, *Il nazionalismo italiano* (Milan, 1914).

J. A. Cramb, *Germany and England* (London, 1914).

W. Cunningham, *Alien Immigrants to England* (London, 1897).

W. Cunningham, *Case Against Free Trade* (London, 1911).

W. Cunningham, *Politics and Economics* (London, 1885).

C. Darwin, *Origin of Species* (Oxford, 1951).

M. Déat, *Le Parti unique* (Paris, 1942).

J. Doriot, *Refaire la France* (Paris, 1944).

P. Drieu la Rochelle, *Socialisme Fasciste* (Paris, 1934).

E. Dührung, *Cursus der National—und Sozialökonomie* (Berlin, 1875).

E. Dührung, *Die Judenfrage als Racen-, Sitten-, und Kulturfrage* (Leipzig, 1881).

A. Espinas, *Les Sociétés animales* (Paris, 1877).

J. Fichte, *Werke* (Berlin, 1845–6).

A. Gobineau, *Essai sur l'inégalité des races humaines* (Paris, 1853–5).

J. Görres, *Das Wachstum der Histoire* (Heidelberg, 1807).

H. Grimm, *Volk ohne Raum* (Munich, 1928–30).

E. Haeckel, *Die Welträtsel* (Berlin, 1899).

F. Haiser, *Die Sklaverei, ihre biologische Begrundung und sittliche Rechtsfertigung* (Nuremberg, 1938).

K. Haller, *Handbuch der allgemeinen Staatenkunde* (Munich, 1938).

E. Hasse, *Weltpolitik, Imperialismus und Kolonialpolitik* (Berlin, 1936).

H. Heiber (ed.), *The Early Goebbels Diaries* (London, 1962).

J. Herder, *Sämmtliche Werke* (Berlin, 1877–1913).

B. Hildebrand, *Die Nationalökonomie der Gegenwart und Zukunft* (Berlin, 1848).

A. Hitler, *Mein Kampf* (London, 1939).

A. Hitler, *Secret Book* (New York, 1962).

T. Hobbes, *Leviathan* (London, 1959).

S. G. Hobson, *National Guilds* (London, 1920).

S. G. Hobson, *Pilgrim to the Left* (London, 1938).

S. H. S. Inglefield, *The Mornings of the King of Prussia* (London, 1897).

International Military Tribunal, *Proceedings* (Nuremberg, 1948–8).

E. Kaufmann, *Das Wesen des Völkerrechts* (Halle, 1911).

H. Keyserling, *The World in the Making* (London, 1927).

B. Kidd, *Social Evolution* (London, 1894).

R. Kjellén, *Staten som livsfom* (Stockholm, 1924).

R. Kjellén, *Die Grossmächte der Gegenwart* (Frankfurt, 1935).

K. Knies, *Die politische Ökonomie vom Standpunkte der geschichtlichen Methode* (Hamburg, 1853).

P. Lagarde, *Deutsche Schriften* (Göttingen, 1878—81).

K. Lamprecht, *Zur jüngsten deutschen Vergangenheit* (Freiburg, 1904).

F. Lassalle, *Gesammtwerke* (Leipzig, 1900).

J. Lee, *Tomorrow is a New Day* (London, 1939).

J. von Leers, *Geschichte auf rassischer Grundlage* (Frankfurt, 1936).

F. Lenz, *Die Rasse als Wertprinzip* (Munich, 1938).

F. List, *Das nationale System der politischen Ökonomie* (London, 1904).

D. Lloyd-George, *War Memoirs* (London, 1934).

N. Machiavelli, *Il principe* (London, 1960).

N. Machiavelli, *The Discourses* (London, 1970).

H. Mackinder, *Democratic Ideals and Reality* (London, 1919).

F. Marinetti, *Futurismo e Fascismo* (Foligno, 1924).

K. Menger, *Untersuchungen über die Methode der Sozialwissenschaften* (Vienna, 1883).

A. Moeller van den Bruck, *Das dritte Reich* (London, 1934).

O. Mosley, *Fascism: 100 Questions Asked and Answered* (London, 1936).

O. Mosley and J. Strachey, *Revolution by Reason* (London, 1925).

A. Müller, *Die Elemente der Staatskunst* (Vienna, 1809).

A. Müller, *Versuche einer neuen Theorie des Geldes* (Vienna, 1816).

F. Naumann, *Mitteleuropa* (Berlin, 1915).

F. Nietzsche, *Complete Works* (Edinburgh, 1909–11).

F. Nitti, *Rivelazioni* (Naples, 1948).

F. von Papen, *Memoirs* (London, 1952).

K. Pearson, *Darwinism, Medical Progress and Eugenics* (London, 1912).

K. Pearson, *National Life from the Standpoint of Science* (London, 1905).

K. Pearson, *The Ethic of Free Thought* (London, 1901).

G. W. Prange (ed.), *Hitler's Words* (Washington, 1944).

L. Ranke, *Sämmtliche Werke* (Leipzig, 1881–90).

H. Rauschning, *Hitler Speaks* (London, 1940).

Lord Roberts, *Lord Roberts' Message to the Nation* (London, 1912).

A. von Rochau, *Grundzüge der Realpolitik* (Berlin, 1853).

K. Rodbertus, *Briefe und Sozialpolitische Aufsätze* (Berlin, 1876).

W. Roscher, *Das System der Volkswirtschaft* (Mainz, 1854).

W. Roscher, *Grundriss zu Vorlesungen über die Staatswirtschaft nach geschichtlicher Methode* (Frankfurt, 1843).

A. Rosenberg, *Blut und Ehre* (Munich, 1939).

A. Rosenberg, *Der Mythus des 20 Jahrhunderts* (Munich, 1934).

C. Saint-Simon, *Oeuvres* (Paris, 1848).

H. Schacht, *Account Settled* (London, 1948).

F. Schleiermacher, *Dialektik* (Berlin, 1811).

G. von Schmoller, *Grundriss der allgemeinen Volkswirtschaftslehre* (Munich, 1923).

A. Schopenhauer, *Die Welt als Wille und Vorstellung* (Frankfurt, 1859).

K. Schuschnigg, *Ein Requiem in Rot-Weiss-Rot* (Zurich, 1946).

R. Schüller, *Schutzzoll und Freihandel* (Vienna, 1906).

A. Schwegler, *Geschichte der Philosophie im Umriss* (Tübingen, 1846).

G. B. Shaw (ed.), *Fabianism and the Empire* (London, 1900).

S. Sighele, *Il nazionalismo e i partiti politici* (Milan, 1911).

J. de Sismondi, *Nouveaux principes d'économie politique* (Geneva, 1819).

W. Skarzynski, *Die Agrarkrisis und die Mittel zu ihrer Abhilfe* (Koblenz, 1935).

A. Smith, *An Inquiry into the Nature and Causes of the Wealth of Nations* (London, 1920).

G. Sorel, *Réflexions sur la violence* (Paris, 1906).

O. Spann, *Der wahre Staat* (Vienna, 1921).

A. Speer, *Inside the Third Reich* (London, 1970).

O. Spengler, *The Decline of the West* (London, 1971).

O. Spengler, *The Hour of Decision* (London, 1963).
W. Stapel, *Der christliche Staatsmann: eine Theologie des Nationalismus* (Hamburg, 1932).
Baron vom Stein, *Briefwechsel, Denkschriften und Aufzeichnungen* (Berlin, 1931–7).
J. Strachey, *The Menace of Fascism* (London, 1933).
W. Sumner, *Social Darwinism: selected essays* (Englewood Cliffs, 1963).
D. Syme, *Outlines of an industrial science* (Melbourne, 1876).

F. Thyssen, *I Paid Hitler* (London, 1941).
H. Treitschke, *Die Politik* (Leipzig, 1899–1900).

R. Wagner, *Werke* (Leipzig, 1883).

S. Zweig, *The World of Yesterday* (Vienna, 1943).

Secondary Sources

A. A. Afrifa, *The Ghana Coup* (London, 1967).
H. Arendt, *The Origins of Totalitariansim* (New York, 1958).

E. Barker (ed.), *The Politics of Aristotle* (Oxford, 1950).
E. Barker, *The Political Thought of Plato and Aristotle* (London, 1906).
M. D. Biddiss, *Father of Racist Ideology: the social and political thought of Count Gobineau* (London, 1970).
R. Bowen, *German Theories of the Corporative State* (New York, 1947).
K. D. Bracher, *Die Auflösung der Weimar Republik* (Villingen, 1960).
A. L. C. Bullock, *Hitler: a study in tyranny* (London, 1964).
R. D'O. Butler, *The Roots of National Socialism, 1783–1933* (London, 1941).

P. Calvocoressi, *World Politics Since 1945* (London, 1968).
R. N. Carew Hunt, *The Theory and Practice of Communism* (London, 1963).
T. Carlyle, *Heroes, Hero-worship and the Heroic in History* (London, 1926).
R. Carr (ed.), *The Republic and the Civil War in Spain* (London, 1971).
G. Carter (ed.), *African One-party States* (London, 1962).
G. Carter (ed.) et al., *South Africa's Transkei: the politics of domestic colonialism* (London, 1967).
F. Chabod, *A History of Italian Fascism* (London, 1963).
W. S. Churchill, *The World Crisis* (London, 1941).
R. T. Clark, *The Fall of the German Republic* (London, 1935).
A. Cobban, *Dictatorship; its history and theory* (London, 1939).
F. M. Cornford (ed.), *The Republic of Plato* (Oxford, 1944).
C. Cross, *The Fascists in Britain* (London, 1961).

R. Debicki, *The Foreign Policy of Poland, 1919–39* (London, 1963).
C. F. Delzell, *Mussolini's Enemies* (Princeton, 1961).

E. S. Forster, *A Short History of Modern Greece* (London, 1958).
C. J. Friedrich (ed.), *Totalitarianism* (New York, 1964).

D. L. Germino, *The Italian Fascist Party in Power* (Minneapolis, 1960).

C. Gide and C. Rist, *A History of Economic Doctrines* (London, 1967).

A. J. Gregor, *Contemporary Radical Ideologies: totalitarian thought in the twentieth century* (New York, 1968).

A. J. Gregor, *The Ideology of Fascism: the rationale of totalitarianism* (New York, 1969).

P. B. Harris, *Studies in African Politics* (London, 1970).

P. M. Hayes, *Quisling* (Newton Abbot, 1971).

K. Heiden, *Der Führer* (London, 1944).

E. Heller, *The Disinherited Mind* (London, 1961).

C. Hibbert, *Benito Mussolini* (London, 1962).

D. L. Horowitz, *The Italian Labour Movement* (Harvard, 1963).

R. Humphrey, *Georges Sorel: prophet without honour* (Harvard, 1951).

G. S. Kirk (ed.), *Heraclitus: the cosmic fragments* (Cambridge, 1954).

B. H. Klein, *Germany's Economic Preparations for War* (Harvard, 1959).

W. A. Lewis, *Politics in West Africa* (London, 1965).

H-D. Loock, *Quisling, Rosenberg und Terboven* (Stuttgart, 1970).

D. Mack Smith, *Italy* (Ann Arbor, 1969).

A. S. Milward, *The Fascist Economy in Norway* (Oxford, 1972).

A. S. Milward, *The New Order and the French Economy* (Oxford, 1970).

G. Mosse, *The Crisis of German ideology: intellectual origins of the Third Reich* (New York, 1964).

J. A. La Nauze, *Political Economy in Australia* (Melbourne, 1949).

F. Neumann, *Behemoth: the structure and practice of National Socialism, 1933–44* (New York, 1966).

V. Nitti, *L'Opera di Nitti* (Gobetti, 1924).

E. Nolte, *Three Faces of Fascism* (London, 1965).

J. Nyerere, *Freedom and Socialism* (Dar es Salaam, 1968).

A. F. K. Organski, *The Stages of Political Development* (New York, 1965).

R. Pascal (ed.), *Thus Spake Zarathustra* (London, 1960).

S. G. Payne, *Falange* (Stanford, 1961).

K. R. Popper, *The Open Society and its Enemies* (London, 1966).

D. Read, *Cobden and Bright* (London, 1967).

R. Rémond, *La droite en France* (Paris, 1954).

A. Rhodes, *The Poet as Superman* (London, 1959).

R. A. H. Robinson, *The Origins of Franco's Spain* (Newton Abbot, 1970).

H. Rogger and E. Weber (eds.), *The European Right: a historical profile* (London, 1965).

R. Rolland, *Péguy* (Paris, 1944).

Lord Rosebery, *Miscellanies: literary and historical* (London, 1921).

C. Schmidt, *The Corporate State in Action* (Oxford, 1939).

J. A. Schumpeter, *History of Economic Analysis* (Oxford, 1954).

L. Senghor, *On African Socialism* (New York, 1964).

B. Semmel, *Imperialism and Social Reform* (London, 1960).

R. J. A. Skidelsky, *Politicians and the Slump* (London, 1970).

F. Stern, *The Politics of Cultural Despair* (New York, 1965).
S. D. Stirk, *The Prussian Spirit* (London, 1941).

H. Taine, *Les Origines de la France contemporaine* (Paris, 1912).
J. L. Talmon, *The Origins of Totalitarian Democracy* (London, 1961).
A. J. P. Taylor, *Bismarck* (London, 1961).
H. Thomas, *The Spanish Civil War* (London, 1961).
H. Tint, *The Decline of French Patriotism, 1870–1940* (London, 1964).

L. Villari, *The Fascist Experiment* (London, 1926).

I. Wallerstein, *Africa: the politics of unity* (London, 1968).
E. Weber, *Action Française* (Stanford, 1962).
W. G. Welk, *Fascist Economic Policy* (Harvard, 1938).
A. Werth, *France in Ferment* (London, 1934).
A. G. Whiteside, *Austrian National Socialism before 1918* (The Hague, 1962).
S. J. Woolf (ed.), *European Fascism* (London, 1970).
S. J. Woolf (ed.), *The Nature of Fascism* (London, 1968).

Z. A. B. Zeman, *Nazi Propaganda* (Oxford, 1964).

Articles and Periodicals

The Clarion.
International Affairs (especially Vols. xvii, xxxviii).
The Journal of Contemporary History (especially Vol. 1, No. 1, 1966).
The Annual Register (especially 1910).
The Fortnightly Review (especially 1931).
Niles' Register.
Revue mensuelle d'économie politique.
Deutsche Wehr (especially 1932).
Der Stürmer.

W. J. Ashley, Political Economy and the Tariff Problem, *Economic Review* (1904).
W. Cunningham, The Economic Basis of Universal Peace — Cosmopolitan or International ?, *Economic Review* (1913).
J. Gallagher and R. Robinson, The Imperialism of Free Trade, *Economic History Review* (1953).
E. W. Gilbert, The Right Honourable Sir Halford J. Mackinder, *Geographical Journal* (1948).
C. J. H. Hayes, Influence of Political Tactics on Socialist Theory in Germany, 1863–1914, in C. Merriam and H. E. Barnes (eds.), *A History of Political Theories* (New York, 1924).
B. J. Hovde, Socialistic Theories of Imperialism Prior to the Great War, *Journal of Political Economy* (1928).
W. Kampmann, Stöcker und die Berliner Bewegung, *Geschichte in Wissenschaft und Unterricht* (1962).

R. Koebner, The Concept of Economic Imperialism, *Economic History Review* (1949).

F. E. Loewenstein, The Shaw-Wells Controversy of 1904–8, *Fabian Quarterly* (1944).

H. J. Mackinder, The Geographical Pivot of History, *Geographical Journal* (1904).

M. Rintala, A Generation in Politics: a definition, *Review of Politics* (1963).

M. Rintala, An Image of European Politics: the People's Patriotic Movement, *Journal of Central European Affairs* (1962).

H. Rogger, Was There a Russian Fascism?, *Journal of Modern History* (1964).

A. Rozsnyói, October 15th, 1944, *Acta Historica* (1961).

Index